HIDDEN BURNE-JONES

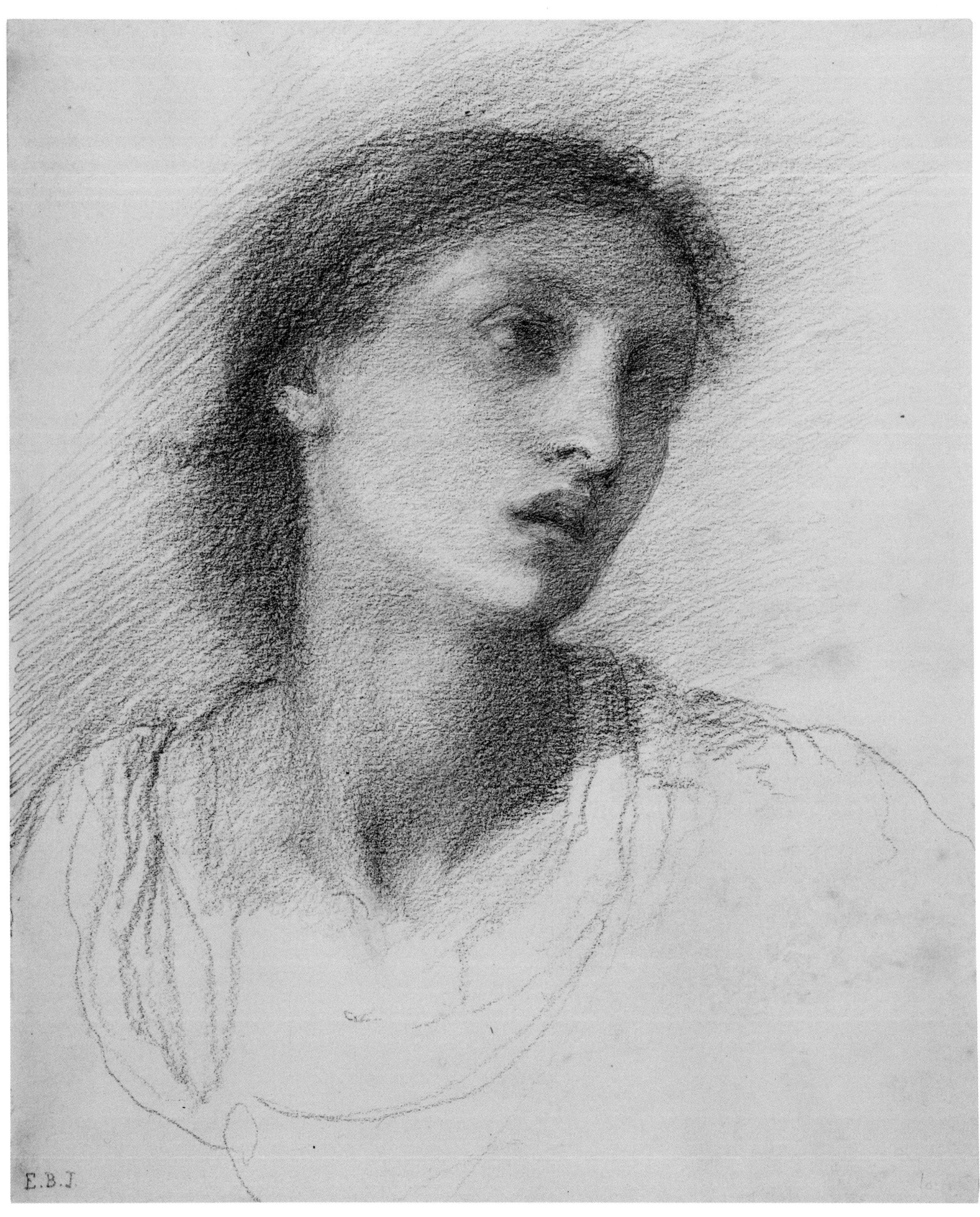
E.B.J.

HIDDEN BURNE-JONES

Works on paper by Edward Burne-Jones from Birmingham Museums and Art Gallery

with essays by JOHN CHRISTIAN, ELISA KORB
and TESSA SIDEY

includes a catalogue of Edward Burne-Jones:
Drawings, Watercolours, Prints and Archive Material
at Birmingham Museums and Art Gallery

D Giles Ltd
in association with Birmingham Museums and Art Gallery

For Gerald and Elaine Korb, and A. E. Whitley

First published in 2007 by GILES
An imprint of D Giles Limited
Kite Studios, Priory Mews
2B Bassein Park Road
London
W12 9RU
www.gilesltd.com

ISBN: 978-1-904832-30-0

For D Giles Limited:
Helen Swansbourne, designer
David Rose, copy-editor and proof-reader
Christine Shuttleworth, indexer
Produced by D Giles Limited, London
Printed and bound in China

Unless stated otherwise, all illustrations are drawn from Birmingham Museum and Art Gallery
Photographs by Luke Unsworth

Front cover: Studies of female Drapery seen from the back, 1867–69 (cat. 34, detail)
Back cover: *King René's Honeymoon: Sculpture*, 1862 (cat. 11)
Frontispiece: Stained Glass Design: Head Study of Maria Zambaco for *St Mark the Evangelist*, 1869–71 (cat. 36)

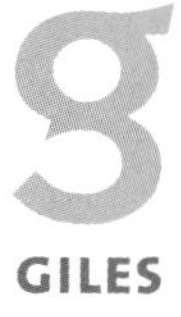

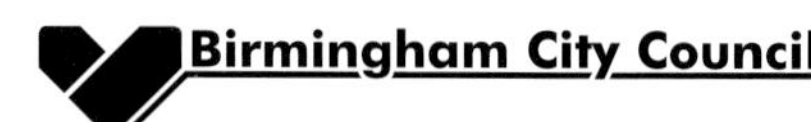

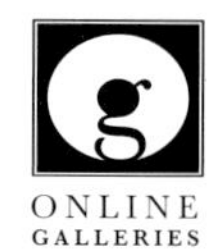

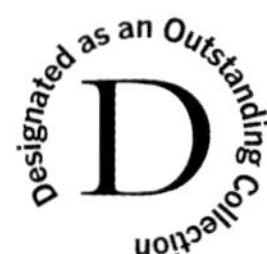

This publication coincides with the following exhibition:

Hidden Burne-Jones
Works on Paper by Edward Burne-Jones from Birmingham Museums and Art Gallery
Birmingham Museum and Art Gallery
Chamberlain Square, Birmingham B3 3DH
4 April – 1 July 2007

Leighton House Museum, London
12 October 2007 – 27 January 2008

Contents

6 Foreword and Acknowledgements

7 *The Compulsive Draughtsman*
JOHN CHRISTIAN

17 Colour Plates

28 *Models, Muses and Burne-Jones's Continuous Quest for the Ideal Female Face*
ELISA KORB

34 *Public Patronage: The Burne-Jones Collection in Birmingham*
TESSA SIDEY

39 Exhibits
ELISA KORB WITH TESSA SIDEY

41 Colour Plates

62 Edward Burne-Jones: Catalogue of Drawings, Watercolours, Prints and Archive Material at Birmingham Museums and Art Gallery
ELISA KORB AND TESSA SIDEY

95 Index

Foreword

Hidden Burne-Jones is very much the result of wanting to expose the less familiar aspects of the unique Pre-Raphaelite collections at Birmingham Museums and Art Gallery, and in particular the considerable draughtsmanship of Edward Burne-Jones. The collection is in every sense an international public resource for this major nineteenth-century artist, with 1183 works, 1137 of which are works on paper and related archive material. Some nine years after the highly successful centennial exhibition of *Edward Burne-Jones Victorian Artist-Dreamer*, seen in New York, Birmingham and Paris, the organisers of this multi-layered research-based project have chosen to focus on the theme of Burne-Jones as draughtsman.

The final realisation has evolved from the research of Elisa Korb, a postgraduate doctoral student at the University of Birmingham, who over the last three years has set about documenting the collection of Burne-Jones works on paper. Her findings will form the basis of a new online Burne-Jones Resource Site to be launched in 2007. She has worked with Tessa Sidey, Curator of Prints and Drawings, over this period and together they have selected the accompanying exhibition to this publication.

Both would particularly like to thank John Christian for his perceptive essay and invaluable reading of the catalogue listing contained in this publication; Online Galleries and Peter Cameron for sponsorship of the aforementioned website; and Peter Nahum for his crucial support of the idea of a Burne-Jones research project. The John Feeney Charitable Trust and The Grimmitt Trust, both long associated with Birmingham, have provided additional financial assistance. Further thanks are due to Leighton House Museum in London and its Keeper, Daniel Robbins, where the *Hidden Burne-Jones* exhibition will be shown after Birmingham; David Elliott, Paul Spencer-Longhurst, Bill Waters and Patricia O'Connor for their guidance and support; Philip Attwood at the British Museum, Sandra Penketh at the Lady Lever Art Gallery, Simon Fenwick at the Royal Watercolour Society; Alison Brisby and Christopher Ridgway at Castle Howard; Luke Unsworth, Gill Casson, Colin Cruise, Paul Goldman, Linda Spurdle, Rachel Cockett, Ben Woodhams, Varshali Patel, David Rowan, Lee Handley, Carl Turner, Pat Welch, Kate Chase, John Woodward, Elizabeth and Robert Smallwood, Gabriela MacKinnon, Nicholas Robinson, Susanna Brown of the National Portrait Gallery and Vivien Knight, now Curator of the Guildhall Art Gallery, London, whose unpublished catalogue of the Burne-Jones collection in Birmingham has remained an important reference source.

Not least, we would like to thank Dan Giles and Sarah McLaughlin at D Giles Limited and the designer Helen Swansbourne for their respective skills and support in bringing this publication to fruition.

RITA MCLEAN
Head of Museums and Heritage Services
Birmingham Museums and Art Gallery

The Compulsive Draughtsman

JOHN CHRISTIAN

To consider Burne-Jones as a draughtsman is an undertaking fraught with implications that hardly arise in conventional studies of artists' drawings. Far from merely focusing attention on a significant aspect of his work, showing, perhaps, how individual drawings shed light on a particular picture or decorative project, the enquiry goes to the heart of his artistic personality, raising questions that have the most profound bearing on his imagination and style.

Many artists (Rembrandt, Manet and Whistler, for example) are first and foremost painters, revelling in the handling of the brush and the mysterious ability of paint to convey information and evoke sensations when it is smeared or dragged over, jabbed at or piled up on canvas. For these artists, drawings tend to be subservient to the painting process, even if they are not actually *aides-mémoires* for some effect that the executant hopes to achieve in the more substantial medium. If the artist is a great one, they may of course be supreme works of art in themselves, but this does not alter their fundamentally dependent relationship to the painted *oeuvre*. There is a sense in which the paintings explain and even justify their existence.

In Burne-Jones's case the dynamics are the exact opposite; he was always a draughtsman first and a painter second. 'He was pre-eminently a draughtsman …', his friend Graham Robertson recalled, 'to draw was his natural mode of expression – line flowed from him almost without volition. If he were merely playing with a pencil, the result was never a scribble, but a thing of beauty however slight, a perfect design'.[1] On the other hand, there tends to be an element of strain and contrivance about Burne-Jones's paintings. 'Certain spaces in his design', Robertson observed, 'were to be filled up with various hues so as to make up a beautiful pattern; he coloured his drawing as a child will colour a black and white outline.'[2] A later writer might have used the phrase 'painting by numbers'. This might be a blasphemous downgrading of effects that, by means of colour and texture, can appeal powerfully to the senses and imagination. The famous *Laus Veneris* (Laing Art Gallery, Newcastle-upon-Tyne), shown at the Grosvenor Gallery in 1878, reminded Robertson of 'clusters of many-coloured gems or stained windows through which shone the evening sun'.[3] But however seductive the results may be, they are emphatically of a different order to the thrilling spectacle of watching a master of the brush at work.

Burne-Jones's tendency to approach his painting like a child filling in an outline chimed perfectly with his perception of himself as a neo-Renaissance artist, employing assistants who transferred his designs to canvas and did some of the groundwork. The design of a picture was everything, the essential hallmark of his authorship, while the execution, though obviously important, was of secondary interest. In an ideal world, moreover, this busy studio would have been employed on frescoes. 'The chance of doing public work seldom comes to me', he complained wistfully in 1888, 'if I could I would work only in public buildings and in choirs and places where they sing.'[4] Easel pictures were a poor substitute for the murals in civic halls and great basilicas that he would have been painting had he lived in a society with the priorities of Renaissance Florence.

With hindsight, this can be read not only as a lament about modern patronage but about the medium it forced him to employ. Fresco would have been far better suited to his talents than oil. You can draw with a brush dipped in water-based paint in a way that you cannot with one charged with viscous, oil-saturated pigment. Fresco lends itself to the definition of form and the articulation of design, both cornerstones of his style; oil is suited to the rendering of light, chiaroscuro, atmosphere and passing mood, with none of which was he primarily concerned.

This dilemma would never be entirely resolved, but a solution of sorts lay in the use of watercolour. Drawing and watercolour have always been closely associated, perhaps finding their purest union in the so-called 'tinted drawings' of the early English watercolour school. Burne-Jones's method, as it happened, could hardly have been more different. Probably inspired initially by the approach advocated in John Ruskin's *Elements of Drawing* (1857), he developed a technique that, far from being a matter of transparent washes and *premier coup*, relied heavily on bodycolour and revelled in the opportunities it offered to make radical revisions. In fact the results, paradoxically enough, closely resembled oil, achieving its richness and density by appropriating the techniques of glazing and scumbling that had characterized its pre-Impressionist practice.

For all this, watercolour enabled Burne-Jones to handle the brush as a truly graphic instrument, and it is for this reason, not because they happen to be 'works on paper', that his pictures in this medium are integral to any account of his development as a draughtsman. The tenacity with which he clung to watercolour speaks volumes about his instinctive feeling for it and its superiority to oil in letting him be true to himself. It was his principal vehicle of expression until the early 1870s, and he continued to adopt it for some of his most important later works. The obvious example at Birmingham is the great *Star of Bethlehem* of 1888–91 (cat. 56, illus. p. 19).

To see Burne-Jones as a 'draughtsman' rather than a painter does not of course in itself go far enough. Hints that more was at stake have already surfaced in references to his neo-Renaissance studio practice and his preference for abstract design as against rendering the transitory appearance of the natural world. As these hints imply, the merely formal divide is subsumed in a more comprehensive distinction between a conceptual or literary approach and one that may broadly be described as realist. Leaving aside the question of how inevitable and invariable these alignments are, we may at least be sure that Burne-Jones represents the literary-graphic mode in a particularly telling form. He was to live to see that mode under siege by a rising generation of realists, and it was their triumph, albeit short-lived, that largely accounts for his long eclipse in the twentieth century.

So great was Burne-Jones's inclination to literary subjects and graphic expression that it is doubtful if any early influences would have altered his course. That possibility, however, hardly arose; he was conditioned to think in such terms from the very start.

Growing up in the heart of Birmingham, the only surviving child of a widowed and self-absorbed carver and gilder, Burne-Jones was left much to his own devices. He was by nature studious, and his lonely circumstances gave him both the need and the time to develop his imagination by a voracious reading of history, travellers' tales and romantic literature. As his widow put it, 'books, books, and always books were the gates of the new world into which he was entering'.[5] From an early age he knew his Shakespeare, Coleridge, Byron, Keats and Scott. At home, he recalled, there were 'very few books, but they were poets all of them', cherished by his father as poignant mementos of his dead wife, who had 'recited poetry well'.[6] In 1844 he entered the local grammar school, King Edward's, then enjoying a golden age under the enlightened headmastership of James Prince Lee, a former adjutant to Thomas Arnold at Rugby who had inherited his master's vision of learning as an essential prerequisite of virtue. This not only opened to him the treasures of the school library but brought him the friendship of two fellow bookworms, Richard Watson Dixon and Cormell Price. Together they continued to explore the heady field of romance, absorbing 'Ossian', Thorpe's *Northern Mythology*, and 'a volume of ballads and translations' that was almost certainly 'Monk' Lewis's *Tales of Wonder*, a celebrated expression of the taste for Gothick horror.

As yet, of course, Burne-Jones had no intention of becoming an artist. If anything, by the late 1840s, like so many young men fired by the Romantic movement, he saw himself entering the Church as a follower of the Tractarians. Nonetheless, he was 'always drawing' as a boy, and would astonish his friends by his ability to 'cover a sheet of foolscap' with figures 'almost as quickly as one could have written'.[7] Most of these juvenilia are known only from descriptions. He was particularly prolific at comic drawings of devils, but there were more serious subjects too: scenes from Roman history, an illustration to G. A. Bürger's well-known ballad 'Lenore', and evocations of such stirring contemporary events as the massacre in the Khyber Pass and the exploits of Lady Sale, the redoubtable heroine of the First Afghan War. Among the few drawings to survive are two illustrations to Alessandro Manzoni's novel

I promessi sposi, or *The Betrothed*, a choice that reflects his clerical ambitions since the book was popular in Anglo-Catholic circles.

Burne-Jones would later dismiss as worthless anything he did prior to his meeting with Dante Gabriel Rossetti, but he could hardly have denied that even at this stage a familiar pattern was emerging. Already he possessed a teeming imagination that found its lifeblood in books and expressed itself in drawing; neither in the handful of surviving sketches nor in the descriptions of lost ones are there any hints of colour. This was hardly surprising, given that what limited sense of style he had was also derived from books, or rather their black-and-white illustrations. Lady Burne-Jones saw in the 'grotesque vigour' of his earliest work the influence of George Cruikshank, the satiric and caricatural illustrator of Dickens.[8] In fact, one of the surviving sketches is a copy of a Cruikshank-like illustration in Thomas Hood's *Comic Album* of 1843. He also owned 'a book of English ballads with engravings'[9] that is probably identifiable with S. C. Hall's *Book of British Ballads* (1842), an ambitious publication lavishly embellished with designs by a galaxy of artists – E. M. Ward, Noel Paton, Richard Dadd, Kenny Meadows, John Tenniel, Richard Redgrave and others. One of those involved, E. H. Corbould, seems to have inspired his drawings of Lady Sale, while his illustration to 'Lenore' may have been prompted by the ones made by Daniel Maclise for an edition of Bürger's poem published in 1847. Maclise was an artist he remembered 'liking' when he was 'little'.[10]

Burne-Jones was not without mentors, but they were hardly challenging and certainly did nothing to awaken any sense of 'painterly' values. His happiest contact was with Frederick Catherwood, the brother-in-law of an aunt who lived in Camberwell. This former pupil of Soane and acquaintance of Keats had made his name as an explorer and topographical draughtsman, risking his life to penetrate the Mosque of Omar in Jerusalem and publishing ground-breaking books on the monuments of Mayan civilisation buried deep in the Central American jungle. Burne-Jones was fascinated by his drawings and first-hand accounts of places that had long haunted his imagination, but Catherwood did little to broaden his formal horizons.

Meanwhile, in Birmingham, such teaching as came his way was actively demoralising. His father's frame-making business attracted men with pretensions to connoisseurship, but their opinions, by all accounts, were woefully ill-informed. One, a retired businessman named Mr Caswell, saw promise in his drawings and tried to encourage him, but his well-meant efforts, which included lending him engravings to copy and setting him exercises in objective drawing, only made the boy into a rebel. Still less fortunate was his experience of Thomas Clark, a minor landscape artist who taught drawing at King Edward's and was director of the Birmingham School of Design. The School had been set up in 1842 as a regional outpost of the government School of Design at Somerset House in London, and had premises not far from King Edward's in New Street. Burne-Jones encountered Clark at both institutions, being among the King Edward's boys whom Lee encouraged to attend evening classes at the School of Design; and Clark, who had lived for many years in London, exhibited at the Royal Academy, and travelled in France, Italy and Egypt in search of subjects, theoretically had much to offer a boy in his position. But Clark was a disastrous teacher and seems to have struck no spark of response in his pupil. In fact so glaring were his deficiencies that he was made to resign from the School of Design in 1851.

Looking back in later life, Burne-Jones remembered 'hating' painting as a boy, associating it with the dreary examples left for framing in his father's workshop or picked up by Mr Caswell at sales.[11] But Birmingham had better things to offer than this, and it would be truer to say that he simply failed to 'see' them, so wrapped up was he in his own pursuits. The chief source of potential enlightenment was the annual exhibitions held by the Society of Artists in Temple Row, wide-ranging surveys that both showcased local talent and represented nearly every well-known artist of the day. Many of the most important pictures were lent by the wealthy industrialists who were now emerging as a new class of patron: men like Charles Birch, the Society's honorary secretary, or Joseph Gillott, the steel-pen manufacturer, who bought extensively from Turner, William Etty, John Linnell, W. J. Müller and others.

Although there are strong hints that these exhibitions were discussed in his father's circle, we never hear of them being seen by Burne-Jones himself. Nor does he seem to have taken much interest in the pictures by David Cox, the most famous Birmingham artist of the day, that he saw at the house of friends in Hereford. Charles Spozzi, a local bank manager, and his wife belonged to a cultured circle and had known Cox well when the artist was living in Hereford in the 1820s. They not only owned good examples of his work but would probably have been willing to introduce their young friend to the elderly artist, with whom they were still in touch. It was an opportunity that many aspirants would have jumped at, but apparently not Burne-Jones. What excited him in Hereford was the experience of living in the land of Celtic romance, the presence of a still unrestored Cathedral, and the company of a young Tractarian priest, the Rev. John Goss, who introduced him to the writings of John Henry Newman.

By the time he went up to Oxford in January 1853 Burne-Jones had formed habits of mind that he never outgrew. He was always to be the literary man (there are said to have been piles of books even on his studio table) who 'drew' his dreams because it was only in this form that he could convey them adequately. Needless to say, Oxford confirmed this mindset. Years later, Henry James imagined a critic complaining that the artist's work was 'not painting, and has nothing to do with painting. It is literature, erudition, ... a reminiscence of Oxford, a luxury of culture'. James considered this 'brutal' but also 'very true ... Oxford occupies a very large place in Mr Burne-Jones's painting'.[12]

Hardly had Burne-Jones set foot in Exeter College than he had the incredible good luck to meet a fellow freshman who would not only prove to be a lifelong friend but a close working partner for well over three decades and, give or take a little, a rock-like source of intellectual and moral support. William Morris came from a very different background but, like Burne-Jones, he was a born romantic with a passion for the Middle Ages. He also shared his religious convictions, being an Anglo-Catholic seeking ordination, and for the first year church affairs monopolised their thoughts. Things began to change, however, in 1854, involving them both in those agonising spiritual crises that clashing ideologies made so characteristic of the time. Reading Carlyle led them to question their clerical intentions and embrace the concept of the 'hero', the prophet or man of vision who interprets for ordinary mortals the transcendental will, while Ruskin took this a stage further, claiming that the artist was uniquely qualified to fulfil the prophetic role since the imagination, using allegory and symbolism based on a painstaking study of nature, could offer profound insights into the nature of God. For a young man who was becoming disillusioned with the Church but was still intensely idealistic and had always enjoyed drawing imaginary subjects, it was an intoxicating argument with an inescapable conclusion, and by the late summer of 1855 Burne-Jones had taken the momentous decision to become an artist. Morris simultaneously chose architecture as his profession.

Ruskin also led them, through *Modern Painters* and the Edinburgh Lectures, to the Pre-Raphaelites, whom he had identified, together with Turner, as the chief contemporary exponents of aesthetic prophecy. They were thrilled to see Holman Hunt's *Light of the World* at the Royal Academy of 1854, and the following summer they visited the Pre-Raphaelite collection of Thomas Combe, the director of the Clarendon Press, in Oxford. Of all the pictures there, Burne-Jones recalled, their 'greatest wonder and delight' was reserved for Rossetti's watercolour *The First Anniversary of the Death of Beatrice* (Ashmolean Museum, Oxford). Its poetic evocation of the Middle Ages corresponded perfectly to their own ardent romanticism, and they at once concluded, rightly enough, that Rossetti was 'the chief figure in the Pre-Raphaelite Brotherhood'.[13]

From then on events moved fast. In January 1856 Burne-Jones went up to London and managed to meet Rossetti, whose magnetic personality proved as fascinating as his work. It was the start of an *annus mirabilis*, and the defining moment of his career. In May, without taking a degree, he settled in London to begin work under his hero's supervision, and in August he was joined there by Morris, who was perhaps even more dazzled by Rossetti than he was himself. Far from being awed outsiders, they were suddenly at the heart of the Pre-Raphaelite circle, meeting Hunt, Millais, Madox Brown, Arthur Hughes and everyone else in this closely-knit community. Ruskin they eventually met in November, when he returned from travelling abroad.

Throughout this turbulent period Burne-Jones continued to draw, making Ruskinian studies of flowers and landscape in the Oxford countryside, illustrating 'The Lady of Shalott' (Tennyson was another hero), and even attempting an allegorical self-portrait. His most ambitious work, however, was a collection of more than eighty designs – title-pages, full-page illustrations, vignettes and borders, tailpieces and 'illuminated' capitals – for Archibald Maclaren's *Fairy Family* (cat. 1, illus. p. 13). Maclaren was a fencing master and pioneer of physical education who ran a gymnasium in Oxford frequented by Morris, Burne-Jones and other members of their undergraduate set. He was also a man of considerable culture, whose 'book of ballads and metrical tales illustrating the fairy faith of Europe', as he described it on the title-page, was very much a product of its time. The Romantic era saw an enormous interest in fairy tales and folklore, and Maclaren's debt to earlier researchers such as Scott, Southey, Thomas Keightley and the brothers Grimm was readily acknowledged in his preface.

Started in the spring of 1854 and continued until late 1856, the drawings span the watershed of Burne-Jones's meeting with Rossetti and show a corresponding development. In many ways they have not moved far from the juvenile sketches. All are in monochrome (pencil, pen-and-ink, grey wash), being intended for reproduction as wood- or steel-engravings. Some continue to rely on Cruikshank, while in some it is tempting to see reflections of Catherwood's accounts of the stifling, mosquito-ridden Mexican jungle. Others again may contain reminiscences of gas-lit fairy tableaux in the 'transformation' scenes of pantomimes that the boy had seen when he visited London theatres. All this is incongruously mixed up with a very obvious influence: the draughtsman's considerable knowledge not only of Gothic and Gothic Revival buildings but of Anglo-Catholic ritual and everything summed up by the phrase 'the beauty of holiness'.

Many drawings, however, could only have been conceived once Burne-Jones had reached Oxford and embarked on a voyage of self-discovery with Morris. The decorated capitals were probably inspired by the illuminated manuscripts they studied in the Bodleian Library. There are first, tentative responses to Dürer's engraving *The Knight, Death and the Devil*, an image fraught with significance for the friends because of its association with two more books revered in Tractarian circles, Friedrich de La Motte Fouqué's *Sintram* and Charlotte Yonge's *The Heir of Redclyffe*. Ruskin, too, is inevitably a pervasive presence, suggesting wild Turnerian skies and such architectural features as a machicolated tower apparently copied from an illustration to the Edinburgh Lectures. Finally, there is a group of drawings that must post-date Burne-Jones's meeting with Rossetti. The figures become larger in relation to their setting, the emotional temperature rises, and an attempt is made to assimilate the master's mannerisms. There is even some borrowing of specific compositional ideas.

Ultimately, contact with Rossetti involved a clash of styles that made it impossible to bring the project to a satisfactory conclusion. Only three of the drawings appeared when the book came out in 1857, and there was no mention of their authorship. The rest remained in Maclaren's possession, and this probably accounts for their survival.[14] Had they returned to Burne-Jones, he would almost certainly have destroyed them, as he seems to have done everything else that pre-dated the Rossettian revelation.

The earliest work that he would allow into the canon was *The Waxen Image*. An elaborate pen-and-ink drawing showing a scene of witchcraft in two compartments, it dated from 1856 and was entirely post-Rossetti. Indeed it was inspired by his poem 'Sister Helen'. Unfortunately it was destroyed during the Second World War, and although a detailed description exists, there is no photograph. It was the first of a series of such drawings, some on vellum and all meticulously worked with the pen, highlights often being scraped out with a knife while shadows are strengthened with grey wash. In all, some ten finished examples are known, the last being *Childe Roland* (Cecil Higgins Art Gallery, Bedford), an illustration to Browning's poem dating from 1861. Apart from various decorative commissions, they were the artist's chief productions during these early years.

The drawings embody the intense medievalism that currently flourished in Rossetti's circle. This was emphatically a joint creation, owing as much to his two disciples as it did to Rossetti himself. They were far more knowledgeable medievalists than he was, and may even have introduced him to Malory's *Morte d'Arthur*, the cult's defining text. Burne-Jones's drawings may be seen as one side of a triangle, the others being Rossetti's 'Froissartian' watercolours of the same period and Morris's first volume of poetry, *The Defence of Guenevere* of 1858.

Technically, the drawings were the product of several forces. The pen-and-ink medium was not only familiar and congenial to Burne-Jones; it was sanctioned by Rossetti, who used it extensively himself. But Burne-Jones's method of handling it was always drier and more finicky than Rossetti's, and this may owe something to Ruskin's *Elements of Drawing*. Echoing advice he was currently giving to his students at the Working Men's College, Ruskin urged his readers to begin with pen-and-ink and to build up tone with minute scratches and dots, then use the pen-knife to soften forms or erase redundant lines. He also told them to study and copy Dürer's engravings. In 1857 Rossetti described his follower's pen-and-ink drawings as 'marvels of finish and imaginative detail, unequalled by anything unless perhaps Albert Dürer's finest works',[15] and this was no idle comparison. There is plenty of evidence that once he was a part of the Pre-Raphaelite circle Burne-Jones's knowledge of Dürer increased dramatically, and that the master's prints not only influenced his drawing style but suggested many a quaint motif.

Unfortunately there are none of these remarkable drawings at Birmingham, but the collection does contain other works of the same period. A number are connected with early decorative projects: the St Frideswide window at Christ Church, Oxford (B941); the 'Ladies and Animals' sideboard (B458–B462); the murals at Morris's newly built Red House (B533); and the triptych for St Paul's Church, Brighton (cat. 5, illus. p. 30). All these pre-date the foundation of Morris, Marshall, Faulkner & Co., 'Fine Art Workmen', in 1861; from then on all such projects were the firm's commissions. They include J. P. Seddon's plan chest (cat. 11, illus. p. 44); a very early tile design that, unusually, admits a touch of humour (B1111); and a group of cartoons for the windows at Selsley in Gloucestershire, Morris's very first stained glass (cat. 10, B853, B874, B964–B965).

When working, as it were, for himself, Burne-Jones was gradually relinquishing pen-and-ink for watercolour, no doubt partly because it was more commercially viable. Birmingham has some fine examples, from the very early *Annunciation*, begun in 1857 (cat. 3, illus. p. 18), to *The Merciful Knight* of 1863 (B520), the picture that closes this early period, or, as Lady Burne-Jones characteristically put it, 'summed up and sealed the ten years that had passed since Edward first went to Oxford'.[16] Two works of about 1862, an unfinished *Fair Rosamund* (B277) and *King Mark and La Belle Iseult* (B452), which is developed as a watercolour on top of a stained-glass cartoon, offer fascinating insights into the artist's working methods.

Although watercolour was a preferable option to oil, he still found the medium harder to handle than pen-and-ink or pencil. It is revealing to compare a quite confident study for *The Annunciation* (cat. 2, illus. p. 18) with the clumsy and patched watercolour itself. A study for *The Blessed Damozel* (B15), another very early watercolour, makes a similar point when put beside the finished work (Fogg Art Museum, Harvard University). But the really significant comparison is between Birmingham's *Backgammon Players*, a watercolour of 1861 (B10), and the large pencil version of the same year (Fitzwilliam Museum, Cambridge). One is a timid and hesitant affair, the other a performance of quite astonishing assurance.

The 1860s were a period of momentous change, not only for Burne-Jones but for his circle in general. Even before the decade had dawned, medievalism was giving way to a softer and more sensuous idiom with obvious references to Venetian painting. Rossetti was one of the new style's chief exponents, responding in part to the advent of a model and mistress who seemed its very embodiment, Fanny Cornforth. For Burne-Jones the pressures were more cerebral. Although Ruskin had inadvertently done much to encourage medievalism, he was dismayed at some of its more tongue-in-cheek excesses, regarding them as a self-indulgent derogation from the high ideals of true Pre-Raphaelitism. Ever the pedagogue, he embarked on a reform programme, and since he was currently obsessed with the sixteenth-century Venetian masters, associating them with his recent conversion to humanism, he tended to see them as an antidote to medievalist preciosity as well. It was on Burne-Jones, whom he both admired as an artist and valued as a friend, that the critic's reforming zeal was focused. Their dialogue extended over many years, reaching a climax but by no means ending in the summer of 1862, when Ruskin took his protégé to northern Italy and made him copy Venetian pictures.

At Birmingham the chief examples of Burne-Jones's Venetian phase are *An Idyll*, a Giorgionesque watercolour of 1862 (cat. 9), a related drawing of the two lovers (cat. 8), and a group of three studies for another, slightly later composition of the same type, *Green Summer* (B415–B417). Venetian influence is apparent not only in the sentiment of the two pictures but the soft black or red chalk employed for the drawings. Significantly, *An Idyll* belonged to the artist George Frederic Watts, who aided and abetted Ruskin's intervention and whose own style, based on a dual allegiance to Titian and the Greek sculptor Phidias, did much to promote a general appreciation of Venetian values. Burne-Jones encountered him at Little Holland House, to which he was introduced by Rossetti, and he came to regard Watts, who was sixteen years his senior, as a guru and father-figure.

One of the things that worried Watts was Burne-Jones's draughtsmanship. As Burne-Jones himself admitted, 'it was Watts … who compelled me to try and draw better'.[17] By 'drawing better', of course, Watts meant academically more correctly, not simply more expressively, the sense in which the phrase might be used today. In an age that put a high premium on early and exhaustive artistic training, Burne-Jones had not only started late but was virtually self-taught. His only tuition was Thomas Clark's dismal instruction in

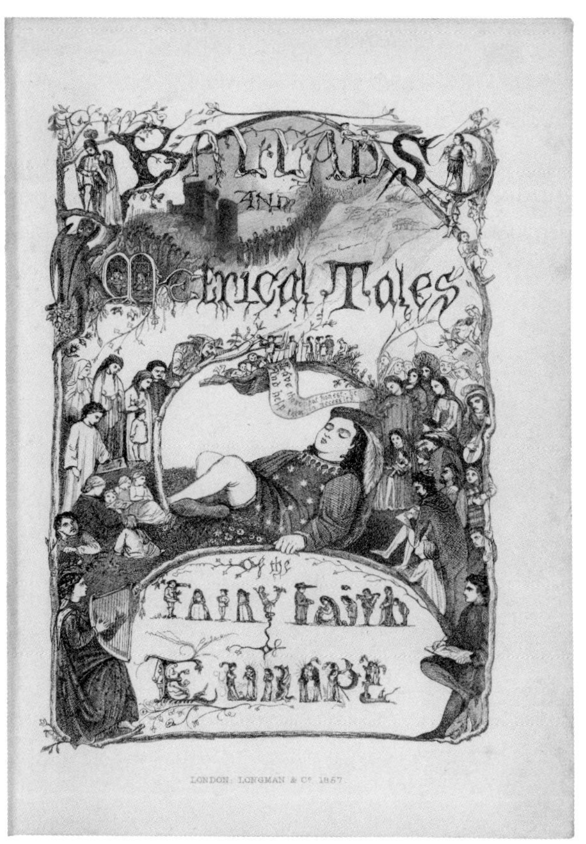

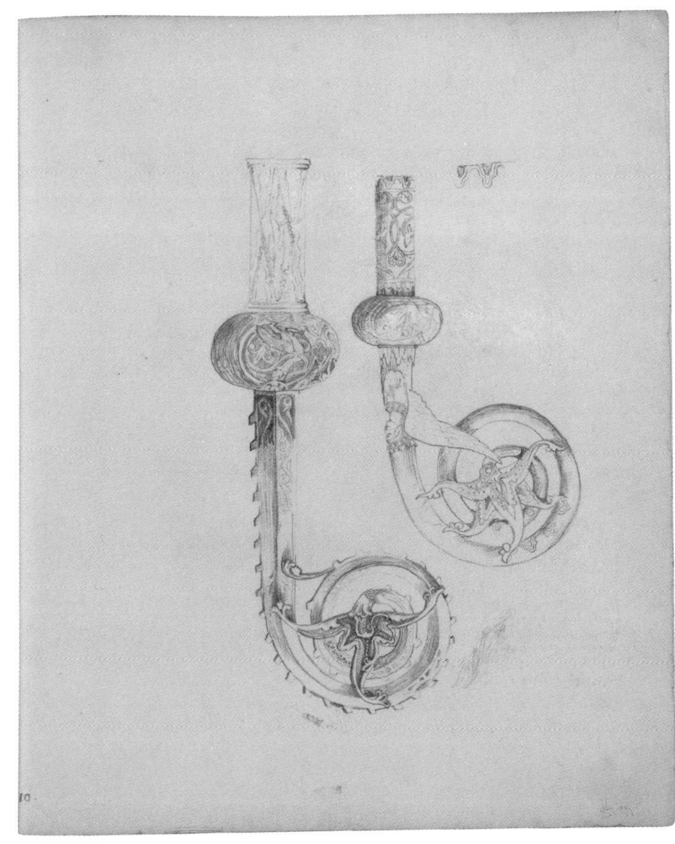

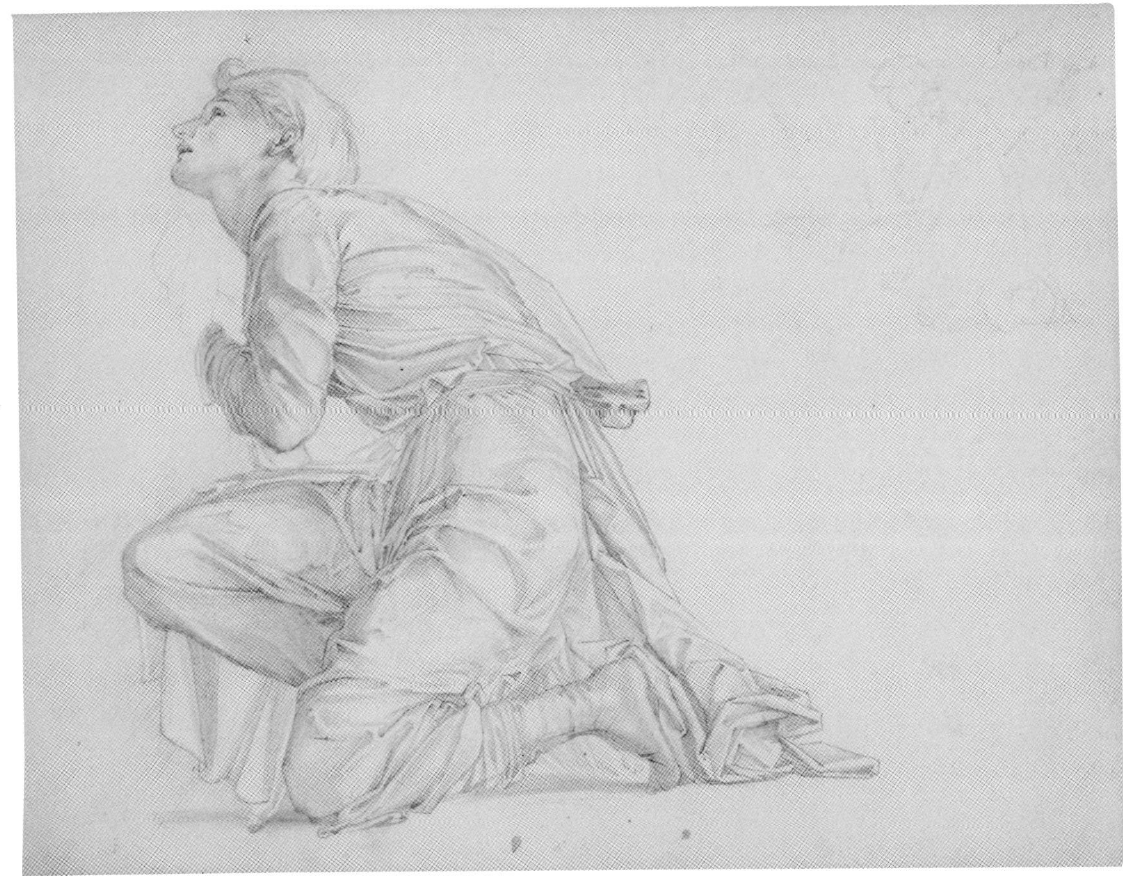

ABOVE: *The Fairy Family: A Series of Ballads & Metrical Tales Illustrating The Fairy Faith of Europe*, pub. 1857 (cat. 1)

ABOVE RIGHT: Sketchbook: Two Studies of Crozier, 1887–94 (cat. 57)

RIGHT: Pygmalion and the Image: Study of Pygmalion for *The Soul Attains*, 1873–75 (cat. 42)

the rudiments of drawing and colour at the Birmingham School of Design, a few informal lessons from Rossetti and, during his early years in London, sporadic life-classes at the art school run by J. M. Leigh, a former pupil of Etty, in Bloomsbury, an experience that he felt taught him 'nothing at all'.[18] His limitations as a draughtsman hardly mattered when he was working among friends not deficient in mutual admiration, or exhibiting at the semi-private Hogarth Club, but in 1864 he was elected to the Old Water-Colour Society (OWCS) and his work was brought before a much wider public. It aroused bitter hostility among the more conservative critics and, while he could afford to ignore their complaints about plagiarism and 'diseased imagination', he had to admit that he was vulnerable when it came to 'anatomical eccentricities'.[19] His awareness of this weakness must have been sharpened by the fact that he was now in competition with artists like Frederic Leighton, Edward Poynter, Albert Moore and James McNeill Whistler, who had received a thorough academic training either at home or abroad. All were his close contemporaries, friends or professional associates on decorative projects. Poynter became his brother-in-law in 1866.

For Burne-Jones, then, the mid-1860s were 'a self-absorbed time' in which he 'set himself hard to make up for lack of earlier training'.[20] Ruskin described him in 1867 as an artist whose pictures, for all their 'power and genius', were 'at first full of very visible faults, which he is gradually conquering'.[21] The truth of these comments is vividly illustrated by the Birmingham collection. One of its outstanding features is the long sequences of studies for works of this period: *The Lament*, *The Hours*, *The Fates*, the St George Series, *St Theophilus and the Angel*, *The Wine of Circe* and others. These drawings vary considerably in quality, but this only makes them more revealing as an exercise in self-improvement. Some are not connected with paintings at all but are independent studies of nudes, heads and drapery. Among the most interesting of the female nudes are a series 'made from a tall model who sat to G. F. Watts' (cat. 28, illus. p. 17).[22] Datable to 1865–67, the drawings must pinpoint the moment when Watts was most active in urging Burne-Jones to 'draw better'. Perhaps they were even made in his studio and under his guidance. The model is no doubt Mary Bartley, 'Long Mary', a housemaid at Little Holland House whose fine physique was celebrated by Watts in many of his more Junoesque nudes.

The drawings of the mid-1860s not only document Burne-Jones's progress as a draughtsman but say much about the stylistic trends of the time. By now the wheel was turning again; the Venetian mode was giving way to a restrained classicism shading into the Aesthetic ideal of 'art for art's sake', in which the emphasis was on abstract arrangements of form and colour at the expense of narrative or symbolic meaning. Burne-Jones never explored this approach as single-mindedly as some of his peers, but he could hardly ignore it in the mid-1860s and it sometimes had a dramatic effect on his pictures' development. *The Wine of Circe* (private collection), a major work conceived in 1863 but not finished and exhibited at the OWCS until 1869, is a key example. According to early sketches at Birmingham (B1122–B1123), the picture originally harked back to the medieval style, showing the sorceress in a claustrophobic interior with massive pieces of Gothic furniture and the sails of her victims' ships filling the window. However, a long series of later studies (B1124–B1132), albeit only for Circe herself, indicate major revisions; and indeed when the picture was eventually finished a transformation had occurred. Light flooded an elegantly appointed room, Circe had become a lithe, classically garbed figure, apparently inspired by the Charioteer from the Mausoleum at Halicarnassus (British Museum), and the chromatic scheme was a harmony in that most Aesthetic of colours, yellow. Appropriately, the picture was bought by Frederick Leyland, the Liverpool shipowner whose patronage did so much to drive the Aesthetic movement.

Circe, for all this, is still a narrative picture; *The Lament* (William Morris Gallery, Walthamstow) is a more thoroughgoing essay in the Aesthetic taste. Again a colour harmony, this time in pink and blue, it has no real subject, being rather an evocation of restrained emotion and mood. The composition is based on the groups of seated deities on the Parthenon frieze (British Museum). Many classical and Aesthetic painters were inspired by these reliefs, but it was characteristic of Burne-Jones, the ideal art-historian's artist, to leave a record of the process in terms of related drawings. First, he copied one of the gods, Ares (Mars), in a sketchbook now in the Victoria & Albert Museum; then, in two drawings at Birmingham, he connected this figure with that of the mourning girl on the right in the painting. One (presumably the earlier) shows her, like her Hellenic prototype, seated upright with her hands clasped on her knees (B463); in the other she bends forward, as she does in the picture, in a pose more expressive of grief (cat. 27, illus.

p. 17). So haunted was Burne-Jones at this period by these seated groups that variations often occur on sheets that bear only a tangential relationship to *The Lament* and have even less narrative content. Invariably executed in white chalk on brown paper, the studies are instantly reminiscent of Moore or Whistler, who both favoured this technique and were equally obsessed with the Parthenon-inspired motif of a group of seated figures. The Birmingham collection includes some fine examples of these interesting and somewhat neglected works (e.g. B332, 368).

But there was more to Burne-Jones's development in the 1860s than the sway of Aestheticism. Ruskin's reform programme had still not run its course. For reasons that lay deep in his private life and his passionate concern about social conditions, the critic had now evolved the concept of 'constant art', an art that moved and uplifted by means of profound symbolism and beautiful, serene forms. Art-historically he associated this with Italian painters active between 1470 and 1520, 'simply the Age of the Masters', as he called it;[23] and he hoped that Burne-Jones, with a little guidance from himself, would be a shining modern exponent. A number of the artist's works of the mid-1860s were meant to embody Ruskin's ideal. *The Wine of Circe* was originally one of them, starting life as a design he commissioned to illustrate *Munera Pulveris*, his controversial papers on political economy that had begun to appear in *Fraser's Magazine* in 1862. Another was a set of large designs for needlework representing the heroines of Chaucer's *Legend of Good Women*, a text in which he saw deep moral significance. Birmingham has an example, *Lucretia* (cat. 30, illus. p. 42), unusual in that, unlike the others, it has been worked up in watercolour and touched with gold. The collection also includes related designs for stained glass from the same period (B52–B63).

In 1864 Ruskin planned to take Burne-Jones to Italy again, their goal this time being Florence. The trip was cancelled due to the death of Ruskin's father, but had it taken place Burne-Jones would no doubt have found himself copying works from 'the Age of the Masters' at his host's instigation. As it was, copies of examples nearer home were soon littering his sketchbooks and finding reflections in his own drawings. A case in point at Birmingham is a group of studies for the Botticelli-like angel in *St Theophilus* (B1069–B1076). Significantly, this important picture, exhibited in 1867 and now destroyed, was another work in which Ruskin took a keen interest. A scene of early Christian martyrdom, it handled its subject with such discretion that Ruskin saw it as the epitome of socially beneficial 'constant' values, claiming that Burne-Jones had a 'special gift of ... seizing the good and disdaining evil'.[24]

The 1860s are indeed a complex period to chronicle. Artists were at the mercy of many powerful cross-currents before finally, like ships after a storm, sailing away on their appointed courses. Burne-Jones's drawings at Birmingham reflect this turmoil, exhibiting a wide variety of styles even within the context of studies for a single picture. But there is one group in which he seems effortlessly himself.

William Morris embarked on *The Earthly Paradise*, the book that was to make his name as a poet, in 1865, and the great narrative cycle was published between 1868 and 1870. Although ambitious plans for a lavishly illustrated edition eventually fell through, Burne-Jones made numerous designs for the project and Birmingham has the single largest holding: well over a hundred for 'The Story of Cupid and Psyche', the first poem to be tackled, smaller groups for 'The Hill of Venus', 'The Ring given to Venus' and 'Pygmalion and the Image'. Stylistically based on the anonymous woodcuts in Francesco Colonna's *Hypnerotomachia Poliphili*, first published in Venice in 1499, the drawings mirror in their sheer abundance the diffuseness of the book itself, rather as the early medieval drawings had found a parallel in *The Defence of Guenevere*. But there is a sense in which Burne-Jones is making these drawings not for the book's sake but for his own. They answer to his deepest needs as an artist, offering relief to a mind overburdened with compositional ideas, a vision that saw not in terms of some salient image into which the essence of a story is distilled, but a whole series of sequential frames laid out like a strip cartoon or the 'stills' of a film. In 1869 Charles Eliot Norton visited The Grange, Burne-Jones's house in Fulham, and saw 'literally hundreds' of drawings lying about or pasted into 'three or four enormous volumes filled with studies of every sort'. The artist's 'lively imagination', Norton observed, 'is continually designing more than he can execute. His fancy creates a hundred pictures for one that his hand can paint. It keeps him awake night after night.'[25] Norton was in exactly the same position as those schoolboys who, years before, had marvelled at their friend's ability to 'cover a sheet of foolscap' with figures 'almost as quickly as one could have written'.

The *Earthly Paradise* designs, many of which would later serve as the basis for easel pictures, are not the only aspect of Burne-Jones's work that resulted from a hyperactive imagination and a passion for drawing. To the same urgent needs we can attribute his caricatures and humorous or whimsical drawings for children, and also to some extent his sketchbooks. It is true that many of these were used for working drawings, testing ideas or defining forms for pictures; the two at Birmingham containing studies for the Perseus Series (cat. 45, 47, illus. p. 23) are of this type. But there are others in which the drawings take off into a world of their own and seem to be made for the sheer joy of wielding a pencil. An example is the little volume taken on holiday in the Haute-Savoie in 1878, and later filled up with drawings of birds copied from a Japanese screen (cat. 48, illus. p. 80). Neither set of studies was useless as raw material for pictures, but neither was top priority either. Much the same goes for the magnificent sketchbook devoted to Byzantine and Romanesque decoration (cat. 57, illus. p. 13). The drawings have an obvious relevance to such works of the period as *Arthur in Avalon* and the Holy Grail tapestries, but Burne-Jones must have known that in practical terms he would need only a tithe of the images. The rest are *jeux d'esprit*; he could not resist committing one more picturesque costume, one more intriguing architectural detail, to paper.

There is even an element of self-indulgence about Burne-Jones's stained-glass cartoons, of which about 130, together with numerous preparatory studies, are in the collection. For many years designing stained glass was his bread-and-butter work. Moreover, his astonishing powers of invention and strong sense of design made him of far greater use to Morris than either Rossetti or Madox Brown. Indeed after 1875, when the original partnership was dissolved, he became entirely responsible for the firm's stained-glass designs. A. C. Sewter calculated that between 1872 and 1878 he drew more than 270 cartoons, an average of 39 a year or approximately one every eight-and-a-half days.[26] But it was more than economic necessity or loyalty to Morris that kept him turning out cartoons until the end of his life. What other successful Victorian artist would have continued to involve himself in such comparatively humble work? True, a rare commission like the four enormous windows in Birmingham Cathedral could be seen as a chance to carry out the large-scale 'public work' for which he yearned, but essentially stained glass just provided one more irresistible opportunity to invent and draw. It was almost like a drug he could not give up. Those frequent complaints in his account book with Morris, whether about irksome, repetitious subjects or indifferent pay, should always be taken with a substantial pinch of salt.

Of all the influences shaping Burne-Jones's development in the 1860s, the one that ultimately proved most formative was his increasingly warm response to the Italian Renaissance. Although Ruskin had done much to encourage his ardour in its early stages, it was to lead to a temporary estrangement between them in 1871 when they fell out over their respective estimates of Michelangelo. An indication of where Burne-Jones stood by 1870 is provided by the well-known *Phyllis and Demophoön* (cat. 38, illus. p. 22), with its entwined figures apparently echoing those of Zephyr and Chloris in Botticelli's *Primavera*. More significant still is his conception that year of the never-to-be-completed Troy Triptych, a secular Renaissance polyptych in which ten mythological and allegorical compositions were to be set in an elaborate architectural frame replete with pilasters, Corinthian columns, numerous putti in free-standing bronze or marble relief, and foliage, drapery and 'chaplets of jewels' festooned above 'in the Crivelli manner'.[27] Two visits to Italy followed in 1871 and 1873, the last he was to make, and the emphasis, far from being on Venice as in 1862, was on Florence, Siena and Rome. 'I belong to Old Florence', he declared after the 1871 journey, '(Italy is) my native country'.[28]

Burne-Jones's work was never more Italianate than in the early 1870s, and the trend is nowhere more apparent than in his drawings. Gone are the soft pencil and red or white chalk he had favoured in the 1860s, to be replaced by a hard pencil suited to exploring the musculature of Michelangelesque nudes or the serpentine rhythms of wind-blown Botticellian hair. Birmingham has many fine examples for pictures of this time: *The Bath of Venus* (B13), *The Days of Creation* (B258), the Pygmalion Series (B589–B590, B592), the Perseus Series (cat. 45, 47, illus. p. 23; B552–B553), and *The Feast of Peleus*, a subject planned for the Troy Triptych but eventually treated as an independent work (B298–B299). Sometimes the Florentine nature of the drawings is underlined by a specific comparison. Malcolm Bell, Burne-Jones's first biographer, related two exquisite illustrations to the *Song of Solomon* (B803–B804), all delicate outlines and linear arabesques, to late fifteenth-century Florentine engravings; and since Bell was a sort of nephew-by-marriage, his comments almost certainly echo conversations with the artist himself.[29] All these drawings

RIGHT: **Studies of a seated Female nude, 1865–67 (cat. 28)**

BELOW: **Two nude Studies for *The Lament*, 1865 (cat. 26)**

BELOW RIGHT: **Study of a crouched female Figure for *The Lament*, 1865 (cat. 27)**

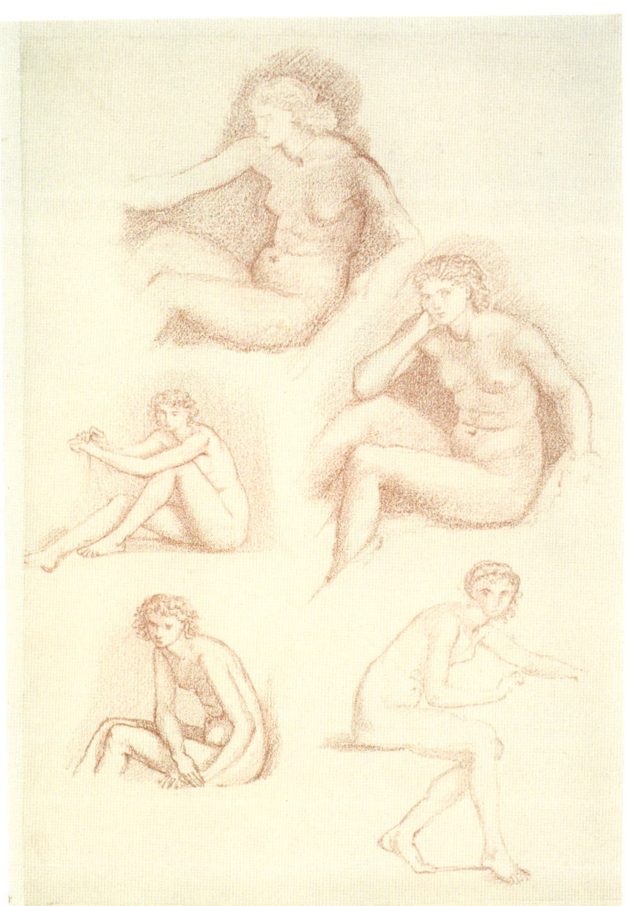

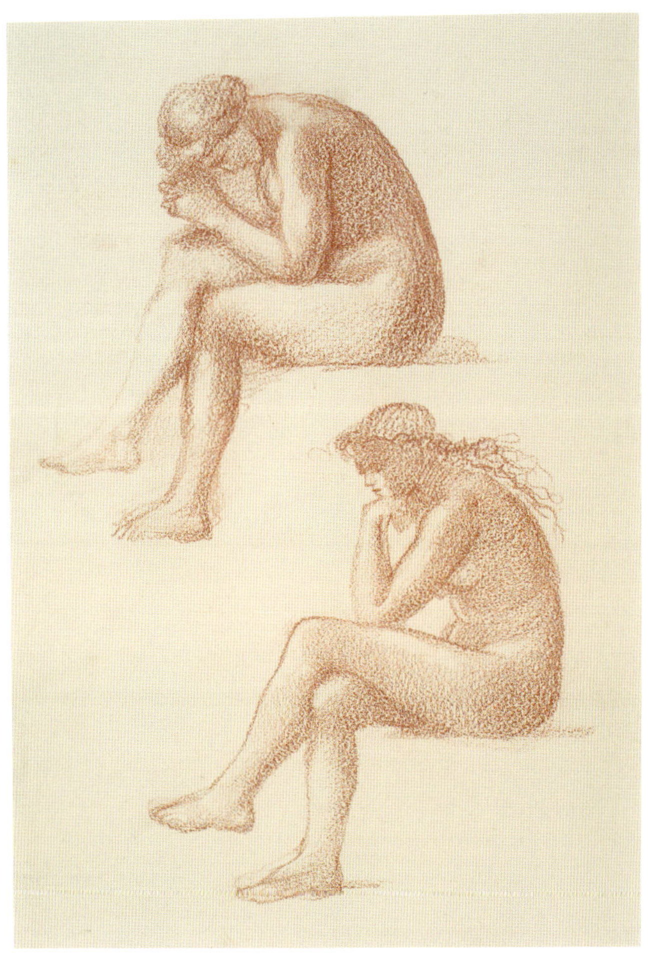

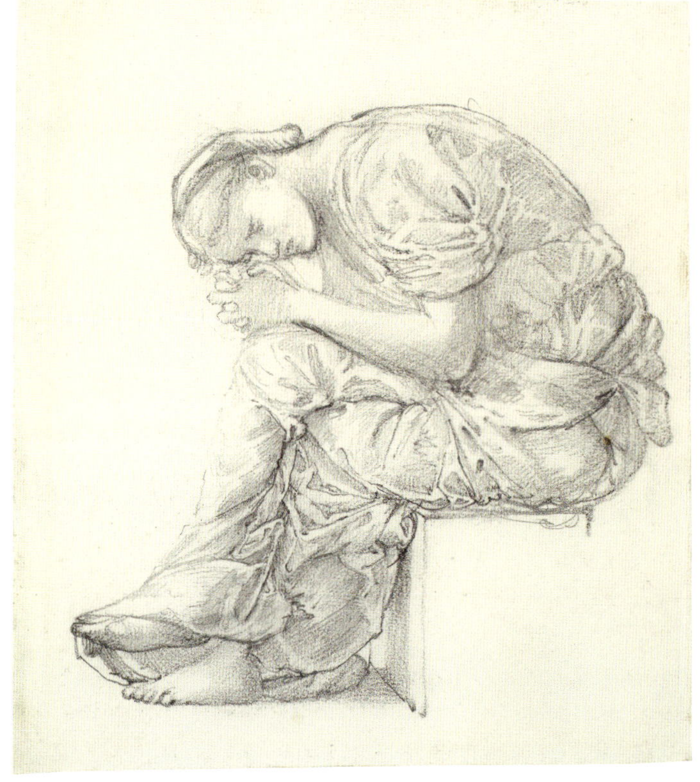

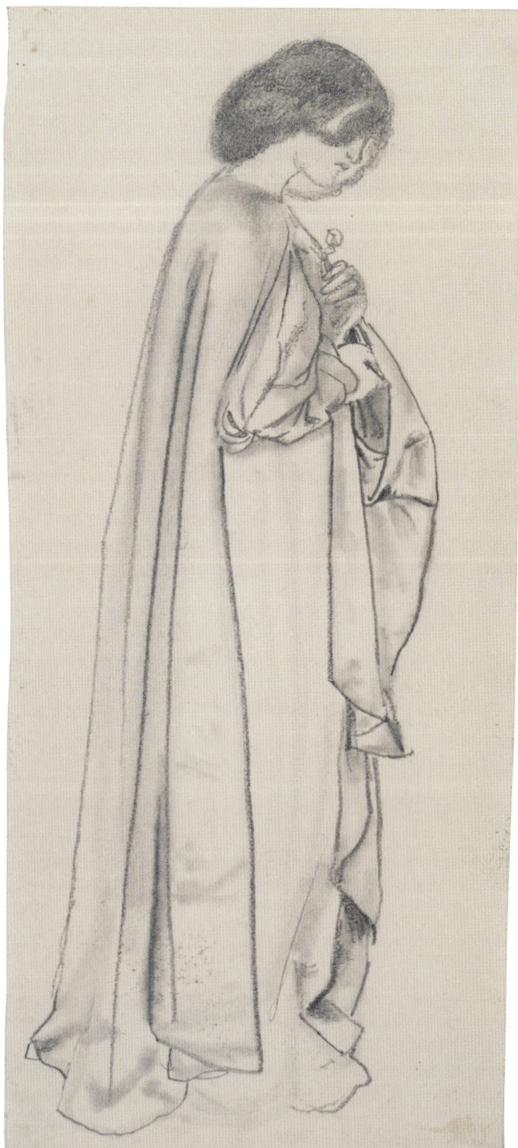

LEFT: *The Annunciation*: Study for the Virgin, 1859–61 (cat. 2)

BELOW: *The Annunciation*, 1859–61 (cat. 3)

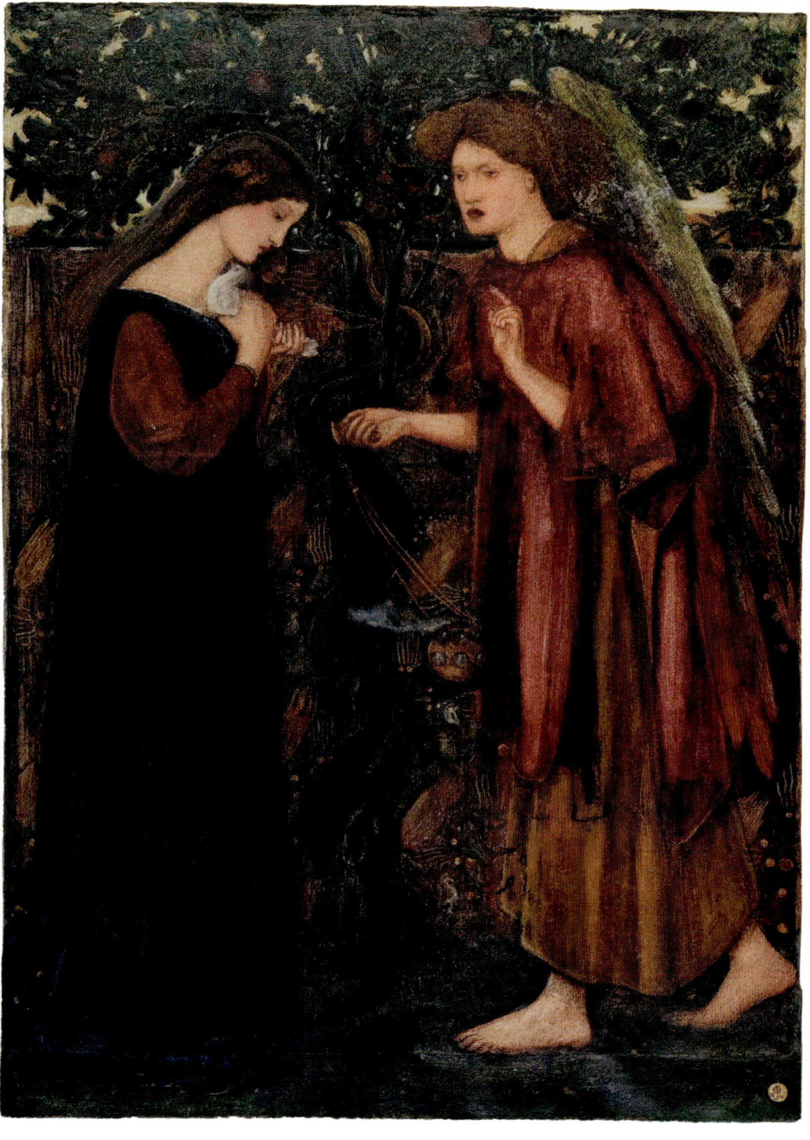

RIGHT: *The Star of Bethlehem*, 1887, 1888–91 (cat. 56)

BELOW: *The Flower Book*: *Star of Bethlehem*, pub. 1905 (cat. 62)

BELOW RIGHT: *The Star of Bethlehem*: Study for the Angel's Head, 1886–90 (cat. 55)

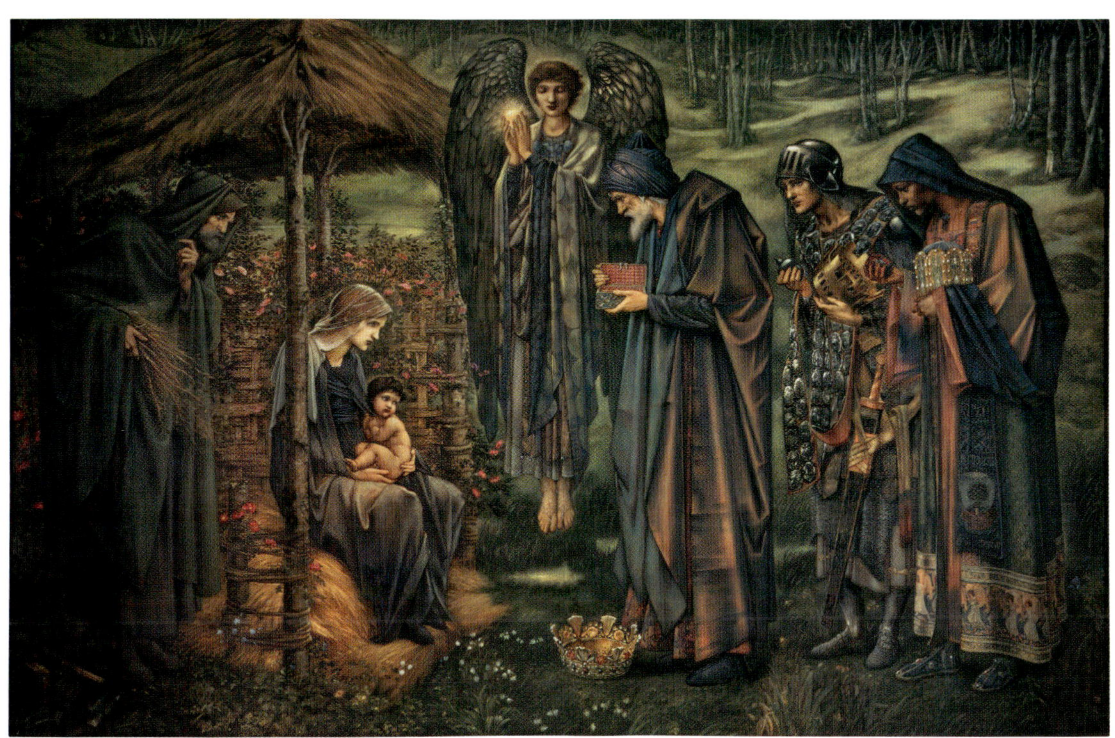

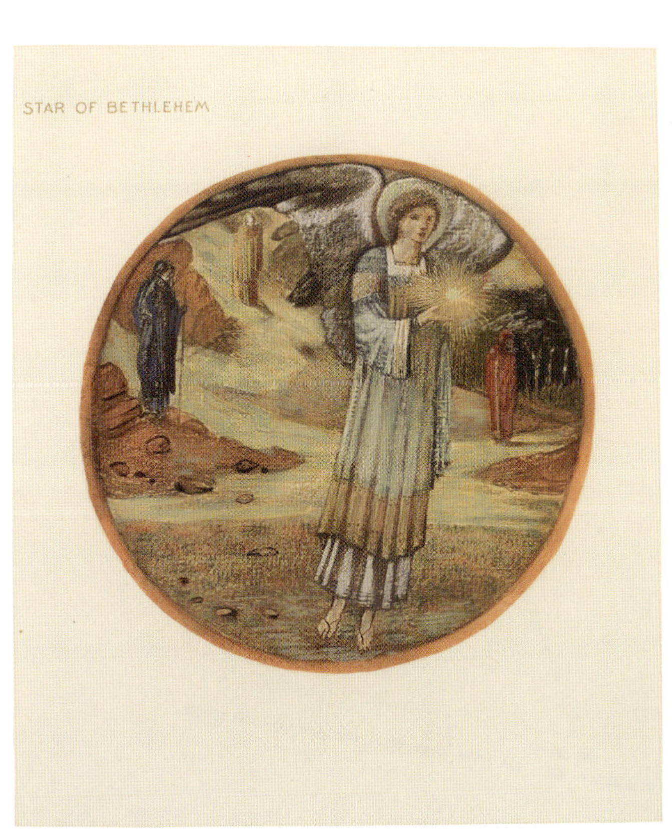

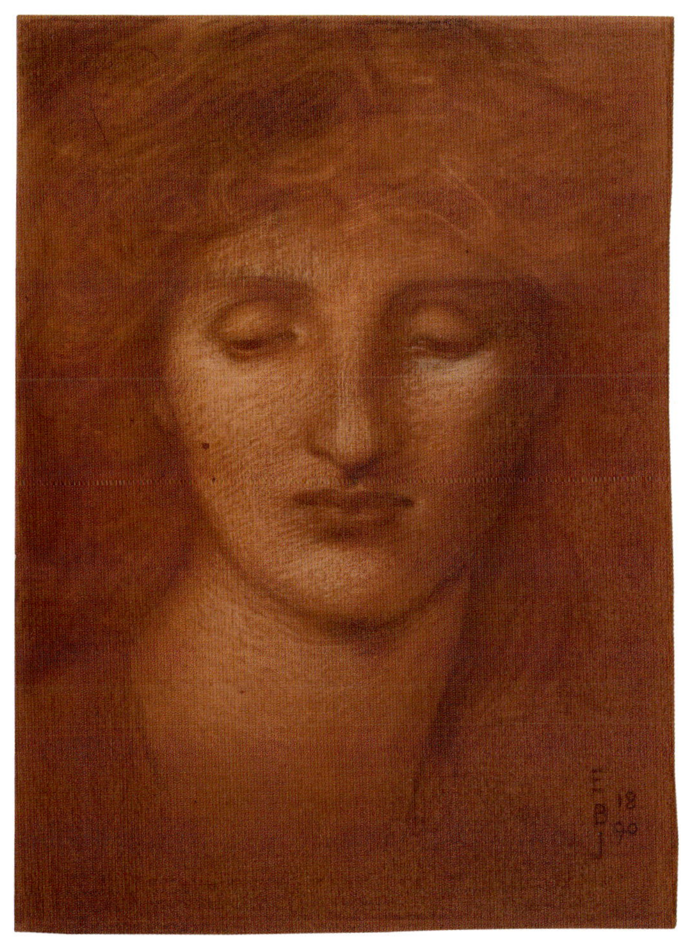

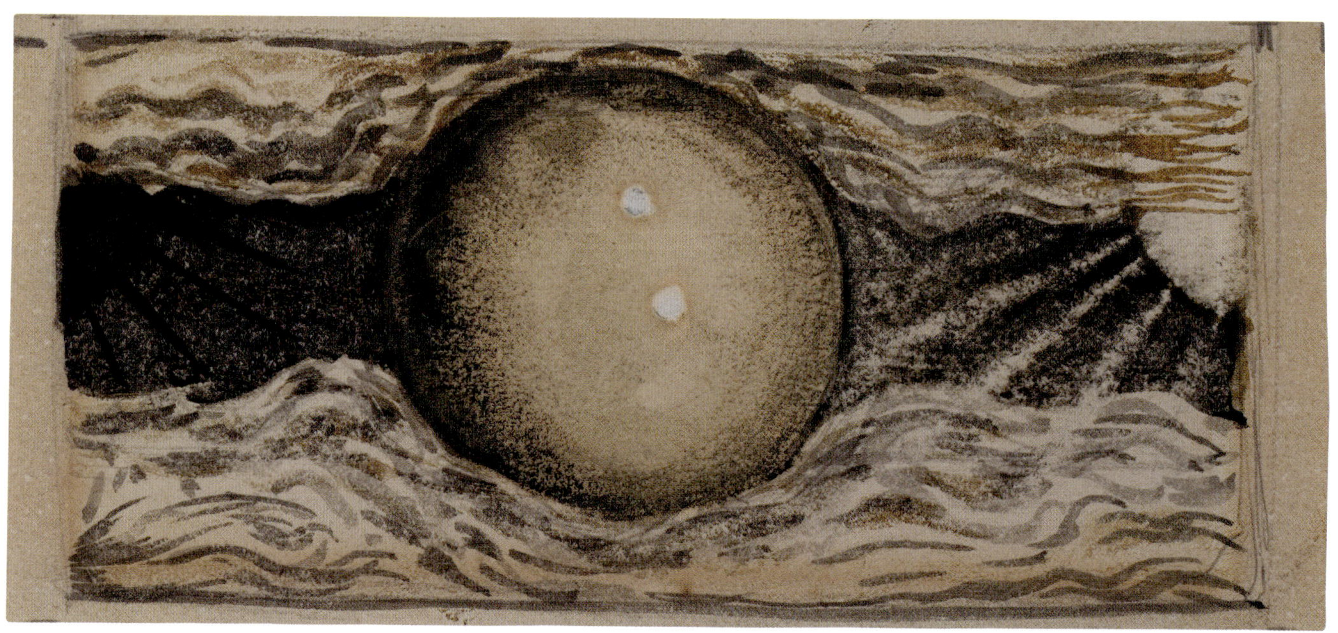

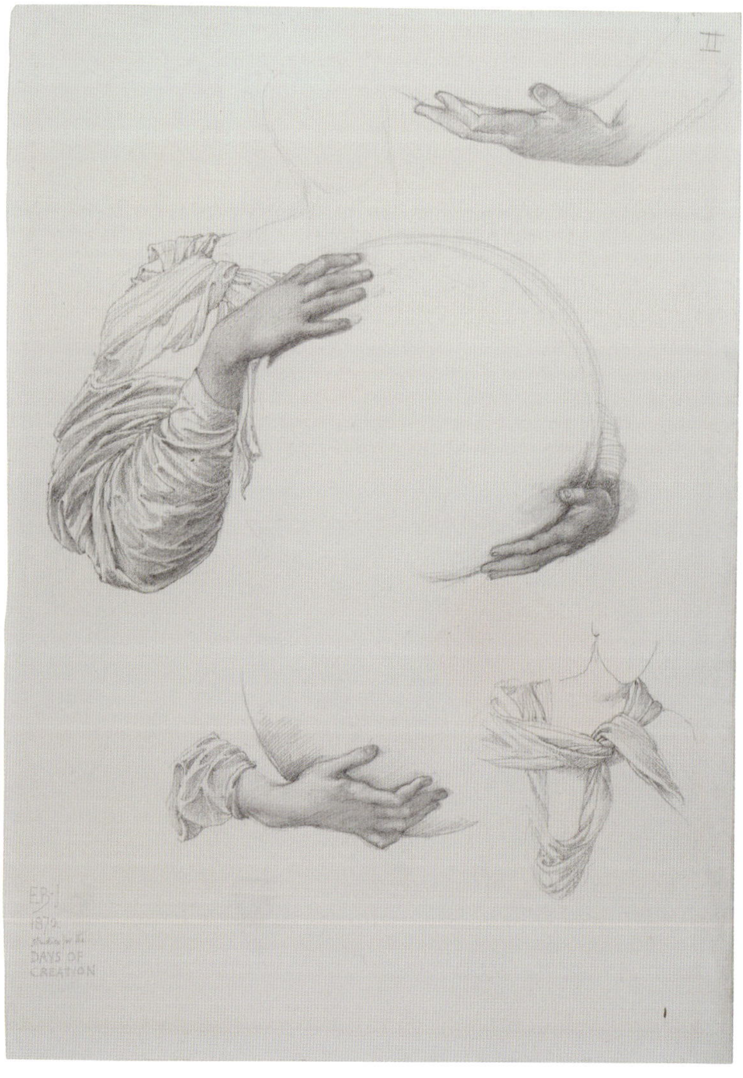

ABOVE: *The Days of Creation: The Second Day*, 1863 (cat. 16)

LEFT: *The Days of Creation*: Study of Hands and Globe for 'The Second Day', 1872 (cat. 39)

BELOW: Stained Glass Design: *The Song of Solomon – 'I charge you, O Daughters of Jerusalem'*, 1862–63 (cat. 14)

RIGHT: *The Song of Solomon: 'Who is it that cometh out of the Wilderness?'*, 1875–76 (cat. 46)

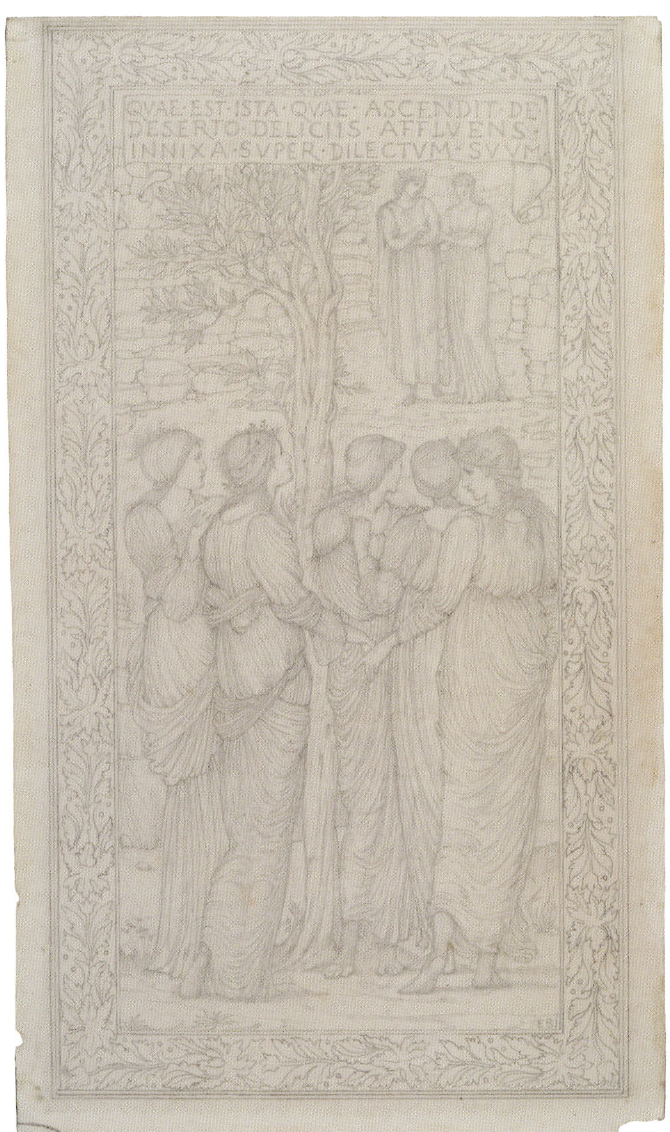

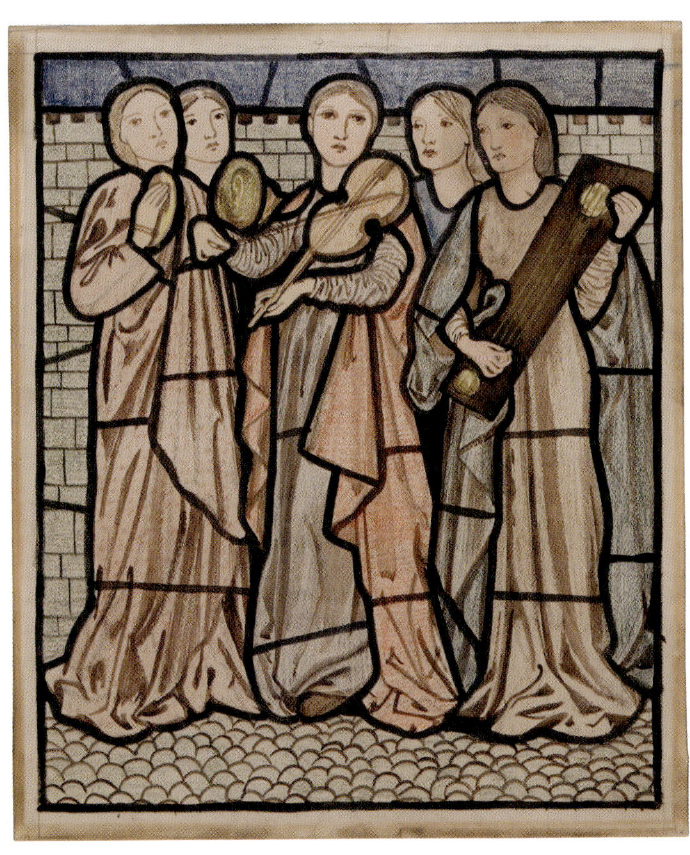

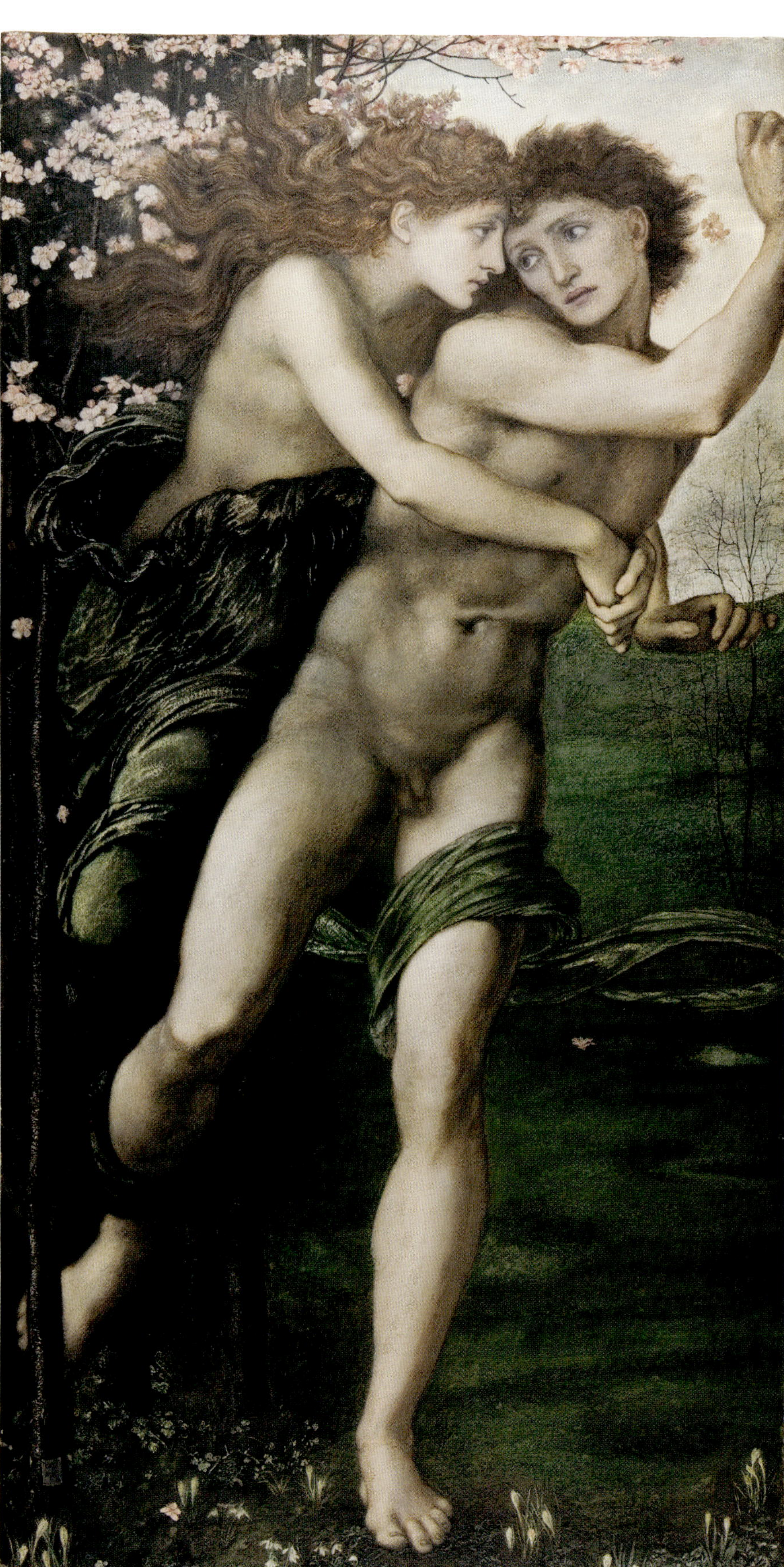

Phyllis and Demophoön, 1870 (cat. 38)

OPPOSITE PAGE

ABOVE LEFT: Stained Glass Design: Two nude Studies for *The Stoning of St Stephen*, 1863 (cat. 18)

ABOVE RIGHT: Study of a Man embracing a Tree, 1868–69 (cat. 35)

BELOW LEFT: Sketchbook: Study of Atlas in *Atlas turned to Stone,* 1875 (cat. 45)

BELOW RIGHT: Sketchbook: Nude Study from Cast for The Perseus Series, 1875–79 (cat. 47)

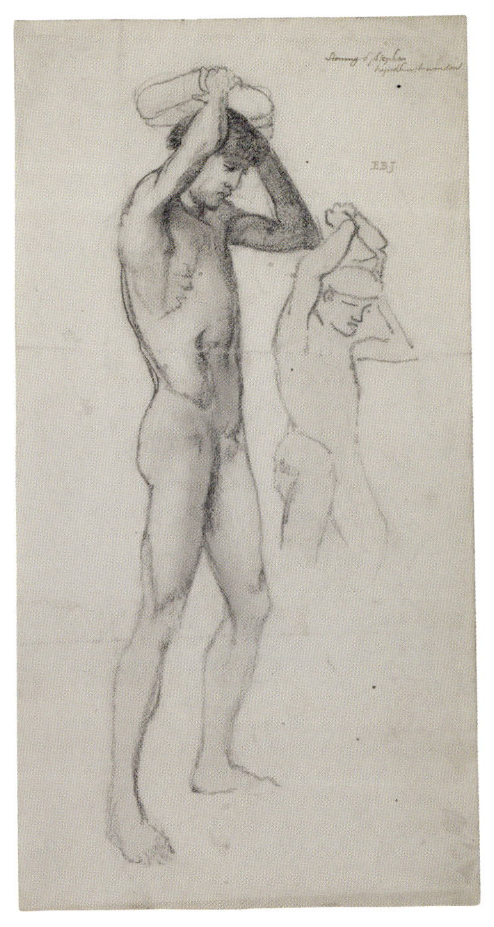

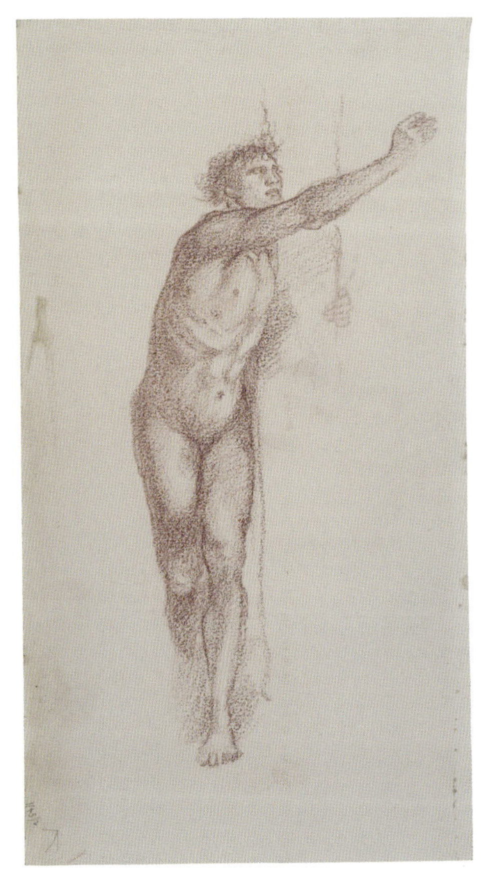

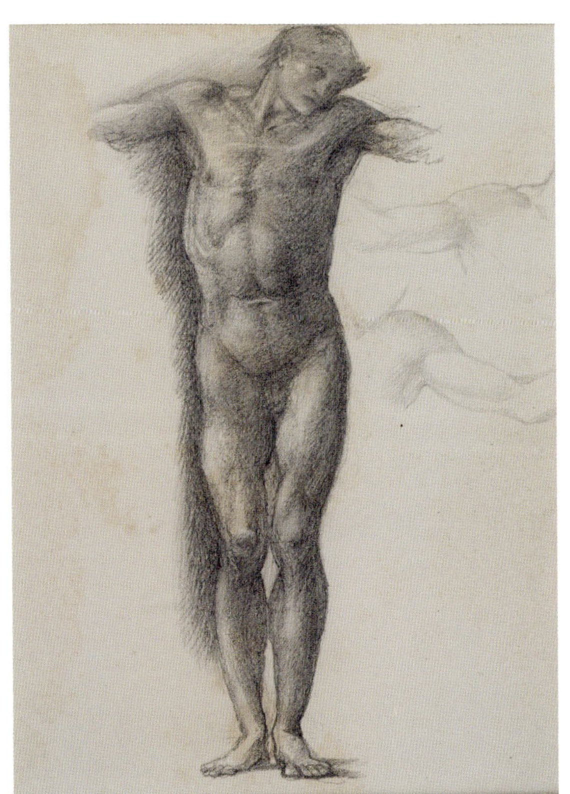

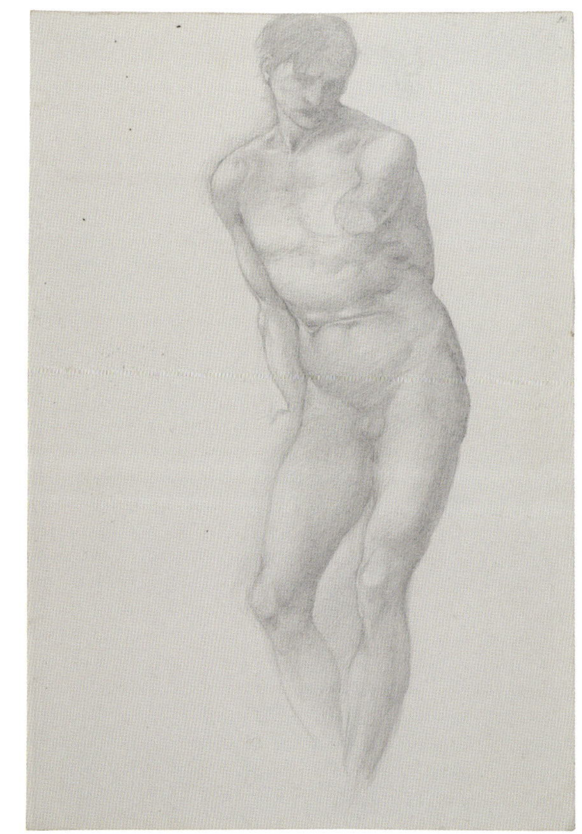

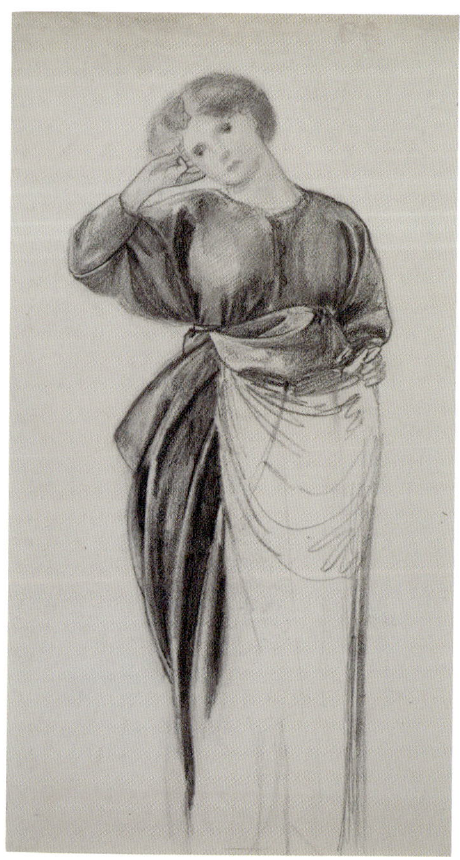

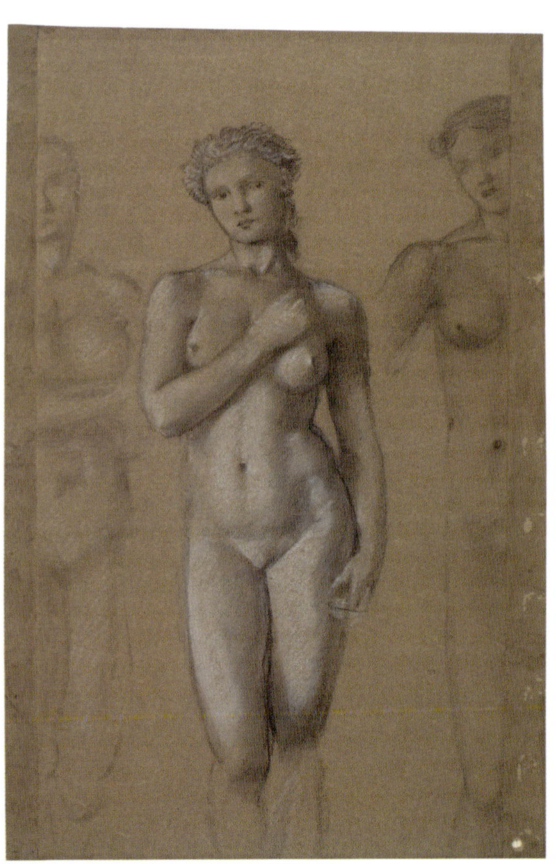

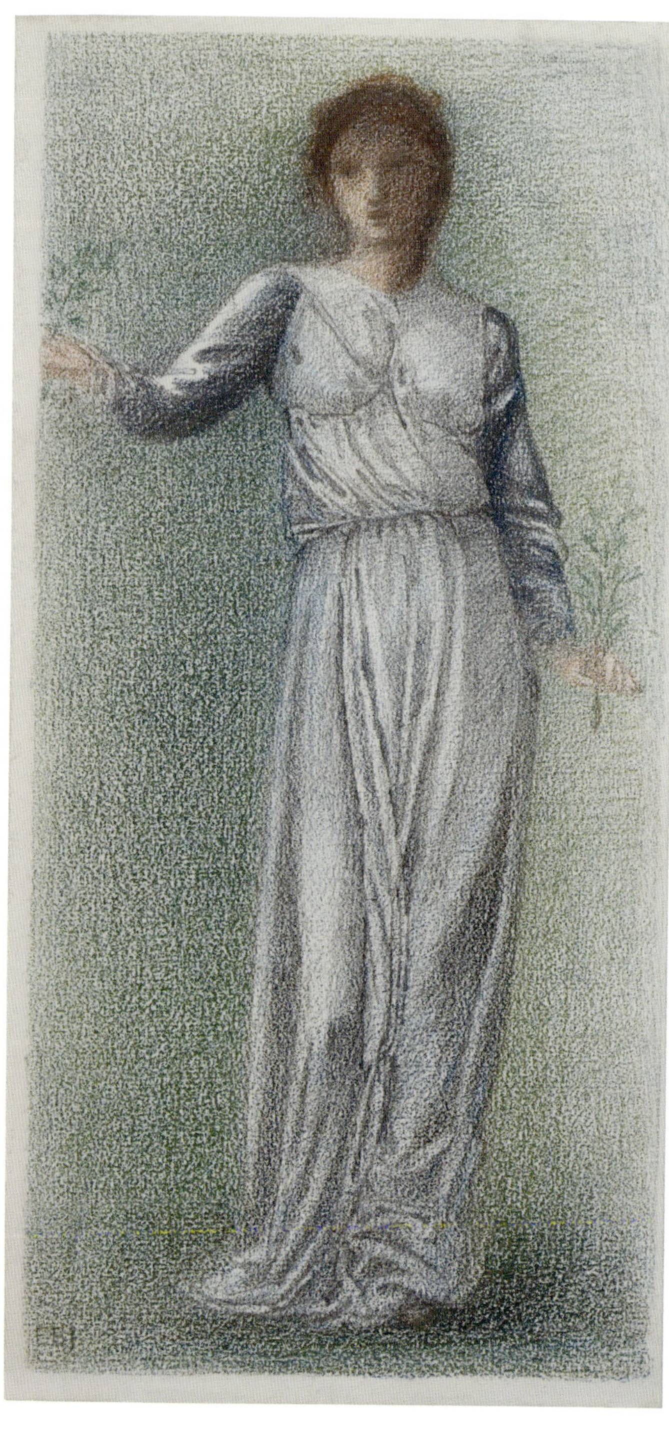

LEFT: Study of *Cinderella,* 1862–63 (cat. 13)

BELOW LEFT: Female Nude: Three Studies, 1865–66 (cat. 25)

BELOW: Full-length Study for *The Garland Weavers,* 1862–66 (cat. 12)

are on stiff white paper, colour being eschewed in this bracing world of formal probity and rigour. But occasionally Burne-Jones would resort to pencil and bodycolour on a toned ground, in the manner of silverpoint drawings by Botticelli or Filippino Lippi – the kind of drawings that his friend A. C. Swinburne had enthused about in his article 'Notes on Designs of the Old Masters at Florence', published in the *Fortnightly Review* in July 1868. Three studies on green grounds for *The Passing of Venus* (B549–B551) represent this notion here.

Phyllis and Demophoön was the last picture Burne-Jones showed at the OWCS. When objections were raised to the male nude, he withdrew the work, waited until the exhibition ended, and then resigned. During the next seven years he rarely exhibited, relying on the support of loyal patrons, but in 1877 a momentous event occurred. The Grosvenor Gallery opened in Bond Street as a liberal alternative to the Royal Academy, a showcase for all that was deemed most adventurous in modern British art and (to mix metaphors) a flagship for the Aesthetic movement.

Burne-Jones showed eight large works and this dramatic revelation of his mature powers caused a sensation. Overnight he was famous, the undisputed star of the Grosvenor and one of the most controversial and talked-about artists of the day. His reputation was sustained by a series of large canvases shown every year at the Grosvenor until 1887 and thereafter at its successor, the New Gallery in Regent Street. Or almost every year: nothing appeared in 1881, causing Henry James to observe that 'a Grosvenor without Mr Burne-Jones is a *Hamlet* with Hamlet left out'.[30] No picture made a greater impact than *King Cophetua and the Beggar Maid* (Tate, London), exhibited in 1884. It was, declared *The Times*, by no means always so friendly in the past, 'not only the finest work that Mr Burne-Jones has ever painted, but … one of the finest pictures ever painted by an Englishman'.[31] *Cophetua* was to score another great success when it was shown at the Exposition Universelle in Paris in 1889. A vogue for Burne-Jones in the French capital lasted well into the 1890s.

Although Burne-Jones's career was at its zenith in the 1880s, his drawing style became less coherent and focused than it had been in the previous decade. That he was still a master of line and capable of great delicacy is evident from *The Rape of Proserpine*, a composition drawing made for Ruskin in 1883 (B593).[32] But his linear sense, once so Botticellian, now tended to derive from the Byzantine sources he was studying in connection with the mosaics in the American Church in Rome, an enormous commission he received in 1881 and worked on for many years. His drawing also lost some lightness of touch, becoming more ponderous and mannered. Good examples at Birmingham are the six cartoons representing Norse gods and heroes executed in 1883 for stained glass in a house at Newport, Rhode Island (B881, B894, B903, B915, B970, B971). It is part of the same development that fine pencil often gives way to a rather florid use of chalks on coloured paper. Some studies for *King Cophetua*, including the full-scale cartoon, are in this idiom (cat. 53 and 54, illus. p. 30; B447).

In 1886 Henry James described Burne-Jones's work as 'growing colder and colder – pictured abstractions, less and less observed'.[33] In 1890 the artist enjoyed a last great triumph when the *Briar Rose* paintings (Faringdon Collection, Buscot Park, Oxfordshire) were exhibited to rapturous acclaim at Agnew's, but from then on his star waned and by 1896 he was admitting to his assistant T. M. Rooke that 'the rage' for him was 'over'.[34] Alienated and out of sympathy with prevailing trends, he retreated into himself, exploring a personal vision that made few concessions to popular taste and letting mannerism and abstraction have their head. In one form or another the phenomenon is common to many elderly artists, including his own hero Michelangelo. It is well known to psychologists, who identify it as the 'third period' in a creative life.[35]

Birmingham has little from this final phase apart from two studies for pictures, *The Sirens* (cat. 59, illus. p. 41) and *Venus Concordia* (B1117), which were still on the easel when Burne-Jones died suddenly in June 1898. In a sense, however, it hardly needs more when it possesses one of his greatest works from only a few years earlier. *The Star of Bethlehem* (cat. 56, illus. p. 19) was painted expressly for the new Art Gallery in 1888–91, and the artist must have been acutely aware of certain obligations: to create a worthy memorial to himself in his native city; to provide an example to local artists, many of whom, the so-called Birmingham Group, were looking to him for leadership; and to make some statement of permanent value to the citizens in general. No-one could say that he failed to meet this challenge. Vast in scale and technically truly astonishing, the picture has the intensely private quality that is so characteristic of his late work. A sort of Arthurian account of the Incarnation, imbued with a brooding mysticism, it leaves no room for doubt that the artist is baring

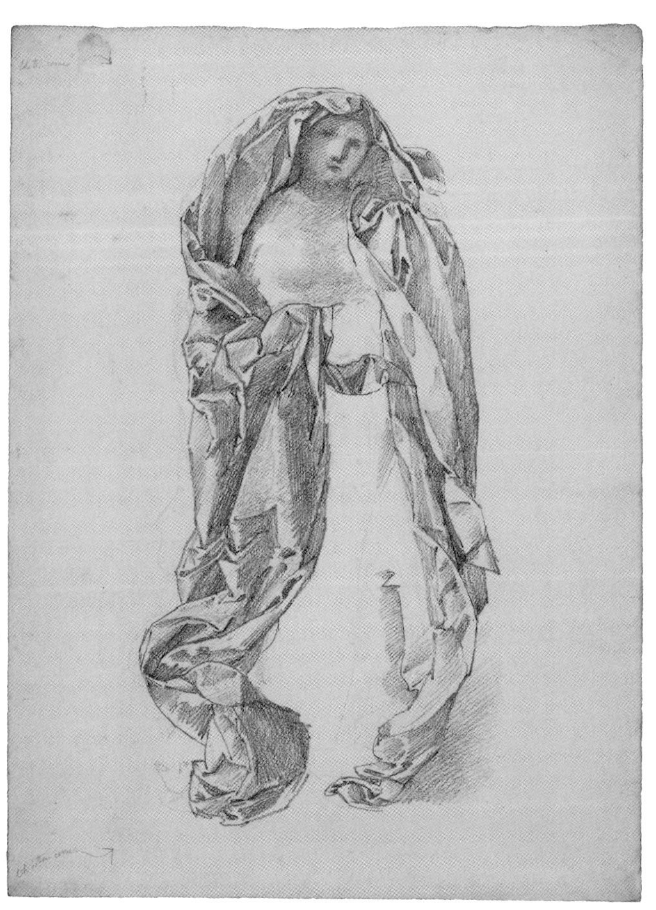

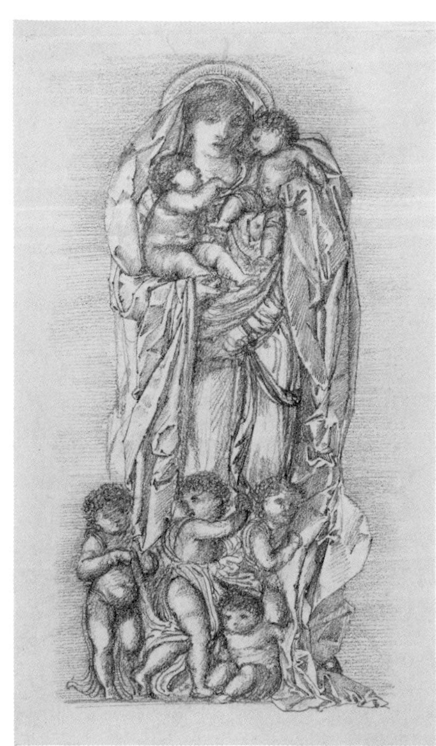

FAR LEFT: Study of Drapery for *Charity*, 1867 (cat. 31)

LEFT: Composition Study for *Charity*, 1867 (cat. 32)

BELOW LEFT: Small Composition Studies for *Charity*, 1870 (cat. 37)

BELOW: *Charity/ Caritas*, pub. 1900 (cat. 61)

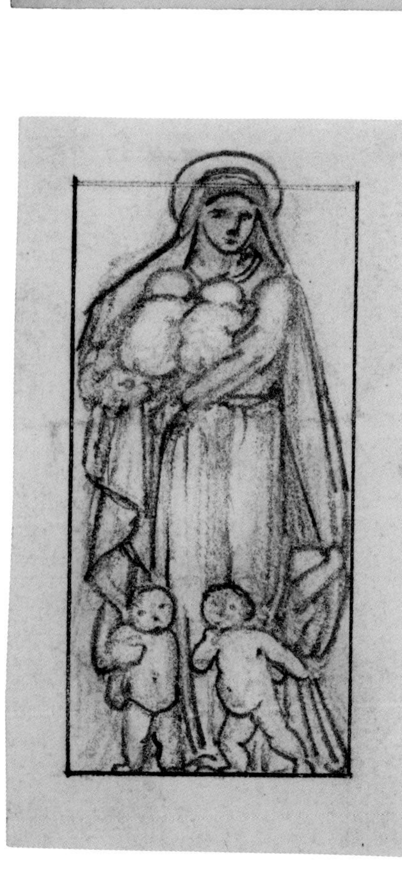

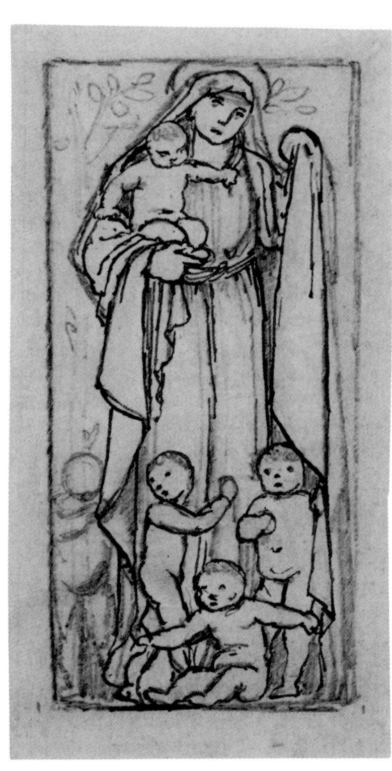

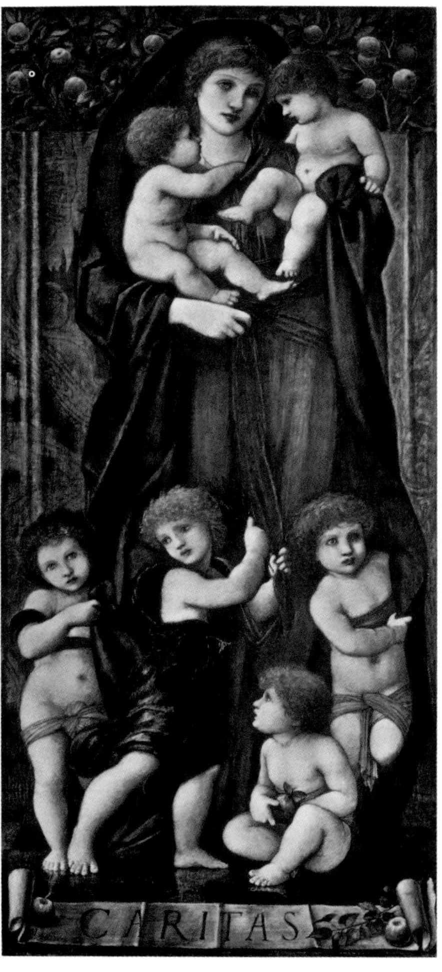

his soul and seeking to touch the heart. It is said to have so moved Bernard Sleigh, one of his avowed followers, that he would lay a floral tribute beneath it on Burne-Jones's birthday (28 August). But if this is a private vision, it has a very public, not to say subversive, purpose; for how else are we to characterize placing so prominently in a centre of capitalism and free enterprise an unforgettable image of the abasement of wealth and power before a higher reality? In this act of silent but surely deliberate bravado, all too typical of the man, Burne-Jones sums up his deepest beliefs and gives enduring expression to the Ruskinian concept of aesthetic prophecy.

1. W. Graham Robertson, *Time Was* (London, Hamish Hamilton, 1931), p. 84.
2. Ibid., p. 82.
3. Ibid.
4. Georgiana Burne-Jones, *Memorials of Edward Burne-Jones* (London, Macmillan, 1904), II, p. 13.
5. Ibid., I, p. 18.
6. Ibid., I, pp. 10, 16.
7. Ibid., I, pp. 8, 38.
8. Ibid., I, p. 44.
9. Ibid., I, p. 57.
10. Mary Lago, ed., *Burne-Jones Talking* (London, John Murray, 1982), p. 155.
11. *Memorials*, I, p. 48.
12. John L. Sweeney, ed., *The Painter's Eye: Notes and Essays on the Pictorial Arts by Henry James* (London, Rupert Hart-Davis, 1956), p. 145.
13. *Memorials*, I, p.110.
14. All the drawings are reproduced in an edition of the book published by the Dalrymple Press, London, in 1985.
15. Oswald Doughty and J. R. Wahl, eds, *Letters of Dante Gabriel Rossetti* (Oxford, Clarendon Press, 1965–67), I, p. 319.
16. *Memorials*, I, p. 262.
17. J. Comyns Carr, *Some Eminent Victorians* (London, Duckworth, 1908), p. 72.
18. *Memorials*, II, p. 294.
19. *Art Journal* (1864), p. 173, and *The Times*, 25 April 1864, p. 14.
20. *Memorials*, I, p. 286.
21. E. T. Cook and Alexander Wedderburn, eds, *The Works of John Ruskin: Library Edition* (London, George Allen, 1903–12), XIX, p. 206.
22. A. E. Whitley, *City of Birmingham Museum & Art Gallery, Catalogue of the Permanent Collection of Drawings in Pen, Pencil, Charcoal and Chalk, etc., including Cartoons for Stained Glass* (Derby, Bemrose & Sons, 1939), p. 106 under acc. no. 48'04.
23. Cook and Wedderburn, eds, *Works* (1903–12), XIX, p. 443.
24. Ibid., p. 208.
25. Sara Norton and M. A. DeWolfe Howe, eds, *Letters of Charles Eliot Norton* (London, Constable, 1913), I, p. 346.
26. A. C. Sewter, *The Stained Glass of William Morris and his Circle* (New Haven, Yale University Press, 1974–75), I, p. 46.
27. *City of Birmingham Art Gallery: Catalogue of the Permanent Collection of Paintings in Oil…* (Birmingham, 1930), p. 31. A full-scale oil sketch for the Triptych, largely by assistants, is in the Birmingham collection.
28. *Memorials*, II, p. 23.
29. Malcolm Bell, *Edward Burne-Jones: A Record and Review* (London, George Bell, 1892), p. 102. Bell was the nephew of Edward Poynter, who was Burne-Jones's brother-in-law.
30. Sweeney, ed., *The Painter's Eye*, p. 205.
31. *The Times*, 1 May 1884, p. 6.
32. A painting of this subject was commissioned by Ruskin, but this drawing did not actually belong to him. He owned another version, now in the Montréal Museum of Fine Arts; see *The Earthly Paradise*, exh. cat., Art Gallery of Ontario, Toronto (1993), pp. 88–91, no. A:39 (illustrated).
33. Percy Lubbock, ed., *The Letters of Henry James* (London, Macmillan, 1920), I, p. 126.
34. Rooke's notes of conversation with Burne-Jones (typescript), National Art Library, Victoria & Albert Museum, London.
35. See Anthony Storr, *The School of Genius* (London, André Deutsch, 1988), chap. 11.

Models, Muses and Burne-Jones's Continuous Quest for the Ideal Female Face

ELISA KORB

Burne-Jones began his search for the ideal female image almost from infancy. Six days after he was born on 28 August 1833, his mother, Elizabeth Coley Jones, died. The family retained one image of the deceased, an ivory miniature, which was accidentally destroyed by Burne-Jones as a very young child.[1] From a Freudian perspective, the maternal figure represents the female archetype against which all other women are measured, and is usually forged during a child's formative years.[2] As a result of Burne-Jones's lack of a mother, and also of a visual representation of her, he had no fundamental standard of feminine beauty. Whether one subscribes to this argument or not, Burne-Jones certainly utilised a series of women who not only inspired and influenced his art but, in some instances, acted as replacements for that which was lost.[3]

The first visually documented muse came in the form of a Methodist minister's daughter, Georgiana Macdonald, whom he became acquainted with through her brother Harry, a schoolmate in Birmingham.[4] The boys remained friendly throughout the years, and by 1856 Burne-Jones was dining with the family when they relocated to London. He had recently decided to become an artist, but was still matriculated at Oxford, and practised drawing and sketching Georgiana and her sisters, Agnes, Alice and Louisa, after dinner.[5] Gradually he fell in love with Georgiana and proposed marriage after a three-week courtship.[6] Several caricatures are extant that show the young Burne-Jones, adoringly portraying the young girl.[7]

His first major work on paper dates from this time: *The Waxen Image* (1856, destroyed or lost; no reproductions exist), executed in pen and ink. Although he had been making numerous studies of Georgiana at the time,[8] it was actually her thirteen-year-old sister Agnes who sat for *The Waxen Image*'s central figure.[9] Several other finished pen-and-ink drawings were completed in the next two years, all featuring either Georgiana or her sisters:[10] both *The Knight's Farewell* (1858, Ashmolean Museum, Oxford) and *Going to the Battle* (1858, Fitzwilliam Museum, Cambridge) were modelled on Agnes, while *The King's Daughters* (1858, Private Collection), *Buondelmonte's Wedding* (1859, Fitzwilliam Museum), *The Wise and Foolish Virgins* (1859, Private Collection) and *Ladies and Death* (1860, National Gallery of Victoria, Melbourne) had figures modelled on each of them.[11] When Burne-Jones's first painting commission came in early 1857, *The Blessed Damozel* (1860, Fogg Art Museum, Harvard University), he enlisted Georgiana alone to model.[12]

It was Georgiana's distinct features that repeatedly reoccur in paintings and drawings of the early to mid-1860s: a small oval face with pointy chin, small lips, serene eyes and generally youthful appearance. Burne-Jones tried to capture the innocence of his teenaged fiancée, engaging her to model whenever he could,[13] sometimes depicting her as the Virgin herself, as in *The Annunciation*, begun in 1859 (B6). The composition may have been started as early as 1857, and an early figure study, most likely for this painting, was modelled on Jane Burden (B5), William Morris's future wife. When the painting was completed in about 1861, the Virgin's face was that of Georgiana, now his wife.

Between 1861 and 1863 Burne-Jones also used Dante Gabriel Rossetti's mistress, Fanny Cornforth, as the model for many of his major works, including the watercolour version of *The Backgammon Players* (B10).[14] Yet it was still Georgiana who was his primary source of female inspiration, and who in 1861 bore their first child, a son, Philip. Burne-Jones celebrated his wife in his first attempt at formal portraiture in 1863 (B412), an awkward picture composed of bodycolour on paper. While the resemblance to the sitter is clear, the painting lacks the colour harmonisation that

Burne-Jones was becoming known for at this time, using the new Aesthetic sensibility. The figure is so stiff and awkward, that not only compositionally, but technically, it owes a debt to the limner-style painters of the English Royal Courts from the fifteenth and early sixteenth centuries. It is so unlike the many other contemporary images Burne-Jones was painting of Georgiana, such as *The Rose Garden* (1862, Private Collection; for studies, see B597–B598), which use a light colour scheme, often with a clearly delineated background.

Around the time Burne-Jones was working on his portrait of Georgiana, he began to hire professional models more frequently. Many of these models sat for other artists in Burne-Jones's circle of friends, such as Rossetti, Simeon Solomon and George Frederic Watts. These women came not only from diverse ethnic backgrounds but also socio-economic classes.[15] There was the Italian beauty Antonia Caiva,[16] a German named Norma,[17] and English girls like Miss Silver, a dancer known as Reserva, a waitress called Ellen Smith, and Mrs Keene with her daughter Bessie.[18] Of the paid models, however, the favourite seems to have been a pretty English girl with a Grecian profile, Augusta Jones, for whom Burne-Jones had 'much regard and respect'.[19] He created a stunning drawing in red-brown chalk of her (cat. 24, illus. p. 41), possibly in preparation for the 1865 body-colour painting *Astrologia* (Private Collection), of which she is the sole figure. She was also *Lucretia* (cat. 30, illus. p. 42), a watercolour probably worked-up from a stained glass cartoon, based on one of Chaucer's heroines from his *Legend of Good Women* (see B70 for the story in The Kelmscott Chaucer). In August 1867 this was given as a wedding gift to John Ruskin's secretary, Charles Augustus Howell.[20]

In 1866 Burne-Jones seemed to have found his quintessential Greek ideal in an English woman of Hellenic heritage, Maria Cassavetti Zambaco. Born in 1843 to Euphrosyne Ionides Cassavetti and her husband, Demetrius, she was a child of privilege, as her father was partner in a large shipping company, and her mother the daughter of one of his competitors.[21] Two years after her father died in 1858, making her equal heiress with her younger brother for his fortune,[22] she married a Greek doctor working in Paris. Demetrius Zambaco was twelve years her senior, and was a specialist in the dermatological effects of syphilis. Two children followed in quick succession, and for reasons unknown she abandoned the marriage in the autumn of 1866, returning to London, with her children, to live with her mother. Dr Zambaco refused a divorce, although, after a considerable amount of pressure from his wife's family, he returned her *prika*, or dowry.[23] When Maria Zambaco died in 1914, her death certificate lists her marital status as 'widow', indicating that her husband went to his grave, a year before, still refusing divorce.[24]

Euphrosyne Cassavetti was a member of the so-called Greek community, living in and around Holland Park, who were great patrons of Burne-Jones and his Pre-Raphaelite and Aesthetic contemporaries. To celebrate her daughter's homecoming, Cassavetti commissioned Burne-Jones to create a painting using her daughter as a model, leaving the subject to his discretion. Burne-Jones made several studies of her in late 1866 for *Cupid Delivering Psyche*, a scene based on ancient Greek mythology, but reworked by William Morris into an epic narrative poem, *The Earthly Paradise*, which Burne-Jones made illustrations for between 1864 and 1866 (B74–B222) The study of Zambaco (B241), in three-quarter view, was probably intended for this watercolour painting of *Cupid Delivering Psyche*, which was completed in 1867 (photogravure, B234).

By the summer of 1868, Burne-Jones and Zambaco had fallen in love, and consummated their relationship;[25] evidence suggests that the sexual relationship continued until about 1875, but a correspondence existed until at least 1888, when Zambaco rented studio space from him.[26] Yet from the late 1860s through the mid-1870s Burne-Jones was constantly using Zambaco's likeness in drawings and paintings, either directly or indirectly: *Maria Zambaco: Profile Study* (B512), *Study for 'The Car of Love'* (B27), *Dorigen of Bretaigne* (photogravure, B265), *Venus Epithalamia* (photogravure, B1118), *Winter* (photogravure, B476), *Summer* (photogravure, B474), *The Wine of Circe* (photogravure, B1121), *The Beguiling of Merlin* (photogravure, B14), *Temperantia* (photogravure, B1102), *Fides* (photogravure, B369), *Study for Venus* and *Galatea* in *'Pygmalion & the Image'* (B589–B590), *Study for St Mark the Evangelist* (cat. 36, illus. p. 60 and on frontispiece), and various figures in both *The Masque of Cupid* (B515–B518) and *Masque of the Four Seasons* (B519). So entranced was he with her face, the large, luminous eyes, the long, gentle slope of her nose, full lips, and pointed chin (B513), that he often used her as a model for more than one figure, sometimes even male, as in *Phyllis and Demophoön* (cat. 38, illus. p. 22). Burne-Jones marvelled at Zambaco's features to Rossetti, stating that she had 'a wonderful head, neither

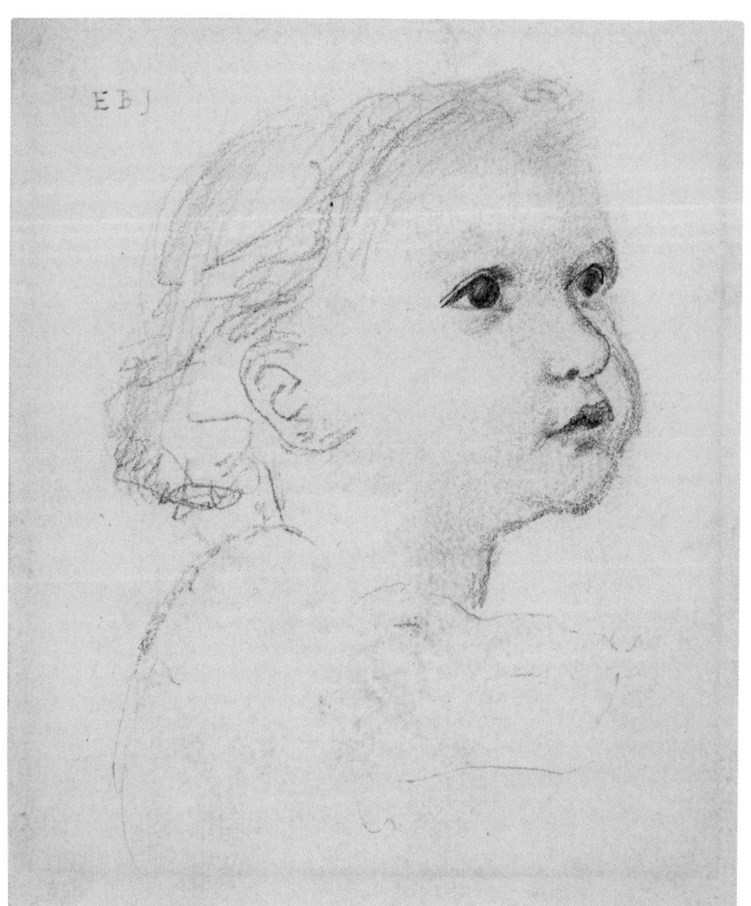

LEFT: *The Adoration of the Kings*: Study of Head for Infant Christ, 1860–62 (cat. 5)

BELOW: *King Cophetua and the Beggar Maid*: Study of a Boy's Head, 1883 (cat. 54)

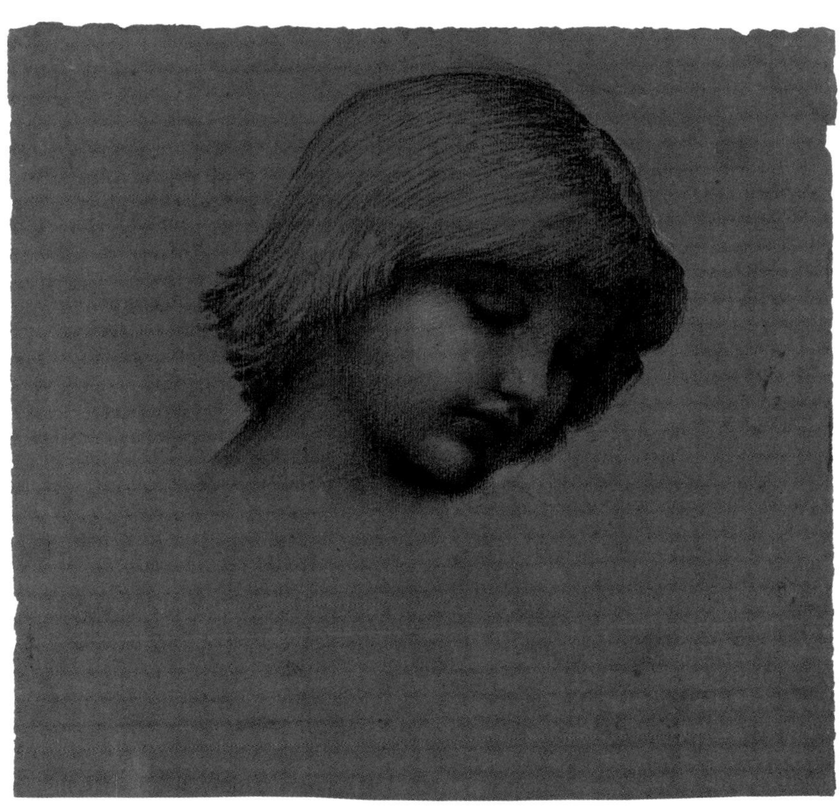

profile was like the other quite – and the full face was different again'.[27]

Phyllis and Demophoön caused a sensation when it was exhibited at the Old Water-Colour Society in 1870, and was the first occasion in its history where an artist withdrew his work,[28] in this instance based on a complaint regarding the nudity of the male figure. Phyllis was directly modelled on Zambaco, for which studies are extant (although currently in private collections). In an 1893 letter to Helen Mary Gaskell, a later muse with whom Burne-Jones was seriously infatuated, he tried to explain the complexity of his feeling for Zambaco:

> The head of Phyllis in the Demophoön picture is from the same Greek damsel and would have done for a portrait ... don't hate – some things are beyond scolding – hurricanes and tempests and billows of the sea – it's no use blaming them ... no, don't hate – unless by chance you think your workmanship was bad; it was a glorious head – and belonged to a remote past – only it didn't do in English suburban surroundings – we are soaked in Puritanism and it will never be out of us and I have it and it makes us the most cautious hypocritical race on earth.[29]

Yet, Zambaco's face was also used for Demophoön (for which there is a study in the Tate London), and in the painting forms a mirror image with Phyllis, almost like a doppelgänger. He next triplicated Zambaco's features that year in another watercolour, *The Garden of the Hesperides* (photogravure, B411), which is basically a visual manifestation of his description of her face to Rossetti.

Sometime in 1875 Burne-Jones's sexual relationship with Zambaco ended; he confided years later, again to Gaskell, that it was she who abandoned the relationship by cheating on her lover,[30] and removed herself to Paris for the next decade. By the following summer, however, Burne-Jones had already found a replacement muse, albeit platonic, for Zambaco: Frances, the eighteen-year-old daughter of his patron, William Graham.

In addition to being a collector of early Italian Renaissance artists, such as Dosso Dossi, William Graham purchased many paintings by Rossetti and Burne-Jones, including the latter's 1865 and 1868 versions of *Le Chant d'Amour* (1868 version, photogravure, B45) and *Laus Veneris* (photogravure, B477). Frances, along with several of her young friends who had been introduced to Burne-Jones, provided the inspiration for his enigmatic masterpiece *The Golden Stairs* (photogravure, B414), begun in 1876. These young beauties are easily identifiable based on a host of studies and sketches Burne-Jones made, and included: Frances Graham (extreme bottom left, with cymbals), his own daughter Margaret (top left, in profile), Morris's daughter May (with violin), Margot and Laura Tennant, daughters of a wealthy Glasgow bleach manufacturer (bending down and with zithern, respectively), Mary Gladstone, daughter of Prime Minister William (above Frances Graham, holding a trumpet), and Mary Stuart Wortley (behind them, turned to the left). The painting was finished in 1880 and was a success when it was exhibited at the Grosvenor Gallery, and was even said to have been the inspiration for the Gilbert and Sullivan operetta, *Patience*.[31]

While Frances Graham acted as his primary confidante in the 1880s, she was by no means his sole source of inspiration, as his wife had been in the 1860s, or Zambaco in the previous decade. He was fascinated with the lively Laura Tennant, now Mrs Lyttleton, whom he referred to as 'the Siren'.[32] She modelled for the mermaid in his second version of the haunting Symbolist oil *The Depths of the Sea* (photogravure, B263), finished shortly before her death in 1886. Frances Balfour, sister-in-law of Arthur, who had commissioned the first version of The Perseus Series (now at Southampton), was also a favourite for a short period of time, and her likeness is observed in some of the studies for the mythological group of paintings. Even Zambaco's closest friend, the artist Marie Spartali, who received the *Venus Epithalamia* (see above) for which Zambaco modelled, upon her marriage to William J. Stillman, sat for *Danaë and the Brazen Tower* (photogravure, B244).

He also forged close friendships with his friends' children, such as his solicitor's daughter, Katie Lewis, having painted portraits of her and her older sister Gertrude (photogravure, B413) in the late 1880s. He greatly admired the family, descended from Sephardic Jews by way of Holland, particularly the girls' lovely ethnic features. When their father, George, was in Paris for the summer of 1883, Burne-Jones amused Katie with a series of caricatures and notes, now known as *Letters to Katie* (British Museum). Katie Lewis never married; she presented to Birmingham Museums and Art Gallery several of Burne-Jones's lavishly finished studies for the *Briar Rose* Series that he had given to her (B16–B21). Later on, in the 1890s, there were:

Venetia Hunt; Violet and Olive Maxse, daughters of artistic friends; Amy Gaskell, daughter of close confidante Helen Mary; and Frances Graham's daughter, Cicely.[33]

His daughter Margaret, born the year he met Zambaco, was almost the perfect physical personification of his Pre-Raphaelite idea of the 'stunner', and looked as though she could have literally walked right out of his pictures (photogravure, B511). They also had a very close friendship, like that which he shared with Katie Lewis, but the whimsical times they enjoyed seem to have ended once she married the brilliant classical scholar J. W. Mackail in 1888. Burne-Jones is presumed to have informed Frances Graham, now Horner, that he had previously presented his daughter with a moonstone, a mineral thought to keep women unto themselves, because he did not want Margaret to 'know love, that she might stay with me'.[34] He dreaded the wedding day at St Margaret's Church, Rottingdean, which stood across a small field from his second house. Two months before the wedding he wrote that he went into St Margaret's to 'try and feel what it would be like when [he had] to take her and hand her over for life to her husband.'[35]

Margaret's marriage left him with a sense of betrayal that was not new to him. When other women seemed to make the same transition from maidenhood to wife, Burne-Jones felt deceived somehow, and often ceased communication with them. In August 1866 Georgiana's sisters, Agnes and Louisa, married in a joint ceremony, the painter Edward Poynter and Alfred Baldwin, respectively. Feeling forsaken by his muses, he refused to attend their wedding in Wolverhampton. He repeated this same exercise later with Frances Graham when she married Sir John Fortescue Horner in 1884, and he did not to write to her for a year after her marriage.[36] For the simple fact that she was his daughter, Burne-Jones did not act accordingly with Margaret and visited her often, as she had set up house within walking distance of his London home, The Grange.

In the 1890s, the last decade of his life, he was still using professional models from years before, such as Bessie Keene, who sat for the *Mona Lisa* homage, *Vespertina Quies*, in 1893 and *Aurora* in 1896 (photogravure, B9). For a worked-up version based on his *Song of Solomon* illustration, *Awake, O North Wind!/ Sponsa de Libano* (B803), he used 'a Houndsditch Jewess, self-possessed, mature and worldly, and only about twelve years old', for a model (autotype, B806).[37] Graham Robertson wrote of another favourite professional sitter of the time, used for the unfinished versions of *The Sirens*: a young woman with 'small eyes which gave her a rather sly expression' (cat. 59).[38]

In 1892 he was introduced to Helen Mary Gaskell by Frances Horner at a dinner party. A few days later, Gaskell visited Burne-Jones at his studio in The Grange and began a rather impetuous, passionate friendship. This lasted until his death six years later, despite the twenty-year age difference. The intensity of his feelings was almost as strong as those he had for Zambaco, although this relationship was entirely platonic, as extant letters seem to indicate. He was in love with her, by his own admission, but also knew the social impossibility of another sexual liaison, particularly at his age, having become a grandfather yet again when Margaret's second child arrived in 1894. While the extensive correspondence exhibited an urgent sensuality, caricatures made for her, and of her in some instances, were wickedly amusing. Yet Gaskell never occupied a position in Burne-Jones's work like Zambaco, whose likeness had appeared in a variety of guises and compositions. In fact, other than actual portrait studies and paintings, Gaskell does not seem to appear anywhere else, although many works of the period were dedicated to her. Strangely, Frances Horner appears in one of the last paintings he ever finished, *The Wizard* (B1135), but Gaskell was visually absent from the remaining works.

When Morris, his best friend for more than forty years, died in 1896, Burne-Jones poured out a lot of his grief to Gaskell. It was also her with whom he discussed his early years, particularly growing up without a mother. To her he revealed that he blamed himself for his mother's death, and since then any hurt he has caused to other women was just as unwilling as that which he felt he did to his mother.[39] He also revealed, indirectly, that he required the attentions of beautiful women because he craved their approval, almost in a maternal sense.[40] Yet while such an interpretation may seem questionable, it does, on the whole, fit the scenario. Burne-Jones utilised so many women, in both his art and his life (often in conjunction), because each of them had a particularly feminine quality that appealed to him. That attraction may have been based on nothing more than aesthetics, but also may be because they were possessors of a wide range of traits, any one of which could have been identical to the woman who was his true ideal, whom he never got to know.

1. Georgiana Burne-Jones, *Memorials of Edward Burne-Jones* (London, Lund Humphries, 1993), I, p. 2.
2. Sigmund Freud, *Three Essays on the Theory of Sexuality*, trans. James Stratchey (New York, Basic Books, 2000), pp. 11, 92–5. See also foreword by Nancy J. Chodorow, xi–xiv.
3. Tammy Clewell, 'Mourning beyond Melancholia: Freud's Psychoanalysis of Loss', *Journal of the American Psychoanalytic Association*, 52/1 (2004), p. 48.
4. A. W. Baldwin, *The MacDonald Sisters* (London, Macmillan, 1960), p. 11. The boys attended King Edward VI Grammar School, then on New Street, in Birmingham.
5. Judith Flanders, *A Circle of Sisters: Alice Kipling, Georgiana Burne-Jones, Agnes Poynter & Louisa Baldwin* (London, Penguin, 2001), p. 48.
6. Penelope Fitzgerald, *Edward Burne-Jones* (London, Michael Joseph, 1975), p. 53.
7. Reproduced in the first edition of *Memorials*, and are in a Private Collection.
8. *Memorials*, I, p. 140.
9. Ibid.
10. Ina Taylor. *Victorian Sisters: The Remarkable MacDonald Sisters and the Great Men They Inspired* (Bethesda, MD, Adler & Adler, 1987), p. 44.
11. Ibid., p. 71, and notes on photograph between pp. 76–7.
12. Ibid., p. 44.
13. Elizabeth Prettejohn, *Art of the Pre-Raphaelites* (Princeton, Princeton University Press, 2000), p. 197.
14. Stephen Wildman and John Christian, *Edward Burne-Jones: Victorian Artist-Dreamer*, exh. cat., New York, Metropolitan Museum of Art; Birmingham Museums and Art Gallery; Paris, Musée d'Orsay (New York, 1998), p. 73.
15. Fitzgerald, *Burne-Jones*, p. 82.
16. Ibid.
17. *Memorials*, I, p. 262.
18. Fitzgerald, *Burne-Jones*, pp. 82–3.
19. *Memorials*, I, p. 302.
20. Unpublished letter from Burne-Jones to George Howard, July 1867. Castle Howard Archives, J22/27/423.
21. Robert Liddell, *Cavafy* (London, Gerald Duckworth & Co., 2000), p.19.
22. Unpublished; Last Will and Testament of Euphrosyne Ionides Cassavetti, 1895.
23. Eileen Cassavetti, 'The Fatal Meeting & Fruitful Passion', *Antique Collector* (March 1989), p. 35.
24. Unpublished; Death Certificate of Maria Cassavetti Zambaco, 1914.
25. Unpublished; Rosalind Howard's Diary for 1869. Castle Howard Archives, J23/102/15.
26. Unpublished; Jeannette Marshall's Diary. Private Collection.
27. Fitzgerald, *Burne-Jones*, p. 114.
28. A survey of the minutes and other archival papers of the Old Water-Colour Society, housed now at the Royal Watercolour Society, confirm this.
29. Liana de Girolami Cheney, 'Burne-Jones: Mannerist in an Age of Modernism', in *Pre-Raphaelite Art in its European Context*, ed. Susan P. Casteras and Alicia Craig Faxon (Teaneck, NJ, Fairleigh Dickinson University Press, 1995), p. 112.
30. Josceline Dimbleby, *A Profound Secret* (London, Doubleday, 2004), p. 93.
31. Fitzgerald, *Burne-Jones*, p. 173. Strangely enough, it was Zambaco's first cousin, Luke Ionides, who suggested the idea to W. S. Gilbert in a letter dated 1 November 1880.
32. *Memorials*, II, p. 148.
33. Burne-Jones became extremely jealous when John Singer Sargent painted Cicely. He wrote to her mother: 'of course I felt a bitter pang when you told me Sargent was going to paint from Cicely – who is mine – who was made to fulfil [sic] a dream of mine – I suffered a great ping.' Richard Ormond and Elaine Kilmurray, *John Singer Sargent*, II: *Portraits of the 1890s* (New Haven, Yale University Press, 2002), p. 164.
34. Fitzgerald, *Burne-Jones*, p. 214.
35. *Memorials*, II, p. 183.
36. Ibid., p. 193.
37. Ibid., p. 215.
38. Graham Robertson, *Letters*, ed. Kerrison Preston (London, Hamish Hamilton, 1953), p. 487.
39. Dimbleby, *A Profound Secret*, p. 93.
40. Ibid., p. 96.

Public Patronage: The Burne-Jones Collection in Birmingham

TESSA SIDEY

In 1939 the then named City of Birmingham Museum and Art Gallery published a pioneering *Catalogue of the Permanent Collection of Drawings*. This publication, long out of circulation, has remained the standard reference source for what its author, A. E. Whitley,[1] described as 'an unrivalled collection of drawings and studies by the English Pre-Raphaelites and their followers'. Here, in the company of his closest contemporaries, Edward Burne-Jones does more than hold his own as a draughtsman: he takes centre stage in terms of commitment to and diversity of graphic media. This includes an extensive group of working designs that chart a remarkable exchange between the fine and decorative arts during the second half of the nineteenth century. The circumstances that gave rise to this collection, and the scope of the 1137 works on paper and archive that it holds, is the subject of this essay.

Burne-Jones had an uneasy relationship with his native city that nevertheless saw him reassess his views in later life. He was first-hand witness as a child to a harsh environment striving for industrial and manufacturing expansion. This undoubtedly contributed to the decision to leave for Oxford in 1853 at the age of twenty. Subsequent years were taken up with visits to see his father. It was not until he began to regain control of his career in 1875, as sole designer of stained glass for Morris & Co., and two years later received critical acclaim at the opening exhibition of the Grosvenor Gallery in London, that Birmingham is seen to make its first official moves towards its 'lost' son and Burne-Jones, in turn, responds to a new climate of public initiatives in Birmingham.

The first official commission was appropriately for stained glass for St Martin's-in-the-Bull-Ring, begun in 1876.[2] Four years later Burne-Jones allowed himself to become an outspoken advocate of a new museum and art gallery.[3] He saw a new found confidence in a 'Birmingham (that) shall be a famous city'[4] and duly worked on 'a colossal design of The Ascension' as the first of four stained glass windows for St Philip's Church, later the Cathedral.[5] A series of formal invitations saw representation at the inaugural exhibition of the new Museum and Art Gallery (BMAG) in 1885, and the Honorary Presidency of the Royal Birmingham Society of Artists, finally accepted in the same year.[6]

The Presidency was officially marked during a week-long visit to the city in October 1885, which by all accounts made a significant impression on Burne-Jones. He was able to check the progress of his own work at St Philip's Church, while also establishing direct contact with the newly opened Art School in Margaret Street. Official reports describe the 'individual conferences ... with a number of the more advanced students' to give 'valuable advice on the prosecution of their work'.[7] The process was repeated some two years later, now as an examiner of local prizes in Life and Antique Drawing for the same institution. The recorded observations might well stand for Burne-Jones's own critical concerns as an essentially self-taught draughtsman of the Figure: 'He observed that in the life drawing more care should be given to the extremities; in nearly all cases the hands and feet being of marked inferiority to the drawing of the body'.[8]

Georgiana Burne-Jones later recalled that during the October week Burne-Jones was the guest of the Liberal MP William Kenrick,[9] and he may well have met another key local patron of the arts, J. R. Holliday, for the first time during this visit. The role of Holliday (1840–1927) as key negotiator for the Museum and Art Gallery in acquiring more than 500 drawings by Rossetti and Burne-Jones in 1903 from Charles Fairfax Murray (1849–1919), and as a major benefactor in his own right principally through his bequest of 1927, has been considered elsewhere.[10] Recent investigations, however, have revealed a closer series of connections and common aspirations between these two outstanding collectors – and in Fairfax Murray's case close associate of Burne-Jones – than has perhaps been realised previously.[11]

The first work by Burne-Jones to enter the new public museum was the extraordinarily scaled watercolour of *The Star of Bethlehem*, commissioned by the Corporation of Birmingham in 1887 and one of the talking points of the important exhibition of *Modern Paintings* at the new Museum and Art Gallery in 1891.[12] It was not until his death in 1898, however, and the first studio sale of the same year, that the Museum made its first outright purchases of Burne-Jones's work.[13] Significantly, Fairfax Murray and Holliday registered their own independent patronage of Burne-Jones at the same time. The latter presented the Museum with *The Last Judgment* triptych as a joint gift with his friend William Kenrick, while, also in 1898, Fairfax Murray donated five stained glass designs and a design for embroidery, followed by sixteen stained glass designs in 1900 and eight in 1901. Both of these donors shared a concern to promote Burne-Jones as a stained glass artist. According to Douglas Schoenherr, the total of seventy-six stained glass designs acquired by BMAG from Fairfax Murray between 1898 and 1912 may have all been purchased or possibly reserved from the firm of Morris & Co. in 1898. Schoenherr's research of *The Cartoon Book* also reveals Holliday as the other outstanding buyer of Burne-Jones's designs from Morris & Co., with sixty-eight stained glass cartoons and five scale drawings acquired for £1697 between 1 July 1901 and 26 January 1904; of these, thirty-five have been traced to the BMAG collection.[14]

A series of notebooks bequeathed by Holliday to BMAG shows the extent of his personal study of Morris & Co. stained glass, and Burne-Jones in particular. Holliday was visiting and producing his own sketches of church windows by 1895 or earlier,[15] and by 1899 was conducting continuous church visits, for example to Elton near Peterborough, Horstead near Norwich, and Langham in Norfolk, all in August 1899. These trips continued into 1916 and 1921, six years before his death, with visits respectively to St James, Brighouse, and the Savoy Chapel, London.[16] A meticulous attention to accuracy and detail is seen in a numerical and alphabetical listing of Burne-Jones's windows,[17] various indexes of Morris & Co. stained glass designs,[18] and a copy of Philip Webb's account book.[19] It is this accumulation of documentation that Sydney Cockerell, Director of the Fitzwilliam Museum, Cambridge, regularly refers to when writing to his friend, and which establishes Holliday as arguably the first dedicated researcher and cataloguer of Morris & Co. as stained glass manufacturers, and of Burne-Jones in particular, more than fifty years before A. Charles Sewter's seminal publication.[20]

A transcription of Burne-Jones's account book with Morris, Marshall, Faulkner & Co. is the most intriguing piece of Holliday annotation to be found in Birmingham.[21] Rather confusingly this notebook includes Charles Fairfax Murray's description of the painting techniques of Rossetti, Burne-Jones and G. F. Watts, and so can quite easily be mistakenly identified. It is quite feasible that Murray dictated the technical notes to Holliday,

> who then tidied them up in prose form; they read like reported conversation, a question and answer dialogue. Alternatively Murray gave Holliday some rough notes to put into better order … What does seem certain is that Holliday is not recalling a conversation, or that Murray wrote the text out in full for Holliday to copy, which would have been out of character of the former.[22]

Possibly dated as early as 1894, it does however confirm that Holliday and Fairfax Murray established direct contact well before 1903 and the purchase of the first group of drawings for BMAG, and were exchanging material of mutual interest in the 1890s.[23]

The often difficult relationship between Sydney Cockerell and Fairfax Murray has been well documented,[24] but surviving correspondence between Cockerell and Holliday also indicates that the latter was very much a part of an inner, even triangular, group of collectors dedicated to the Pre-Raphaelite legacy and inspired by 'our mutual friend Fairfax Murray'.[25] The inevitable clash of interest at auctions appears to have been handled with pragmatic diplomacy on at least one occasion, as indicated by Cockerell when writing to Holliday in 1917,

> On my way to Christie's, I fortunately looked in at Murray's and found your telegram. I would have bid for the Sandys in any case, and it is well that we should not bid against each other. Your telegram says 'I want Sandys 45' for which I concluded that you had not actually given a commission and that I had better do so on our joint behalf.[26]

The Fairfax Murray-Holliday association comes into its own when considering the authorship of a substantial number of inscriptions on small-scale Burne-Jones drawings at BMAG. These typically consist of an *E.B.J.* in sepia ink, clearly not in the artist's hand but in the style of the celebrated monogram, followed by a descriptive title in the same sepia ink.[27] Significantly all but one of these drawings is part of the Holliday Bequest of 1927, and so similar inscriptions can be found in other Burne-Jones collections with the same provenance, for example the Whitworth Art Gallery, University of Manchester. The immediate inclination is to see the legally trained Holliday as the author of this neat script rather than Murray, who was criticized at various stages for his untidy handwriting. The similarities with Holliday's writing are certainly there, but a closer comparison with the tidied-up hand that, according to David Elliott, Fairfax Murray began to employ around 1875 confirms him as the author.[28]

The implication of this identification is to ask how a good number of Burne-Jones drawings (as opposed to those by Rossetti or Millais) bequeathed by Holliday came to be captioned by Fairfax Murray. The answer may well be the simplest, that Holliday purchased the inscribed drawings in question from Murray, perhaps as a single batch. No surviving correspondence or documentation supports this proposition, though it is known that Holliday acquired material from Fairfax Murray.[29] Another possibility may be:

> that Holliday had accumulated a collection over the years, but did not know what all of these were … and he asked Fairfax Murray who had an encyclopaedic knowledge of Burne-Jones's work to sort through and tell him what finished work the sketches were for. The captions appear to have been added as a batch rather than over time … Although Fairfax Murray was increasingly out of England from c. 1907 there was plenty of time for Holliday to consult him between Burne-Jones's death in 1898, and the negotiations [with BMAG] of 1903 and 1906 if he acquired any drawings at that time; and of course earlier.[30]

Together Fairfax Murray and Holliday were the sources for BMAG acquiring just under 700 works on paper by Burne-Jones,[31] with the latter undoubtedly benefiting from his close working knowledge of the former's collection.[32] Fairfax Murray made the most of his early Pre-Raphaelite connections, though he only began to establish a drawing collection seriously in the 1880s. He was the first to make purchases of stained glass cartoons from Morris & Co. in 1898 and, not unexpectedly, chose mainly designs from the early 1860s.[33] Holliday, in contrast, bought later from Morris and Co., with the result that he purchased largely from the 1870s and 1880s. The notable results included designs for Jesus College, Cambridge (1873), Leigh, Staffordshire (1874), St Helen's Church, Welton, Yorkshire (1879), and Newport, USA (1883).

Fairfax Murray bought in bulk when the opportunity arose. This saw him acquire some 300 drawings from Burne-Jones in exchange for an illuminated choral book. Studies for *St Theophilus and the Angel* and The St George Series were among this group.[34] Intentionally or not, this began to shape a collection that aspired to be all-encompassing, and was very much about drawing as a creative process rather than a selective representative of the realised. Both Fairfax Murray and Holliday appear to have been like-minded about this approach. The accumulative result is no less than thirty-three drapery and twenty-five nude sketches dating from the mid-1860s and largely drawn in the red-brown chalk characteristic of this period. This private work in progress takes its place alongside composition sketches, head studies, caricatures, watercolours, and working designs for tile, stained glass, embroidery and book illustration from virtually all the other main phases of Burne-Jones's career, the notable exception being the early pen-and-ink drawing.

At the same time the collection provides an in-depth representation of major preoccupying themes. The St George Series, *The Lament*, *The Garland Weavers* and The Cupid and Psyche Series are cases in point, the latter occupying Burne-Jones over thirty years and represented in all its diverse forms: from sketch, tracing, woodblock and engraved illustration to watercolour and mural painting. The sequence of composition sketches and individual studies for *The Fates* and *St Theophilus and the Angel* has become the main visual source for two projects that were respectively unrealised and lost.

Such was the impact of Fairfax Murray and Holliday's patronage that it levered the support of contemporaries as well as later generations. Six large studies for *The Briar Rose*, bequeathed by Katie Lewis in 1961, and sketchbooks presented by Mrs Angela Thirkell, the artist's grand-daughter, in 1952, followed by landscapes in 1954, are two outstanding examples. As Chairman of the John Feeney Charitable Trust, Holliday ensured that the key watercolour of *Phyllis and Demophoön* came to Birmingham[35] and, six years before his death, is credited by Philip Burne-Jones with rescuing the unfinished painting of The Troy Triptych.[36] At the same time, the concept of an expansive collection has continued to find space for the unexpected and the neglected, for example, the purchase of *The Flower Book* portfolio in 1953 (B371–B409), all too easily dismissed as reproductive, and a miscellaneous group of caricatures and letters in 1980 (cat. 51, B40–B41, B478–B479).

It is such depth of material and the visual connections revealed through drawings made over a forty-year period that marks this collection. It has in turn provided the framework for this exhibition, and the selectors with a platform for profiling the less familiar. The result aspires to be a fitting testament to those who created an extraordinary public resource for Burne-Jones in Birmingham.

1. A. E. (Eric) Whitley was appointed Junior Assistant at Birmingham Museum and Art Gallery in 1925. On the death of the Keeper of the Art Gallery, Sir Whitworth Wallis, in 1927 and the subsequent resignation of A. E. Chamberlain, he took over administration of the art department before being duly appointed Assistant Keeper under the Keepership of S. C. Kaines Smith. The administration of the J. R. Holliday Bequest was one of the duties that Whitley undertook with Kaines Smith in 1927, no doubt laying the foundation for his painstaking *Catalogue of Drawings* published in 1939.
2. A. C. Sewter, *The Stained Glass of William Morris and his Circle* (New Haven, Yale University Press, 1974–5), I, p. 19.
3. G(eorgiana) B(urne)-J(ones), *Memorials of Edward Burne-Jones* (London, Lund Humphries, 1993), II, pp. 99–101.
4. Ibid., p. 156.
5. Burne-Jones in his Account Book for February 1884, now in the Fitzwilliam Museum, Cambridge. BMAG acquired J. R. Holliday's copy of this account book as part of the Holliday Bequest in 1927 (2006.1447). The somewhat exaggerated entry reads: 'For St Philip's Church, Birmingham (my native town) a colossal design of the Ascension perhaps my fiftieth treatment of this subject involving much physical fatigue in addition to mental weariness'.
6. The following works by Burne-Jones were shown at the inauguration exhibition of the Museum and Art Gallery in 1885–6: *Love in the Ruins*, lent by F. A. Craven; *Temperantia*, lent by Hon. Lady Wantage; *Danaë and the Brazen Tower*, lent by J. Graham; *Pan and Psyche*, lent by George Hamilton; and *The Hours*, lent by F. Austen.
7. Report of the Museum and School of Art Committee, 4 January 1887, p. 32.
8. Report of the Museum and School of Art Committee, 8 January 1889, p. 16.
9. *Memorials*, II, p. 156.
10. Tessa Sidey, 'Charles Fairfax Murray, J. R. Holliday and the Birmingham Collection of Millais Drawings', in Paul Goldman, *John Everett Millais Illustrator and Narrator* (Aldershot, Lund Humphries, 2004), pp. 49–54.
11. Charles Fairfax Murray was Burne-Jones's assistant between 1866 and 1870/71, but he remained 'a kind of friend' up until Burne-Jones's death in 1898. His concern that the work of Burne-Jones, Rossetti and the other Pre-Raphaelites should enter public collections was an ideal shared by Holliday.
12. *Permanent Collection of Paintings with Special Loan Collection of Modern Paintings*, City of Birmingham Museum and Art Gallery (1891), no. 183; *The Wheel of Fortune* and *Flamma Vestalis* by Burne-Jones were shown in the same exhibition.
13. BMAG purchased in 1898 *Mars* (B906), *Helen Captive in Burning Troy* (B1113), and *Study of the Three Graces* (B1117), all from the first studio sale at Christie's in the same year.
14. Douglas E. Schoenherr, 'The "Cartoon Book" and Morris & Company's Sale of Burne-Jones's Cartoons in 1901–1904', *Journal of the British Society of Master Glass Painters*, XXIX (2005), pp. 82–134. The thirty-five works listed by Schoenherr as now in the BMAG collection include six designs for Dundee Council Chamber, which Holliday bought from Morris & Co. on 11 July 1901 and 'must have sold to John Feeney soon afterwards since the latter gave them to BMAG in 1901' (B869, B893, B900, B917, B919, B928).
15. Holliday Notebook (BMAG: 2006.1331).
16. Holliday Notebook (BMAG: 2005.1332).
17. A numerical list by J. R. Holliday of Burne-Jones windows from *Adam and Eve after the Fall* for Bradfield College, Berks (1857), through to no. 821 (1898) for St Deiniol, Hawarden (BMAG: 2006.1336).
18. Holliday Notebooks: Index to Morris & Co. Photographs (2006.1333); Index of Burne-Jones stained glass designs (2006.1334).
19. Copy by J. R. Holliday of Philip Webb Account Book (BMAG 2006.1337).
20. Letters, Sydney Cockerell to J. R. Holliday, 2 November 1915, 'What a blessed work you will be doing in setting down methodically all you know about the windows' (Fitzwilliam Museum, Cambridge, 469-1977); and 26 June 1917, 'Do annotate your existing photographs of the Morris windows and set down all you know, you and no other, except Murray, who is not likely to communicate what he can remember to anyone who will set it down' (Fitzwilliam Museum, 490-1977).
21. Holliday Notebook (BMAG: 2006.1330).
22. Notes by David Elliott to the author, following a visit to BMAG, 6 July 2006.
23. Precisely when Fairfax Murray and Holliday met remains unclear, although the first studio sale of 1898 would have provided ample opportunity.
24. Wilfred Blunt, *Cockerell* (London, Hamish Hamilton, 1964); David Elliott, *Charles Fairfax Murray: the Unknown Pre-Raphaelite* (Lewes, E. Sussex, Book Guild Ltd, 2000); Christopher de Hamel, 'Cockerell as Entrepeneur', *The Book Collector* (Spring 2006), pp. 49–72, and 'Cockerell as Museum Director', *The Book Collector* (Summer 2006), pp. 201–223.
25. Letter, Sydney Cockerell to J. R. Holliday, 19 October 1916 (Fitzwilliam Museum, Cambridge, 485-1977).
26. Letter, Sydney Cockerell to J. R. Holliday, 25 January 1917 (Fitzwilliam Museum, Cambridge, 489-1977).
27. The interpolated *E B J* monogram usually includes three dots (occasionally fewer) between the letters. This makes a clear distinction with Burne-Jones's own monogram, where there are no dots or, less frequently, a dot or small hyphen between the B and the J.
28. Notes by David Elliott to the author, 6 July 2006.
29. A rare volume of *The Fairy Family* with Burne-Jones's earliest published illustrations, and a volume of eighty-six Burne-Jones designs for *Cupid and Psyche* were both owned by Fairfax Murray before being acquired by Holliday, and subsequently bequeathed by him to BMAG in 1927.
30. Notes by David Elliott to the author, 6 July 2006.
31. Fairfax Murray and Holliday were respectively responsible for the acquisition of 368 and 310 works on paper by Burne-Jones. This includes two works now attributed to Philip Webb.
32. Holliday writes to Cockerell on 25 March 1925 in reference to Selsley Church, 'As to the 2 cartoons at the Gallery [BMAG] referred to by Letheby … when Murray gave the cartoons they were badly framed and the three pieces of the cartoons were loose behind the glass' (Fitzwilliam Museum, Cambridge, 31-1986).
33. Douglas Schoenherr, 'The "Cartoon Book"', p. 86, where the following cartoons are listed: for Selsley; Lyndhurst; St Michael's, Brighton; Harden Grange; Darley Dale; Bradford Cathedral; Kentish Town Parish Church; Cheddleton; and St Edmund Hall, Oxford.

34. Charles Fairfax Murray diaries, Collection Fitz Lugt, Institut Néerlandais, Paris, for 17 November 1887, and quoted in Sidey, 'Charles Fairfax Murray, J. R. Holliday and the Birmingham Collection of Millais Drawings'.
35. Cockerell to Holliday, 27 November 1916: 'I thought I detected your hand in the sale of the *Phyllis & Demophoön*, or rather in its purchase. You would hardly let so important an example slip through your fingers' (Fitzwilliam Museum, Cambridge, 487-1977).
36. Cockerell to Holliday, 15 December 1921, where he refers to Philip Burne-Jones on The Troy Triptych: 'He not only speaks of the picture having been rescued by you, but he states that it is given in recognition of your long services to the Gallery and your dedication to EBJ's work'. The Troy Triptych was officially presented by Sir Philip Burne-Jones, Mrs J. W. Mackail and J. R. Holliday in 1922 (1922P178).

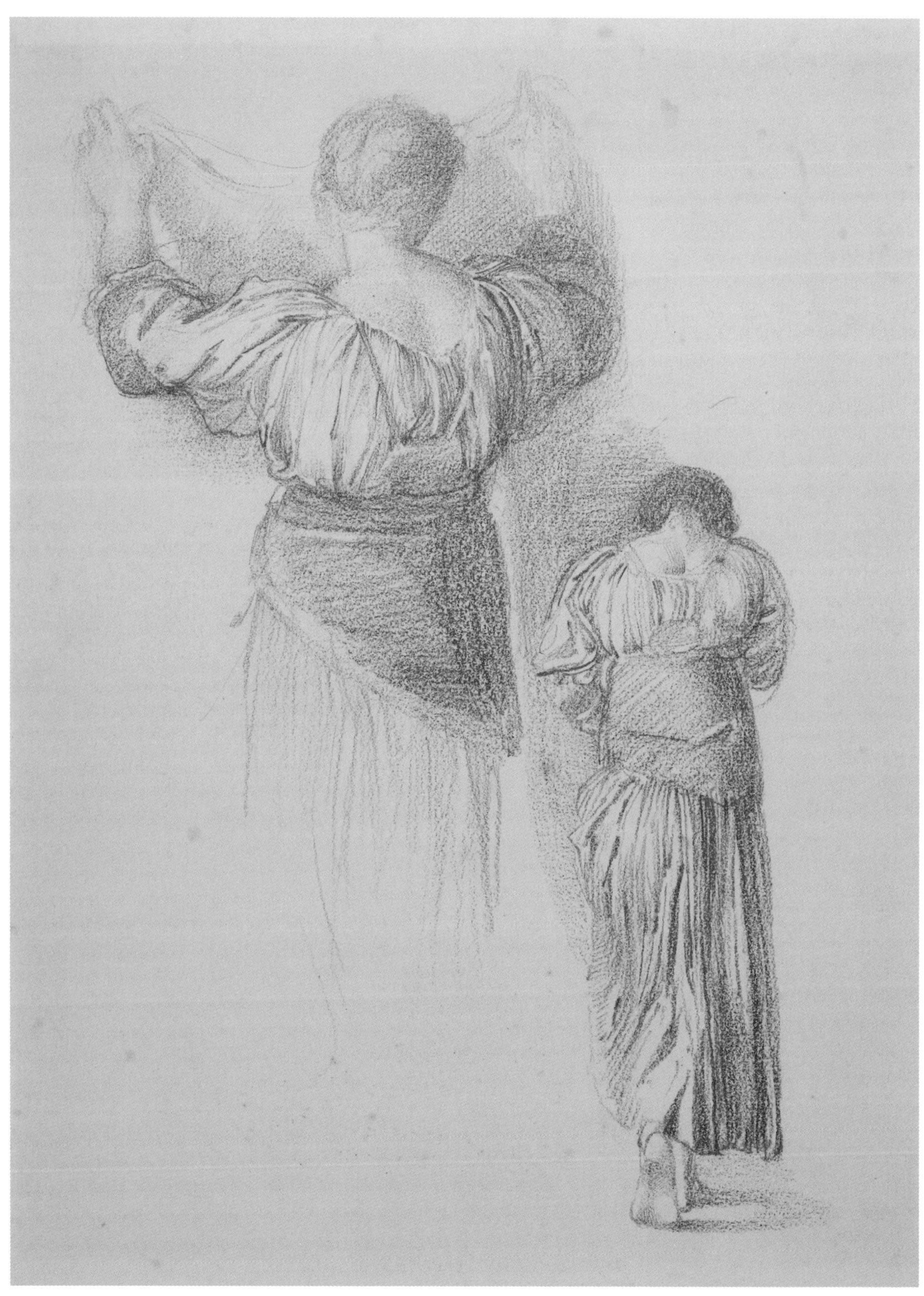

Studies of female Drapery seen from the back, 1867–69 (cat. 34)

Exhibits

The catalogue entries are organised in the following sequence: reference number, title of work, date, medium, size in millimetres (height × width), the main literature and exhibition references, and finally provenance details with the collection reference/ accession number. Birmingham Museums and Art Gallery is abbreviated to BMAG.

Abbreviated References

Arts Council *Burne-Jones: The Paintings, Graphic and Decorative Work of Sir Edward Burne-Jones 1833–98*, catalogue by John Christian, London, Hayward Gallery, and tour, 1975

Ash Russell Ash, *Sir Edward Burne-Jones* (London, Pavilion, 1993)

Bell Malcolm Bell, *Sir Edward Burne-Jones: A Record and Review* (London, George Bell & Sons, 1892)

Birmingham *City of Birmingham Museum and Art Gallery, Catalogue of the Permanent Collection of Paintings in Oil and Water Colours and a Special Loan Collection of Modern Pictures,* compiled by Whitworth Wallis and Arthur Bensley Chamberlain (Birmingham, 1891)

Dalziel George Dalziel and Edward Dalziel, *The Brothers Dalziel: A Record of Fifty Years' Work in Conjunction with Many of the Most Distinguished Artists of the Period 1840–1890* (London, Methuen, 1901)

Harrison and Waters Martin Harrison and Bill Waters, *Burne-Jones* (London, Barrie & Jenkins, 1973)

Hong Kong Richard Lockett, *Pre-Raphaelite Art from the Birmingham Museums and Art Gallery*, exh. cat., Hong Kong Museum of Art (Hong Kong, 1984)

Myers Richard Myers and Hilary Myers, *William Morris: The Tile Designs of Morris and His Fellow-Workers* (Shepton Beauchamp, Richard Dennis, 1996)

New Gallery *Exhibition of the Works of Edward Burne-Jones*, exh. cat., London, New Gallery, 1892–3

Reality and Vision *Reality and Vision: English Drawings* (London, Roland, Browse and Delbanco, 1945)

Rome *Burne-Jones, dal Preraffaellismo al simbolismo,* exh. cat., ed. Maria Teresa Benedetti and Gianna Piantoni, Rome, Galleria Nazionale d'Arte Moderna (Milan, 1986)

Schoenherr Douglas E. Schoenherr, '"The Cartoon Book" and Morris & Company's Sale of Burne-Jones's Cartoons in 1901–1904', *The Journal of the British Society of Master Glass Painters,* XXIX (2005), pp. 82–134

Sewter A. Charles Sewter, *The Stained Glass of William Morris and his Circle,* 2 vols (New Haven, Yale University Press, 1974–5)

Sheffield *Burne-Jones*, exh. cat. by W. S. Taylor, Sheffield, Mappin Art Gallery, 1971

Solomon Colin Cruise, *Love Revealed: Simeon Solomon and the Pre-Raphaelites*, exh. cat., Birmingham Museums and Art Gallery (London, Merrell, 2005)

_V&A_ *Catalogue of an Exhibition in Celebration of the Centenary of William Morris,* London, Victoria & Albert Museum, 1934

Victorian Artist-Dreamer Stephen Wildman and John Christian, *Edward Burne-Jones Victorian Artist-Dreamer*, exh. cat., New York, Metropolitan Museum of Art; Birmingham Museums and Art Gallery; Paris, Musée d'Orsay (New York, 1998)

Victorian Nude Alison Smith, *Exposed: The Victorian Nude* (London, Tate Publishing, 2001)

Visions *Visions of Love and Life: Pre-Raphaelite Art from the Birmingham Collection*, exh. cat., ed. Stephen Wildman (Alexandria, VA, Art Services International, 1995)

Whitley A. E. Whitley, *City of Birmingham Museum & Art Gallery, Catalogue of the Permanent Collection of Drawings in Pen, Pencil, Charcoal and Chalk, etc., including Cartoons for Stained Glass* (Derby, Bemrose & Sons, 1939)

Whitworth *William Morris and the Middle Ages*, exh. cat., ed. Joanna Banham and Jennifer Harris, Manchester, Whitworth Art Gallery (Manchester University Press, 1984)

1. *The Fairy Family: A Series of Ballads & Metrical Tales Illustrating The Fairy Faith of Europe*, pub. 1857 (illus. p. 13)

By Archibald Maclaren (1819–1884)
Bound volume with frontispiece, title-page and tailpiece engraved from pen and ink drawings by Edward Burne-Jones; published by Longman & Co., 1857
185 × 130 mm
Lit.: *Arts Council* (8), *Victorian Artist-Dreamer* (1)
Prov.: bought by Sydney Cockerell at the suggestion of William Morris, 1895; Charles Fairfax Murray; returned to Sydney Cockerell, 1917, and presented to J. R. Holliday, Christmas 1920
Bequest of J. R. Holliday, 1927 (1927P1616)

Sydney Cockerell's annotations on the inside cover of this rare copy of Burne-Jones's earliest published illustrations provide an insight into the unease that he felt about this publication and which he never officially acknowledged. This was in spite of the large number of drawings that he produced for his friend, Archibald Maclaren, from 1854.

> This book I bought in 1895 at the suggestion of/ William Morris who pointed out to me the/ description in a bookseller's catalogue and said, 'Don't let Burne-Jones know that I told you, but/ that book contains his earliest illustrations'. A/ year or so later I gave it to C Fairfax Murray/ who today gave it back to me/ Sydney Cockerell/ Cambridge Oct 24 1917/
>
> The author was Archibald Maclaren of Summertown, Oxford/ See Lady Burne-Jones's *Memorials*, vol I, pp. 80, 100, 120 etc. On/ p. 135 she refers to the abandonment of the scheme, and she nowhere states that the book, which is now very rare, was issued with three/ out of the many designs that Burne-Jones made for it between 1854 and 1856. She reproduces two more of them opposite p. 120/ A second edition/ with Maclaren's name, was published by Macmillan/ in 1874.

2. *The Annunciation: Study for the Virgin (Woman Holding a Flower)*, 1859–61 (illus. p. 18)

Pencil; 313 × 135 mm
Lit.: *Whitley*, p. 117
Bequest of J. R. Holliday, 1927 (1927P586)

This may be an early drawing of Jane Morris. It is now thought to be a study for the Virgin in the *Annunciation* (see cat. 3).

3. *The Annunciation*, 1857–61 (illus. p. 18)

Watercolour and bodycolour with gum on two sheets of paper; 524 × 374 mm
Insc.: *E B J/ 1861* (in gold circle)
Lit.: *Bell*, 1892, pp. 29, 35, 107; *Whitley*, p. 36
Bequest of J. R. Holliday, 1927 (1927P441)

The composition was begun in 1857 but not finished until four years later. The figure of the Virgin may have originally been based on Jane Morris (see cat. 2), but the face, as finally realised, was most likely modelled on the artist's fiancée, Georgiana Macdonald. A more finished study for this figure is in the Fitzwilliam Museum, Cambridge.

The composition may have proved difficult for Burne-Jones, both compositionally and technically. The impasto is fairly thick in some places, uncharacteristic for him even at this early stage. Several areas have also been patched and reworked, particularly the Angel Gabriel.

4. *Stained Glass Design: The Tree of Jesse (Triptych)*, 1860–61 (illus. p. 48)

Sepia pen and ink over pencil; 307 × 420 mm
Insc.: see catalogue entry for B976
Bequest of J. R. Holliday, 1927 (1927P437)

This is an elaborate stained glass design for the east window of Waltham Abbey, executed by James Powell & Sons in 1861. A version of the central panel was exhibited in 1862 at the International Exhibition in London, and is now also at BMAG (1977M1). *The Tree of Jesse* is an allegorical representation of the genealogy of Christ, where the tree is rooted in Jesse, father of King David, and culminates either in the Nativity or Crucifixion of Christ.

Each figure is identified by the artist. The left light, from bottom to top, are: Adam (holding fruit, with serpent to his left), Noah (holding a small ark; name spelled 'Noea' or 'Noeh'); Jacob (holding a ladder); Gideon (holding fleece); Joshua (in armour holding the sun and moon); Samson (with flowing tresses); and Moses (unlabelled by the artist, but holding the two stone tablets of the Ten Commandments).

The middle light, with the actual Tree of Jesse, features (from bottom to top): the four anamorphic symbols of the Evangelists with scrolls around them quoting the first lines of their respective Gospels (the man's scroll, St Matthew, reads 'Generations of Jesus Christ of the book of'; above him is the eagle of St John, whose Gospel begins 'In the beginning was the Word'; opposite is the ox of St Luke, with 'There was in the days of Herod'; the lion is St Mark, with 'The beginning of the Gospel of Jesus Christ'). These creatures flank the sleeping body of Jesse, from which the tree springs. The first branch holds (from left to right): Achaz (kneeling in front of an altar with a statue); Solomon (holding the Temple); David (playing a lyre); Roboam (or Roboham, stringing a bow). The next branch supports: Hezekiah (the king, holding a sundial (?); Manassas (imprisoned and in chains); Josias (the king, holding tablets (?)); Jecunias (bound and chained). The third branch shows two roundels recounting the birth of Christ, with the Nativity scene on the left and the Adoration of the Shepherds on the right. At the top of the tree is Jesus crucified, flanked by his mother and Mary Magdalene, in mourning.

The right panel is incomplete, and features the ancient Hebrew prophets with symbols associated with them. They are from bottom to top: Esaias (or Isaiah); Jeremias (Jeremiah); Ezekiel (with the eyes of the seraphim in wheels behind him); Daniel (with a lion sleeping at his feet); Malachai; and an unfinished rough sketch, in pencil, of Micah. At the very top is John the Baptist, outlined in pen.

RIGHT: *Georgiana Burne-Jones*, 1863 (cat. 20)

FAR RIGHT: *Astrologia*: Profile Study of Augusta Jones, 1865 (cat. 24)

BELOW: Maria Zambaco in traditional Greek Costume, 1867–68 (cat. 33)

BELOW RIGHT: Head Study for *The Sirens*, 1895 (cat. 59)

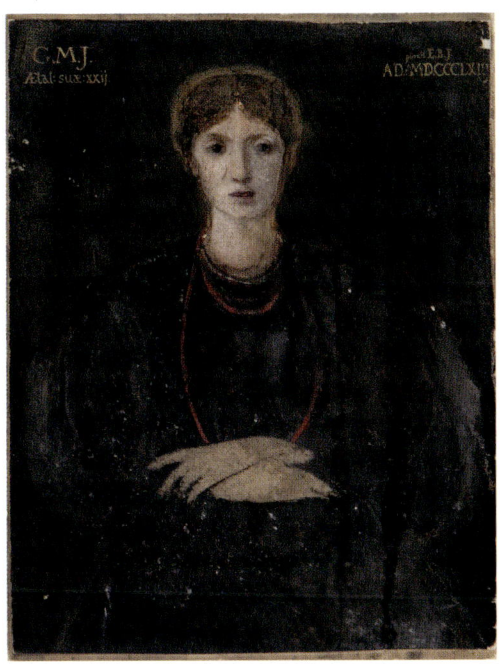

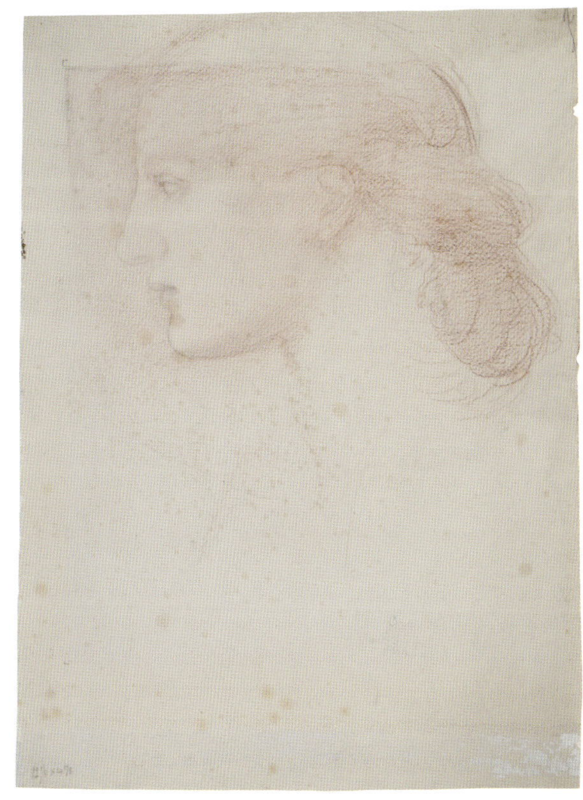

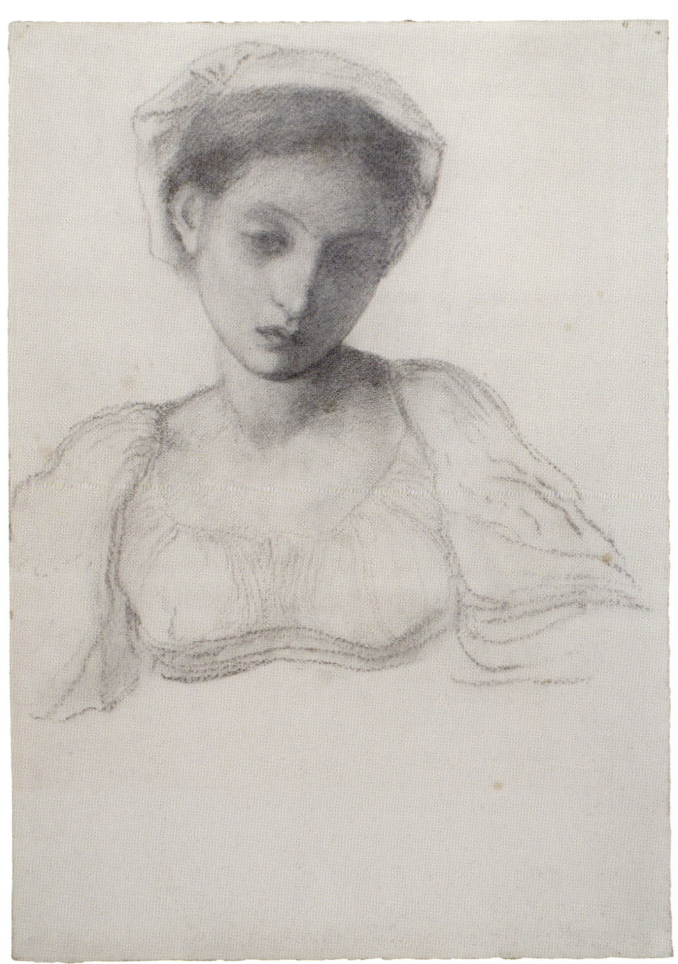

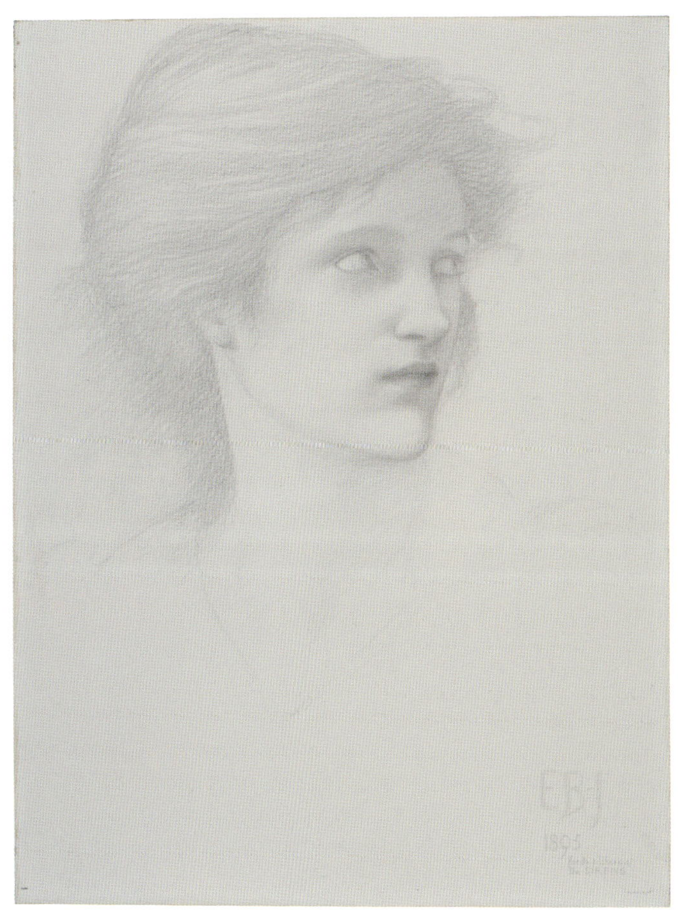

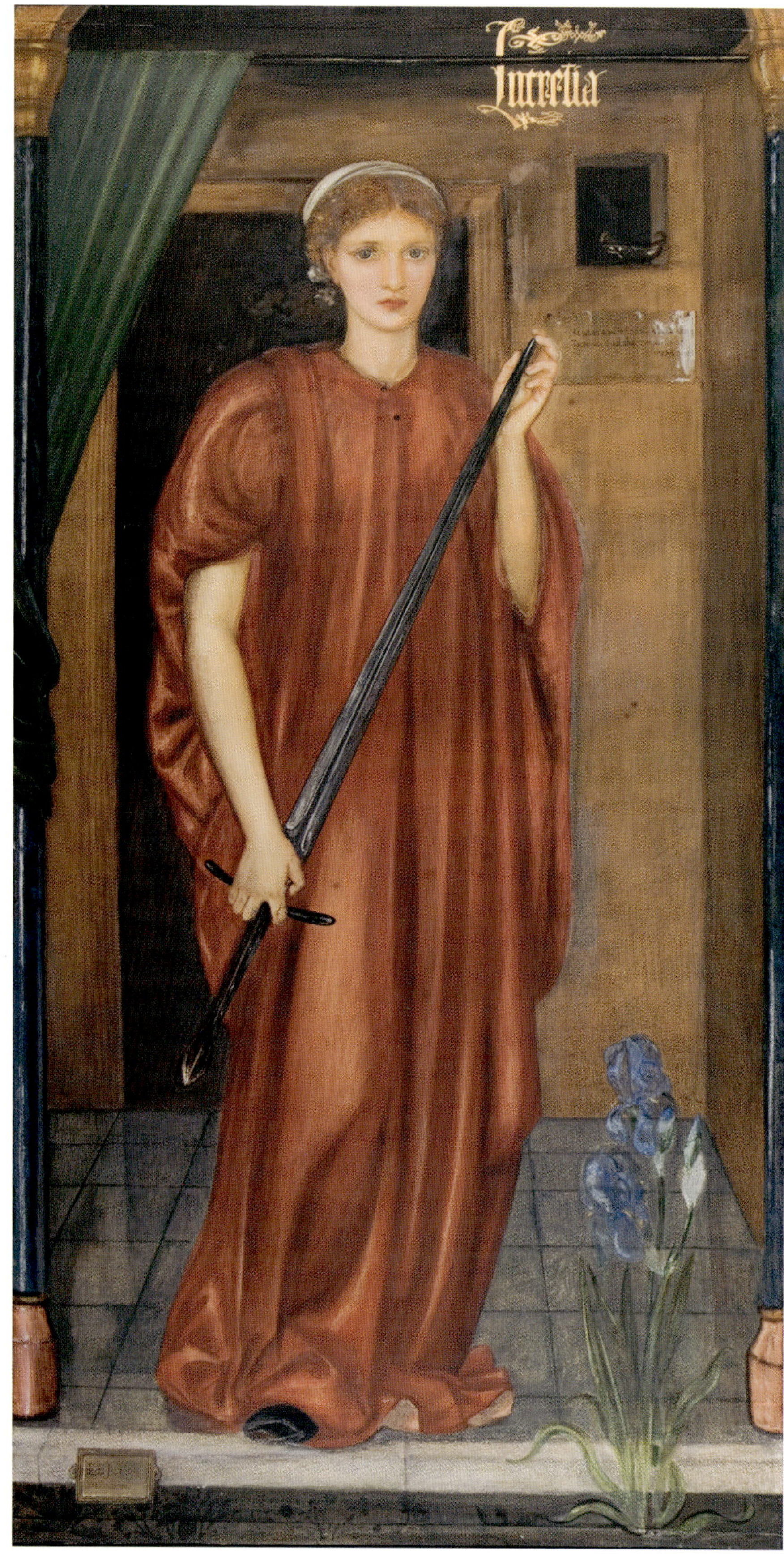

Lucretia, 1867 (cat. 30)

RIGHT: *The Works of Geoffrey Chaucer Now Newly Imprinted: Legend of the Roman Martyr Lucretia*, pub. 1896 (cat. 60)

BELOW: Drapery Study of *Lucretia* for *Chaucer's 'Legend of Good Women'*, 1863 (cat. 19)

BELOW RIGHT: Chaucer's 'Legend of Good Women': *Ariadne and Lucretia*, 1864 (cat. 23)

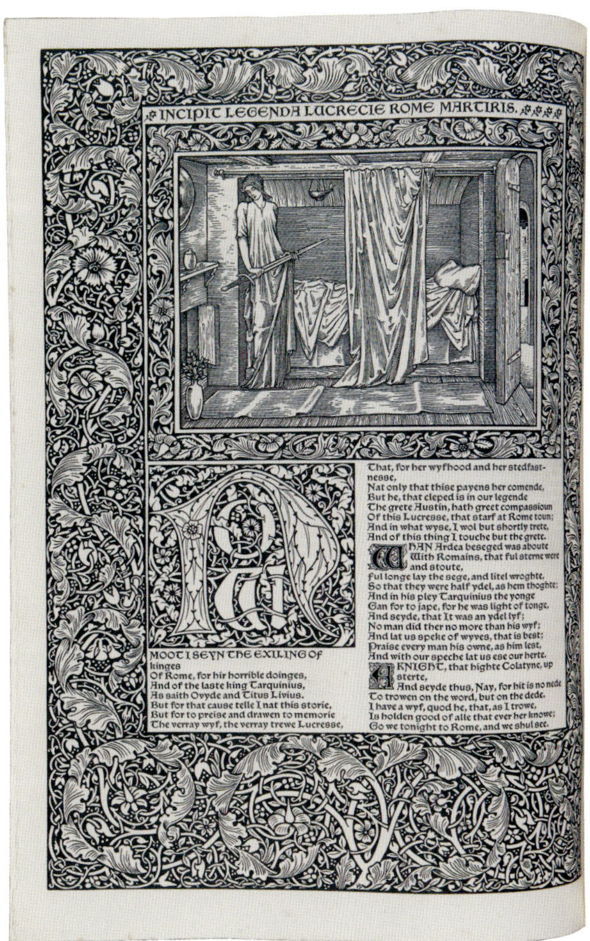

INCIPIT LEGENDA LUCRECIE ROME MARTIRIS.

NOOT I SEYN THE EXILING OF kinges
Of Rome, for hir horrible doinges,
And of the laste king Tarquinius,
As saith Ovyde and Titus Livius.
But for that cause telle I nat this storie,
But for to preise and drawen to memorie
The verray wyf, the verray trewe Lucresse,
That, for her wyfhood and her stedfastnesse,
Nat only that thise payens her comende,
But he, that cleped is in our legende
The grete Austin, hath greet compassioun
Of this Lucresse, that starf at Rome toun;
And in what wyse, I wol but shortly trete,
And of this thing I touche but the grete.

WHAN Ardea beseged was aboute
With Romains, that ful sterne were and stoute,
Ful longe lay the sege, and litel wroghte,
So that they were half ydel, as hem thoghte;
And in his pley Tarquinius the yonge
Gan for to jape, for he was light of tonge,
And seyde, that It was an ydel lyf;
No man did ther no more than his wyf;
And lat us speke of wyves, that is best;
Praise every man his owne, as him lest,
And with our speche lat us ese our herte.

A KNIGHT, that highte Colatyne, up sterte,
And seyde thus, Nay, for hit is no nede
To trowen on the word, but on the dede.
I have a wyf, quod he, that, as I trowe,
Is holden good of alle that ever her knowe;
Go we tonight to Rome, and we shul see.

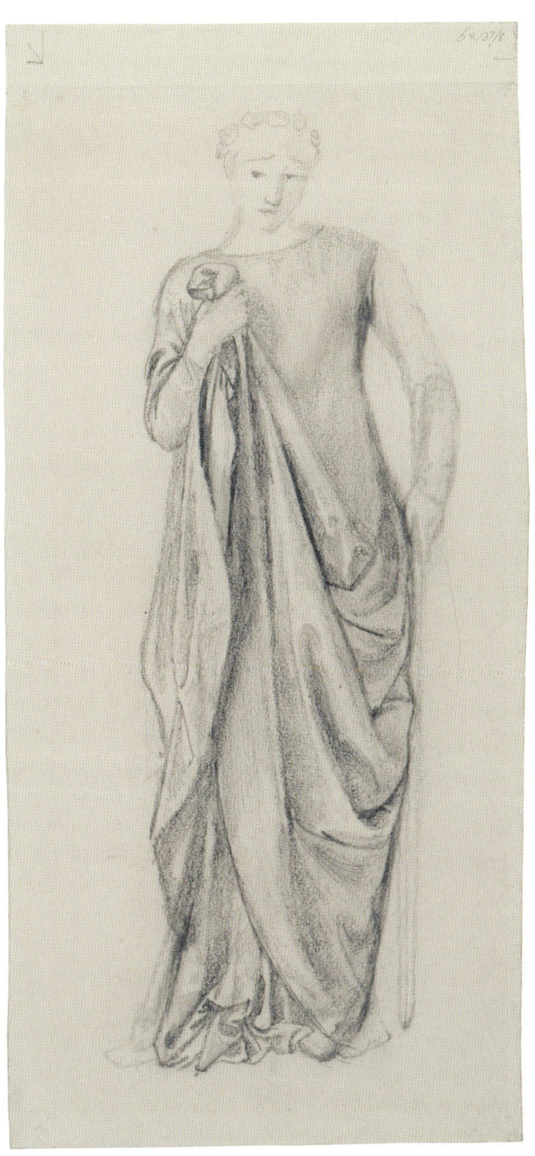

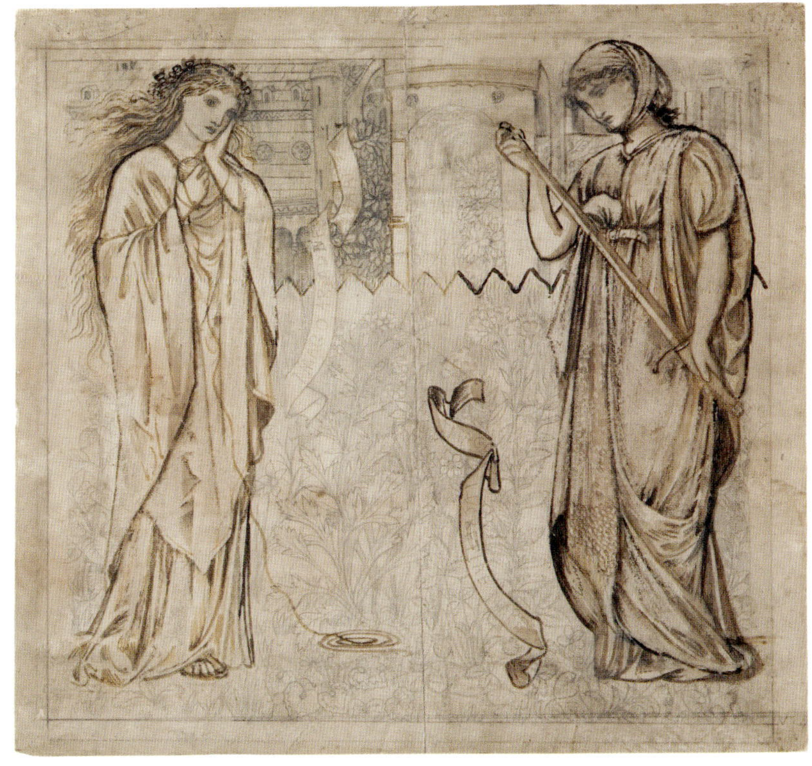

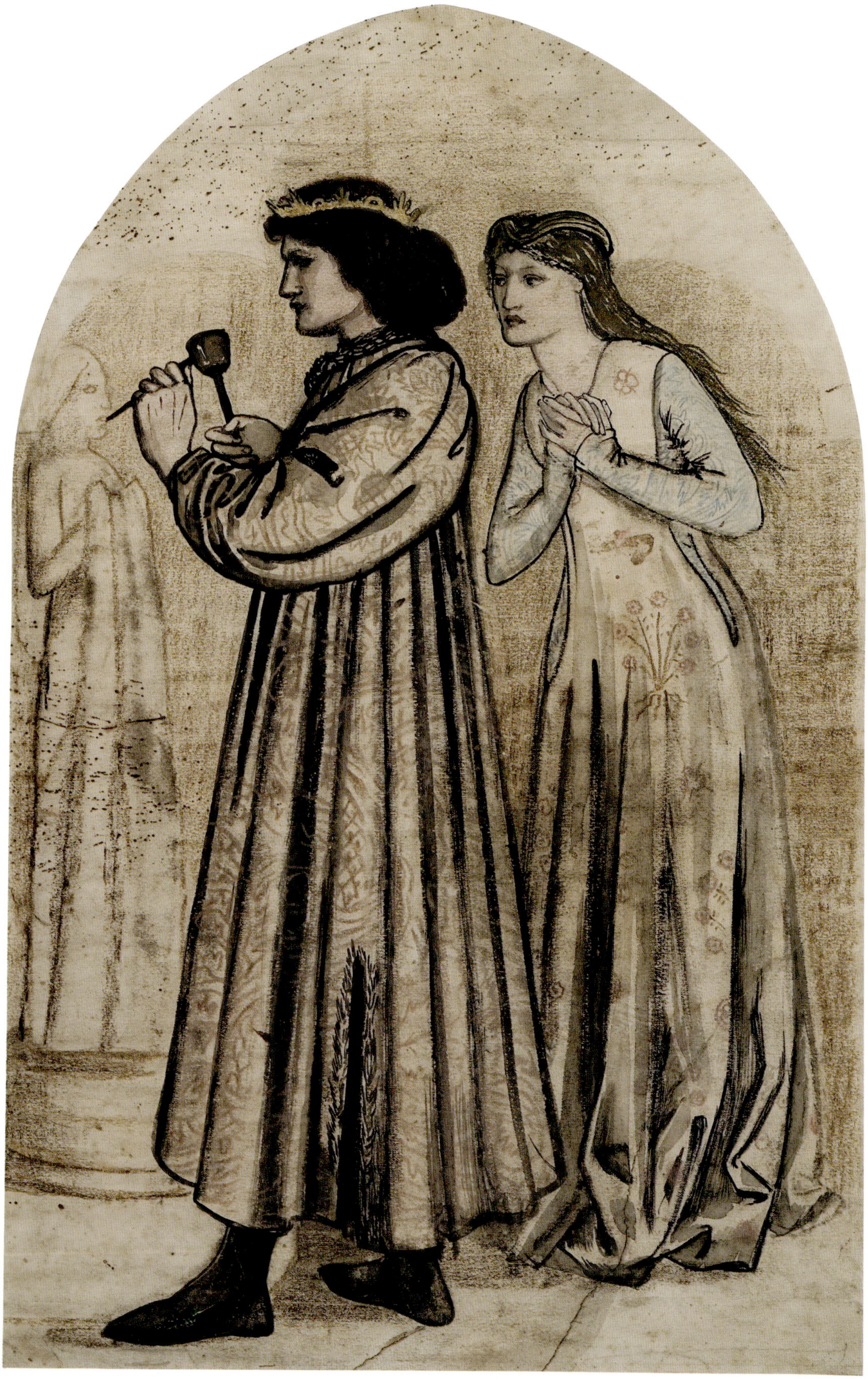

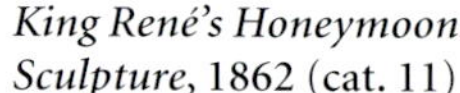

King René's Honeymoon: Sculpture, 1862 (cat. 11)

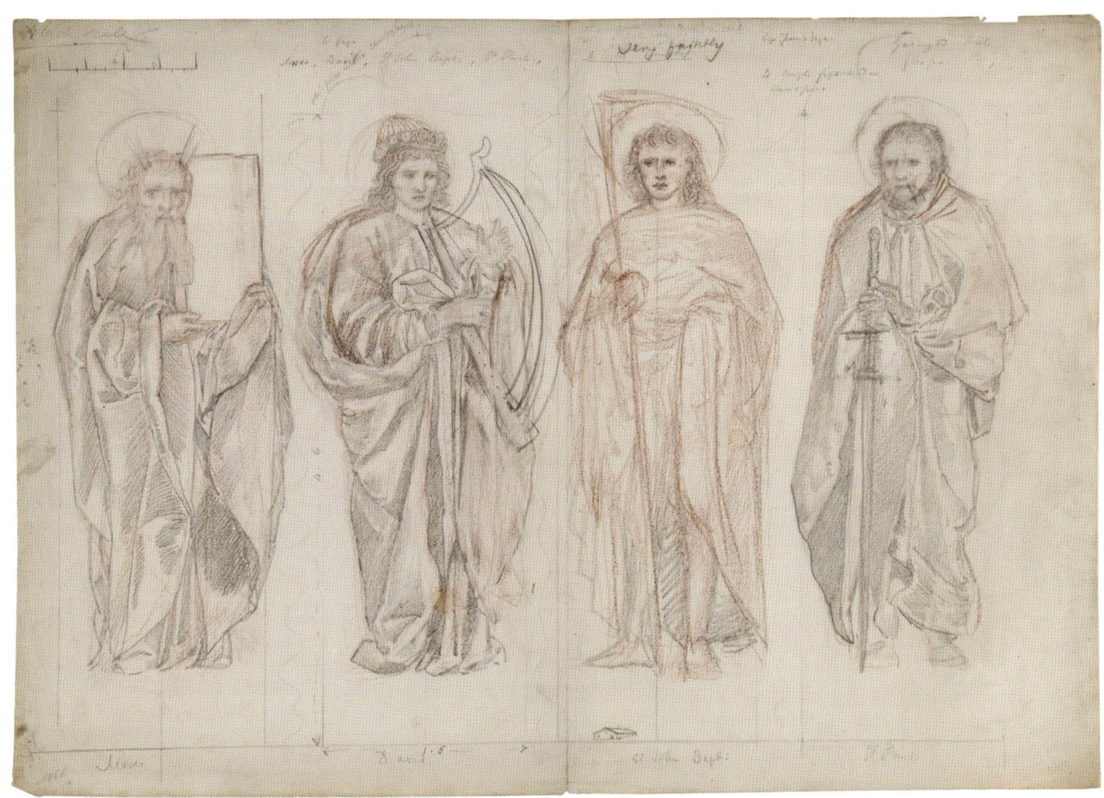

RIGHT: Working Drawing for Stained Glass: *Moses, David, St John the Baptist and St Paul*, 1866 (cat. 29)

BELOW: *The Masque of the Four Seasons*, 1873–75 (cat. 41)

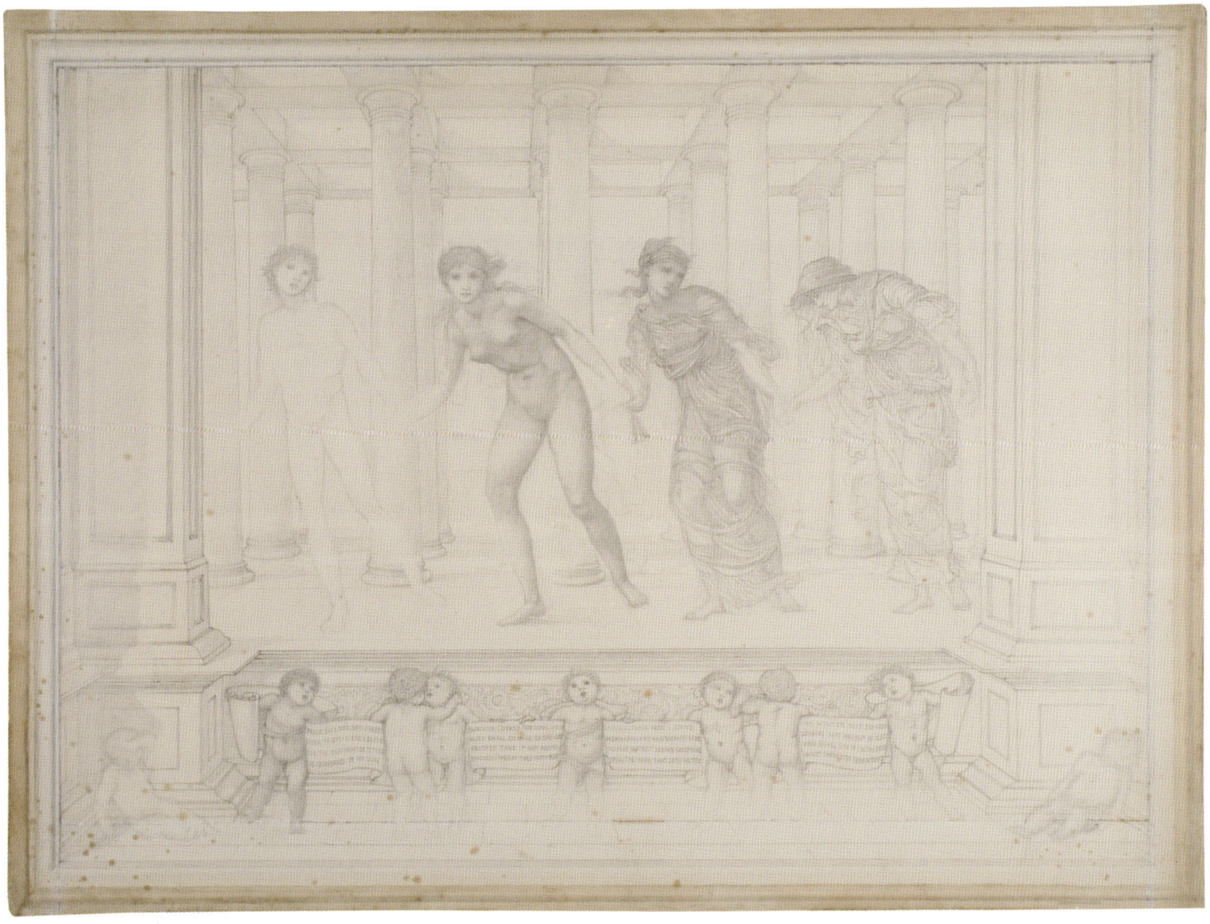

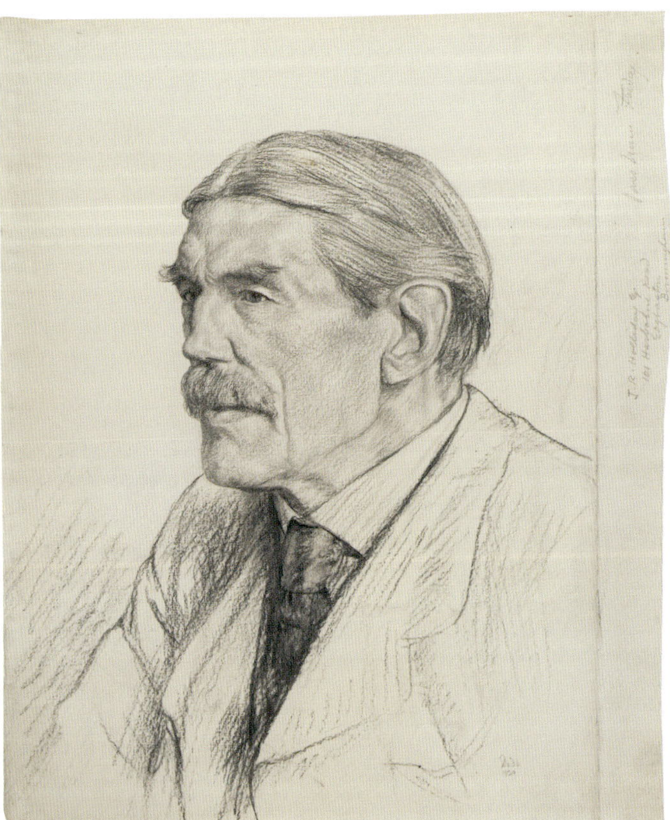

LEFT: *Portrait of J. R. Holliday*, after Francis Dodd, autotype

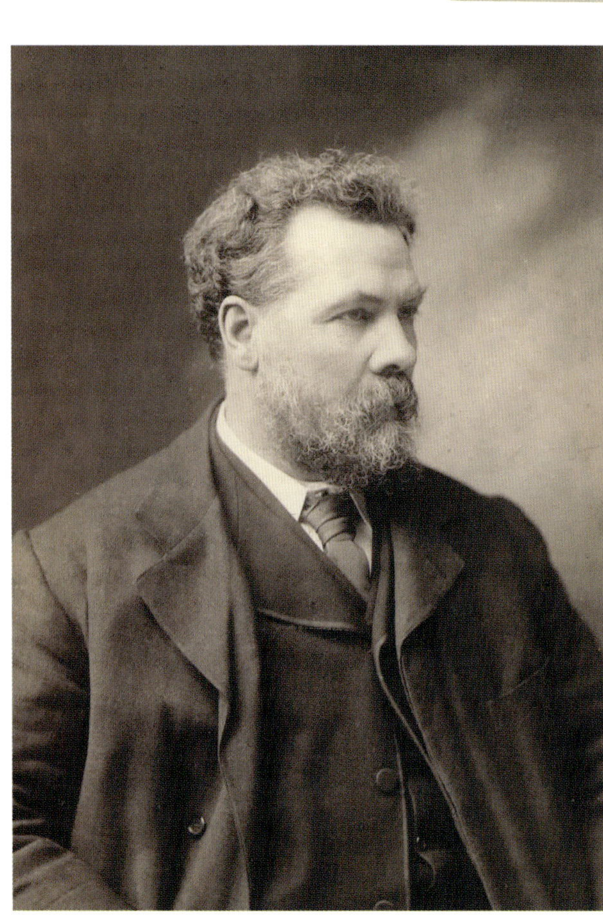

BELOW LEFT: *Charles Fairfax Murray*, photograph by Braun, c. 1902 (courtesy of David Elliott)

RIGHT: *The Briar Rose Series: Study for 'The Garden Court'*, 1889, bequeathed by Miss Kate Lewis, 1961 (B19, ex cat.)

BELOW: *Landscape*, 1863 (cat. 17)

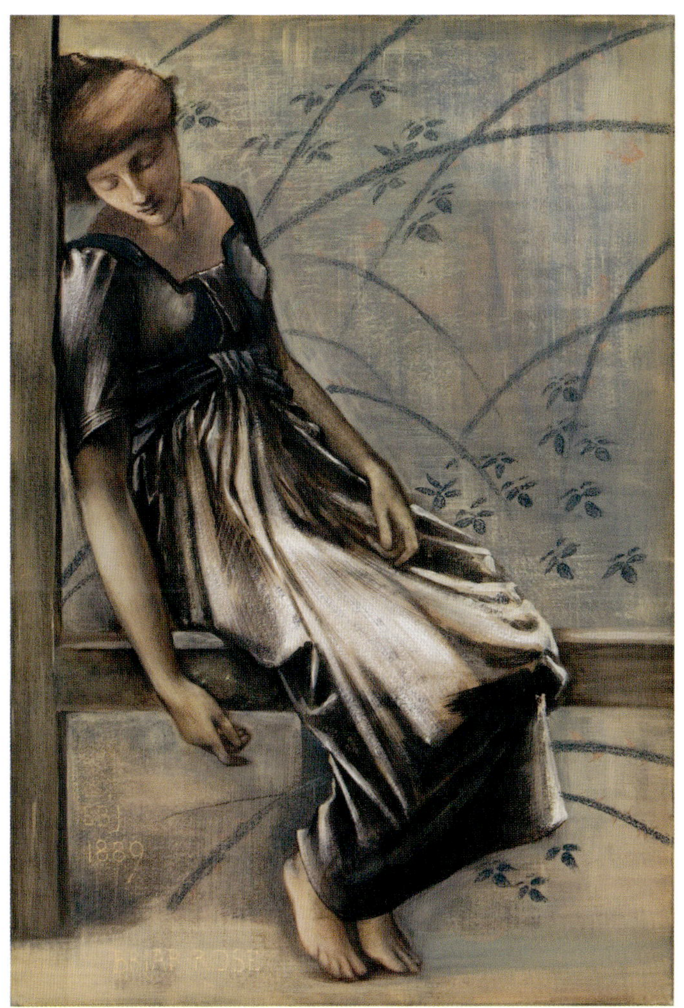

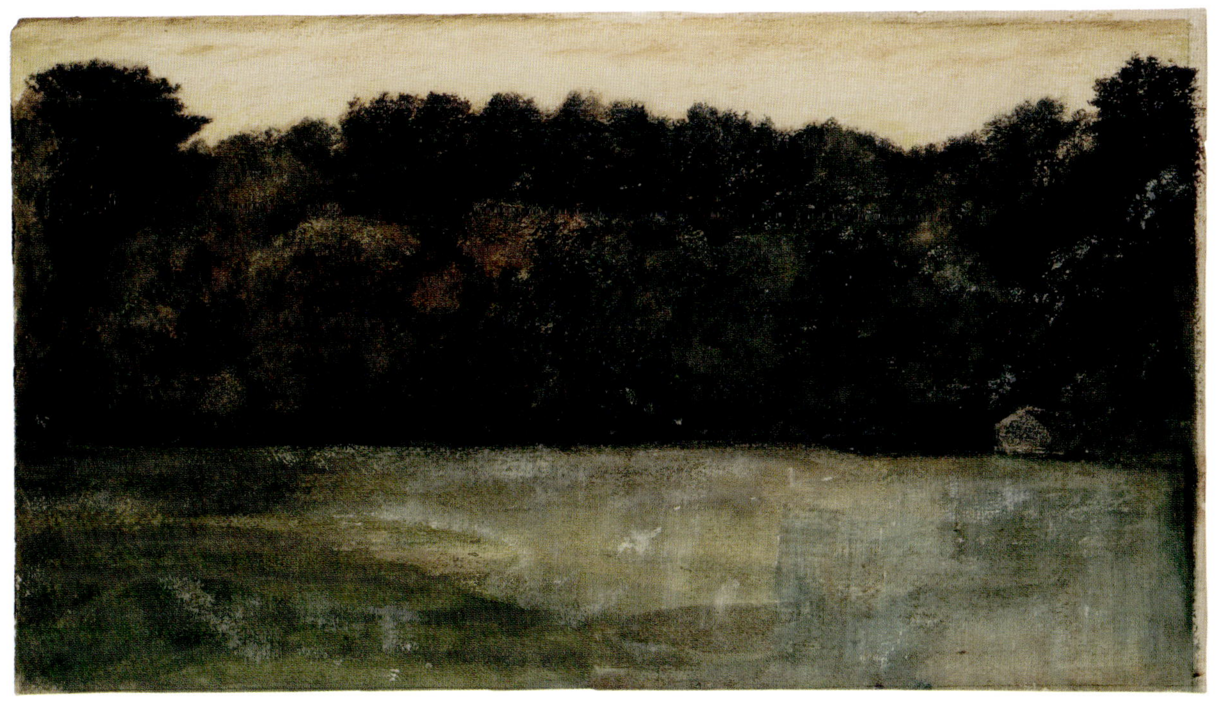

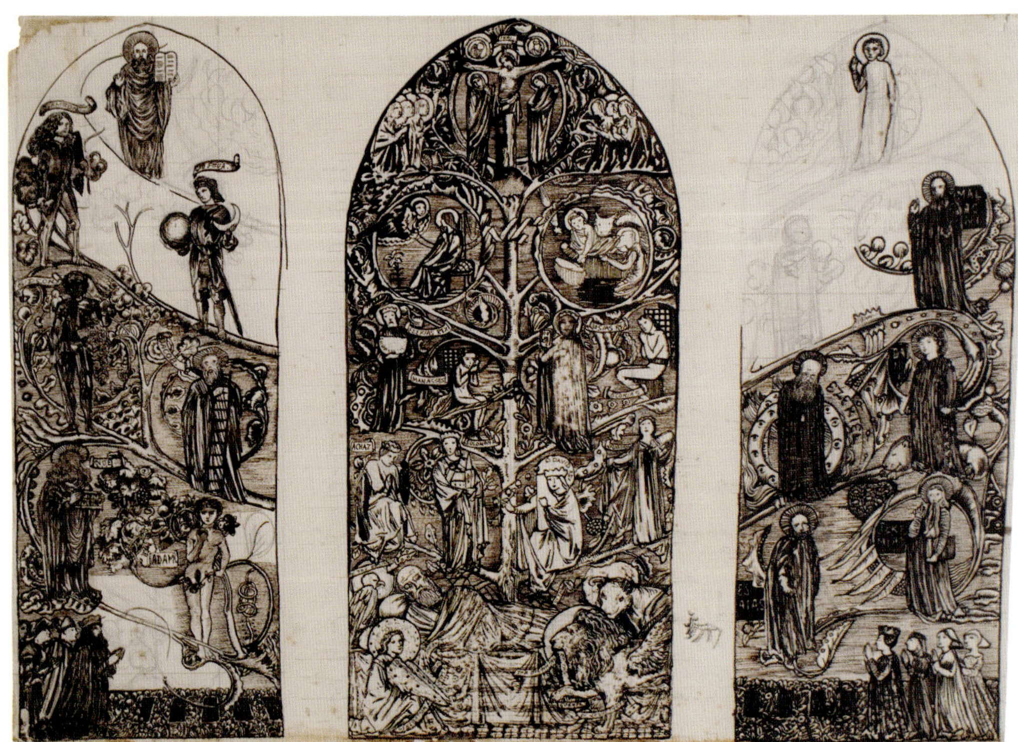

LEFT: Stained Glass Design: *The Tree of Jesse*, 1860–61 (cat. 4)

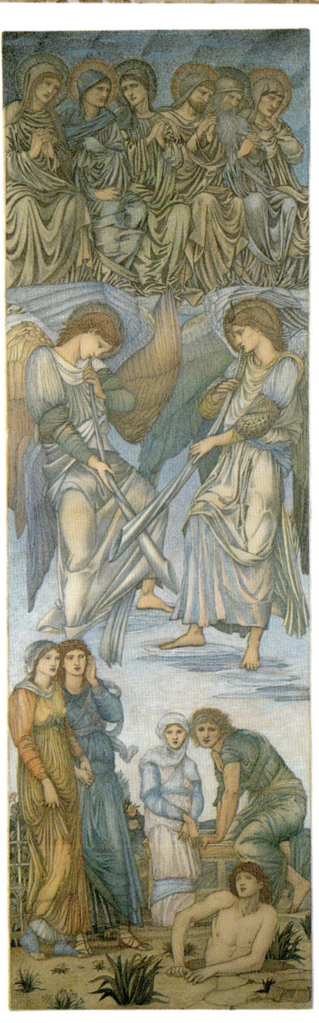

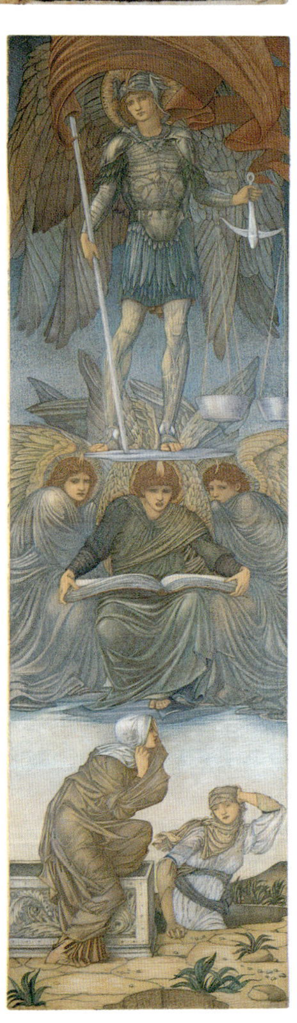

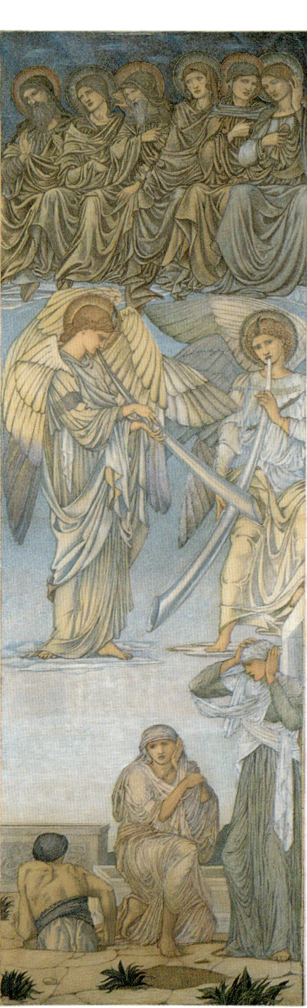

BELOW: *The Last Judgment*, 1874–80 (cat. 44)

5. *The Adoration of the Kings (with Annunciation): Study of Head for Infant Christ*, 1860–62 (illus. p. 30)

Pencil; 134 × 110 mm
Insc.: *E.B.J.**
Bequest of J. R. Holliday, 1927 (1927P559)

This is an intimate study of a small child, very unlike later drawings of children and putti made for works like the Troy Triptych. It is a study for the infant Christ in the second version of *The Adoration of the Kings* (1860–62), now in the collection of Andrew Lloyd Webber and done in oils; the first oil version of the triptych dates from 1860 (Tate, London). The model for the infant in each triptych is markedly different from the other, most notably in the pose and age of the child. Burne-Jones's sensitive treatment of these young models may be due to the fact that he became a father, for the first time, in October 1861, when his son Philip was born.

6. *Composite Drawing of a bewigged Figure*, c. 1861–63 (illus. p. 53)
verso: *possibly William Morris*

Thought to be by Ford Madox Brown and William Morris, with Edward Burne-Jones and Dante Gabriel Rossetti
Pencil; 136 × 79 mm
Purchased from Sotheby's Belgravia, 25 March 1980 (1980P38)

7. *Composite Drawing of a Stunner*, c. 1861–63 (illus. p. 53)
verso: *Girl with Ringlets*

Thought to be by Dante Gabriel Rossetti and Edward Burne-Jones, with William Morris and Ford Madox Brown
Pencil; 21 × 90 mm
Purchased from Sotheby's Belgravia, 25 March 1980 (1980P37)

The composite or *exquisite corpse* drawing was made famous in the early twentieth-century by the Surrealists, though the idea was based on an old parlour game played by several people. Each would write a phrase or, in this case draw on a sheet of paper, fold the paper to conceal the drawing, and pass on to the next player. The attribution and dating to Burne-Jones and his friends has been largely suggested by the envelope accompanying these drawings. It reads: *Early meetings at Burne-Jones in Gt Russell Street* (with *Lucy Falkener* [sic] in another hand).

8. *Study for 'An Idyll'*, 1862

Charcoal over pencil; 221 × 329 mm
Lit./ Exh.: *Whitley*, p. 53; *Arts Council* (34); *Visions* (67)
Purchased from Charles Fairfax Murray and presented by Subscribers, 1904 (1904P36)

This is a study for the watercolour, also in BMAG's collection (see cat. 9), which combines both strength and delicacy through the technique of Burne-Jones smudging the charcoal. It belongs to a group of timeless landscapes that followed Burne-Jones's visits to Italy in 1859 and 1862, and takes inspiration from the Venetian painters of the sixteenth century.

9. *An Idyll*, 1862

Watercolour, bodycolour, gum arabic, scraping on paper stretched onto canvas; 295 × 277 mm (sight)
Insc.: *E B J/ 1862*
Lit./ Exh.: *Whitley*, p. 36; *Harrison and Waters*, pp. 58, 66; *Arts Council* (33), *Solomon* (56)
Prov.: George Frederick Watts
Presented by Mrs George Frederic Watts, 1924 (1924P91)

An Idyll is one of the first of many such watercolours of this early period, where the influence of Giorgione is evident in both the landscape and the enigmatic subject matter. This painting can also been viewed as one of the first Aesthetic works of art with its harmonisation of colours and lack of a narrative element, seeming to just be a beautiful image and nothing more – art for its own sake. There is a question as to whether it was painted before or after Burne-Jones's trip to Venice in the summer of 1862.

10. *Stained Glass Design: Adam*, 1862

Indian ink and wash over pencil; 600 × 315 mm (sight)
Lit./ Exh.: *Whitley*, p. 131; *Harrison and Waters*, p. 50, pl. 65; *Sewter*, I, fig. 44; II, p. 173; *Myers*, p. 26, fig. 48; *Schoenherr*, p. 96
Purchased from Charles Fairfax Murray and presented by Subscribers, 1904 (1904P500)

One of a pair, with *Eve* (B874), of stained glass designs for the west wall of the vestry (under the tower) in All Saints' Church, Selsley, Gloucestershire, the first stained glass commission received by Burne-Jones from the newly founded Morris, Marshall, Faulkner & Co. (later Morris & Co., by 1875). The first study of Adam was drawn by William Morris and intended for tiles (William Morris Gallery, Walthamstow). Burne-Jones then adapted Morris's tile design into this stained glass cartoon of *Adam*, although it has been suggested that the lead lines may have been drawn by Morris. The tiles themselves were executed around this time as well, for a fireplace in John Roddam Spencer Stanhope's Surrey home, Sandroyd.

11. *King René's Honeymoon: Sculpture*, 1862 (illus. p. 44)

Pen and ink with wash over coloured chalk and pencil; 550 × 342 mm (sight)
Lit./ Exh.: *Whitley*, p. 53; *Harrison and Waters*, p. 47, fig. 51; *Whitworth* (66)
Purchased from Charles Fairfax Murray and presented by Subscribers, 1904 (1904P528)

This watercolour was originally one of two designs executed by Burne-Jones for a painted panel cabinet designed by the architect John P. Seddon (now in the Victoria & Albert Museum), the other being *King René's Honeymoon: Painting* (1862, watercolour, Private Collection). There were also designs by Ford Madox Brown, Dante Gabriel Rossetti, and decoration by Morris, all illustrating the various artistic pleasures of the fifteenth-century King René of Anjou, father-in-law of Henry VI of England. The lavishly painted cabinet was one of the main exhibits in the Medieval Court of the International Exhibition of 1862 held in South Kensington. The panels by all the artists involved were later executed as stained glass windows in 1862, made by Morris, Marshall, Faulkner & Co., and now in the Victoria & Albert Museum.

There is a variation in the colours used in the cabinet and this particular cartoon. The drawing was worked up in watercolour and chalks subsequent to the execution of the painted panel, which accounts for the differentiation in the palettes employed by Burne-Jones.

12. ***Full-Length Study for 'The Garland Weavers'***, **1862–66, coloured later** (illus. p. 24)

Coloured chalks; 340 × 159 mm
Insc.: *E B J/ 1862/ E B J*
Lit.: *Whitley*, p. 115
Bequest of J. R. Holliday, 1927 (1927P454)

The Garland Weavers is a series of six stained glass windows executed in 1867 for the Green Dining Room at the South Kensington Museum, London (now the Victoria & Albert Museum), by Morris, Marshall, Faulkner & Co., and designed by Burne-Jones. This study appears to be an early design for the figure in the fourth panel of this series. Although the drawing is dated 1862, it was probably worked up as late as the 1880s, when Burne-Jones would colour old drawings to sell, exhibit or present as gifts. The contrapposto of the figure, coupled with the style of the garment, is identical to other preliminary designs and studies for this series, although none is as finished as this (see B882–B892). Additionally, there are three watercolour studies of the fourth panel, all presently in private collections, dating from about 1864–65, as well as a finished watercolour that dates from 1865–66 (Private Collection).

13. ***Study of Cinderella***, **1862–63** (illus. p. 24)

Pencil; 408 × 214 mm
Lit.: *Whitley*, p. 54
Bequest of J. R. Holliday, 1927 (1927P585)

A nearly whole-length study, with Cinderella standing, turned slightly to the right, with her head resting on her right hand, as in the 1863 finished watercolour now in the Museum of Fine Arts, Boston. There is another similar study in BMAG's collection (B72), as well as in the Whitworth Art Gallery, University of Manchester, which also came from the Holliday collection. Another design, of Cinderella sweeping, is in BMAG's collection (B71), but the composition is considerably different from this and B72.

The differences between the figure of Cinderella in this study and the finished watercolour are revealing. Here, her figure is bulkier in size, indicating that perhaps a different model was used. It has been suggested that Fanny Cornforth, Rossetti's primary model and mistress at this time, sat for the figure of Cinderella, which may explain the differentiations in the size of the figure in the studies. In the finished watercolour, however, Burne-Jones uses the small, delicate facial features, and perhaps body as well, of his wife, Georgiana.

14. ***Stained Glass Design: The Song of Solomon – 'I charge you, O Daughters of Jerusalem'***, **1862–63** (illus. p. 21)

Sepia wash and ink with crayon over pencil on paper laid onto board; 569 × 467 mm
Lit./ Exh.: *V&A* (15a); *Sewter*, I, figs. 107, 110; II, pp. 59–60
Presented by Charles Fairfax Murray, 1900 (1900P173)

Burne-Jones designed this cartoon to illustrate this verse from *The Song of Solomon* (or *Song of Songs*): 'I charge you, O daughters of Jerusalem, if ye find my beloved, that ye tell him, that I am sick of love' (5:8). It was one of eight stained glass designs Morris, Marshall, Faulkner & Co. executed for the south transept of St Helen's Church, Darley Dale, Derbyshire, all of which are in BMAG (B929–B936). Of the eight images, this is one of the few that has been coloured in, an infrequent occurrence, as Burne-Jones usually left the colouring of the glass to Morris.

15. ***Ezekiel and the boiling Pot***, **1862–63** (illus. p. 57)

Pencil; 182 × 140 (i.), 190 × 179 mm (p.)
Insc.: *Ezekiel and the Boiling Pot**
Bequest of J. R. Holliday, 1927 (1927P511)

The drawing of *St Theophilus and the Angel* on the reverse helps to date this little-known design to about 1863. Here Burne-Jones establishes, through the use of deep shadowing, the confrontation between his main protagonists: the infuriated Ezekiel in the foreground with the boiling pot, and the hedonistic bed scene in the background. This particular parable is drawn from Ezekiel 24:10–14. Drawings in Tate, London, indicate that Burne-Jones first began to draw this scene as early as 1861, but slowly made changes to the figures. This drawing has the main elements of the finalised design with a framed edge indicating the shape of the woodblock for which it is intended.

16. ***'The Days of Creation': The Second Day***, **1863** (illus. p. 20)

Watercolour, gold and bodycolour over pencil; 62 × 134 mm (each)
Lit./ Exh.: *Dalziel*, pp. 164, 166; *Sheffield* (205); *Harrison and Waters*, pp. 67, 72; *Arts Council* (259)
Bequest of J. R. Holliday, 1927 (1927P466)

In 1863 the Dalziel Brothers commissioned seven images, of which this is one, for their original *Illustrated Bible* project. Burne-Jones's designs for *The Days of Creation* were the only ones executed in watercolour. It has been suggested that these were influenced by his reading of *The Life of William Blake* by Alexander Gilchrist, which appeared in the same year, although other research has indicated that the designs derived from sources as various as Samuel Palmer or the Renaissance sculptor Luca della Robbia. Previously, in 1861, Burne-Jones had executed a set of *The Days of Creation* for James Powell & Sons, as the east rose window at Waltham Abbey. He returned to the designs again, substantially altering the composition around 1870 (cat. 39). These later designs were much more elaborate, but basically utilised the same media of 1863. They were exhibited at the Grosvenor Gallery in 1877, and are now in the Fogg Art Museum, Harvard University.

17. ***Landscape***, **1863** (illus. p. 47)

Watercolour and gouache with gum arabic; 257 × 448 mm
Exh: *Arts Council* (247)
Presented by Mrs Angela Thirkell, 1954 (1954P61)

A small group of extant landscapes were made by Burne-Jones in 1863, three of which are in BMAG (see also B470–B472). These images are probably as close to pure Pre-Raphaelite naturalism as Burne-Jones ever got, being drawn from woods at Cobham, Surrey, while visiting John Roddam Spencer Stanhope. Although it is a scene taken from an actual location, there is a romantic and mysterious atmosphere in the way the picture is composed and, like *An Idyll* (cat. 9), owes a debt to Giorgione and Venetian painting.

It has been suggested that these landscapes served as background studies for Burne-Jones's 1863 masterpiece, *The*

Merciful Knight, a watercolour and bodycolour painting also in BMAG's collection (B520). His granddaughter, Angela Thirkell, who presented these landscapes to Birmingham, stated that these were in fact used for the 1864 watercolour *Green Summer* (Private Collection).

18. *Stained Glass Design: Two nude Studies for 'The Stoning of St Stephen'*, 1863 (illus. p. 23)

Pencil; 353 × 181 mm
Insc.: *Stoning of Stephen/ Lyndhurst Window/* E.B.J.*
Lit.: *Whitley*, p. 120; *Sewter*, II, p. 125
Bequest of J. R. Holliday, 1927 (1927P539)

This is a study for the executioner standing on the bottom left of the stained glass cartoon for *The Stoning of St Stephen*, also in BMAG's collection (B967), which was executed by Morris, Marshall, Faulkner & Co. in 1863 for the south transept window at St Michael and All Angels Church, Lyndhurst, Hampshire. The drawing is a good example of Burne-Jones's early attempts at anatomical precision for the movement of figures. This is evident by the way the figure holds the giant stone, the weight of which causes his lower body, specifically his buttocks, to contract.

19. *Drapery Study of Lucretia for Chaucer's 'Legend of Good Women'*, 1863 (illus. p. 43)

Pencil with secondary strip of paper along the top edge; 358 × 170 mm
Lit.: *Whitley*, p. 127
Purchased from Charles Fairfax Murray and presented by Subscribers, 1904 (1904P15)

Burne-Jones first designed images of Geoffrey Chaucer's heroines from *Legend of Good Women* in 1862 for tiles executed by Morris & Co. This study dates from about a year later, when Burne-Jones had been commissioned by John Ruskin to design embroidered hangings depicting all of the women (see B56 for the entire scheme). Lucretia was a married Roman noblewoman who was raped by a prince and, in her shame, killed herself with a sword. There is a slight sketch of the weapon visible at her right side.

This composition was not used in the final embroidery cartoons, which were executed in stained glass, as seven individual panels, by Morris, Marshall, Faulkner & Co. in 1864, first for the home of Myles Birket Foster, then for the Combination Room at Peterhouse College, Cambridge. The design for needlework was never realised. All the finished cartoons are in BMAG's collection (B57–B63).

20. *Georgiana Burne-Jones*, 1863 (illus. p. 41)

Bodycolour on paper laid on board; 357 × 267 mm
Insc.: G.M.J./ *Ætat: suae: xxii// pinxit* E.B.J./ AD MDCCCLXIII
Presented by Colin MacInnes, 1956 (1956P3)

This was one of Burne-Jones's first attempts, if not the first, at formal portraiture. The sitter is Georgiana, his wife of three years. Stylistically, the painting is unique in the artist's *oeuvre*, as the composition is entirely reminiscent of early limner-style Northern Renaissance portraiture, particularly those found in the English Royal Courts of the late fifteenth and early sixteenth centuries. This is especially evident with the solid background against which the sitter is placed, combined with the particular type of inscription seen on the panel, which gives the sitter's details.

The figural composition of Georgiana does, however, bear a resemblance to two contemporary paintings, both titled *Hope*, of which there is a version in oils (Private Collection) and a version in bodycolour (Collection of the Duke of Wellington, known as *If Hope were not, Heart should break*). But, unlike these two versions of *Hope*, the portrait of Georgiana was never intended for exhibition, and *Hidden Burne-Jones* marks the painting's public debut. It has never been exhibited previously due to its condition, and has recently undergone conservation work.

21. *Ezekiel and the boiling Pot*, c. 1863 (illus. p. 57)

Woodblock engraved by the Dalziel Brothers after Edward Burne-Jones; 176 × 133 mm
Insc.: see entry for B276
Acquired through J. N. Hart, c. 1965 (2006.1040.68)

The most comprehensive exhibition of Victorian illustration, *Book Illustrations of the 'Sixties'*, toured to Birmingham in 1924, featuring drawings and watercolours owned by Harold Hartley, and woodblocks for *Dalziels' Bible Gallery* (pub. 1881) and the expanded *Art Pictures from the Old Testament* version published by the Society for Promoting Christian Knowledge in 1894, as well as Millais's *Parables*, all belonging to John Napthali Hart. On Hart's death in 1965, as discussed by Robin de Beaumont, the woodblocks were offered to the Victoria & Albert Museum. Upon their refusal, Hart's executors were instructed to approach the then Tate Gallery and the British Museum, who also turned them down. The final acquisition of ninety-three Dalziel Bible project woodblocks by Birmingham was no doubt linked to the 1924 exhibition as well as the Museum's declared interest in nineteenth-century Arts & Crafts. Hart himself was probably unaware of the related sketch by Burne-Jones for the woodblock at BMAG (cat. 15).

22. *Stained Glass Design: St Mark the Evangelist*, 1863–64 (illus. p. 60)

Sepia and Indian ink, squared up in pencil on paper laid onto board; 964 × 390 mm
Insc.: *lining/ lining/ lining/ figure should digress/* FP*190/ 16/ 5*
Lit.: *Whitley*, p. 124; *Sewter*, I, fig. 183; II, p. 28
Presented by Charles Fairfax Murray, 1900 (1900P185)

St Mark was executed in 1864, for the east window of Bradford Parish Church, now Cathedral Church of St Peter. Of the twenty-eight lights that comprise the window, Burne-Jones designed only three, *St Mark*, *King David* (B899), and *Virgin Mary* (B979). The other lights were divided among Peter Paul Marshall, Philip Webb, Ford Madox Brown, Rossetti and Morris.

Also, about 1864, Burne-Jones designed four more cartoons for the church, intended for the chancel south window. BMAG has two of these designs in the collection as well (see B937 and B966).

23. *Chaucer's 'Legend of Good Women': Ariadne and Lucretia*, 1864 (illus. p. 43)

Sepia wash over pencil on brown washed paper; 423 × 445 (i.), 460 × 486 mm (p.)
Insc.: *drawing? from/ buildings up/ Ard?/ N 3/ W/ Imago Ariadnes Mart/ Imago Lucretiae Mart/ lining/ lining/ SP12?*

Purchased from Charles Fairfax Murray and presented by Subscribers, 1904 (1904P523)

Ariadne and Lucretia is one of seven highly detailed drawings at BMAG for Chaucer's *Legend of Good Women* (B57–B63), originally intended for Ruskin as an embroidered tapestry (B56). Aside from the 1863 drapery study for the figure of Lucretia, which may have originally been meant for this particular drawing (see cat. 19), there is also a finished watercolour dated 1867 in the BMAG collection (see cat. 30), which may have been compositionally based on this cartoon, as there are similarities in both the headdress and garment worn by Lucretia.

24. *Astrologia: Profile Study of Augusta Jones*, 1865 (illus. p. 41)

Red chalk over pencil; 483 × 350 mm
Lit.: *Whitley*, p. 104; *Ash*, pl. 2
Purchased from Charles Fairfax Murray and presented by Subscribers, 1904 (1904P202)

Augusta Jones (no relation to the artist; later Johnson) was a favourite model of Burne-Jones in the mid-1860s, and the sister of Frederick Sandys's wife, Mary. This drawing may be an early study made for *Astrologia*, a gouache of 1865 (Private Collection) for which Jones modelled. BMAG also has another head study of Jones (B335), as well as several studies for the first panel of the St George Series, *The Princess in the Garden* (oil, 1866, Musée d'Orsay, Paris), for which she also posed (B985–B988).

25. *Female Nude: Three Studies*, 1865–66 (illus. p. 24) (possibly *'Psyche at Her Bath'* from the **Cupid and Psyche Series**)

Black and white chalk on brown paper with additional strips of paper along the side edges; 510 × 331 mm
Lit.: *Whitley*, p. 106
Purchased from Charles Fairfax Murray and presented by Subscribers, 1904 (1904P9)

These three studies seem to be based on Burne-Jones's prevailing interest at the time in Greco-Roman sculpture, such as the Capitoline *Venus*. In the pose of the body, it certainly owes a debt to his continuing fascination with Florentine Renaissance art, such as Sandro Botticelli's *The Birth of Venus* (c. 1485, Uffizi, Florence). These nude figures may have been intended for the figure of Psyche in the illustrations of 'The Story of Cupid and Psyche' from Morris's epic narrative poem, *The Earthly Paradise* (B74–B233), as the finished drawings seem to bear a closer resemblance to her rather than to Venus.

26. *Two Nude Female Studies for 'The Lament'*, 1865 (illus. p. 17)

Brown chalk; 348 × 233 mm (sight)
Lit.: *Whitley*, p. 65
Purchased from Charles Fairfax Murray and presented by Subscribers, 1904 (1904P206)

There are seven studies at BMAG (see B463–B469) for the first version of the watercolour, *The Lament* (1865–66, William Morris Gallery, Walthamstow). The subject marks Burne-Jones's artistic development from Rossetti's Medievalist and Pre-Raphaelite influence, to a more Italianate and Aesthetic sensibility. *The Lament*, like Burne-Jones's earlier 1864 watercolour, *Green Summer* (1864, Private Collection), as well as the contemporary *Chant d'Amour* (watercolour, 1865, Museum of Fine Arts, Boston), are pure Aesthetic pieces, lacking clearly delineated subjects, truly demonstrating 'art for art's sake'. These studies were most likely drawn directly from a live model, and differ from some of the other BMAG drawings for *The Lament* (see cat. 27).

27. *Study of a crouched female Figure for 'The Lament'*, 1865 (illus. p. 17)

Pencil; 227 × 247 mm
Lit.: *Whitley*, p. 65; *Rome* (13)
Purchased from Charles Fairfax Murray and presented by Subscribers, 1904 (1904P204)

In 1861 Burne-Jones and his growing family lodged in rooms at 62 Great Russell Street, across from the British Museum. Probably at the prompting of both Ruskin and the artist George Frederic Watts, who revered the Elgin Marbles, Burne-Jones began seriously to consider classical sculpture. Sketchbooks from this period until the mid-part of the decade are filled with drawings based on works from antiquity (most of these are in the V&A). This study has its direct antecedents in the Elgin Marbles themselves, particularly in fragments of *The Fates* taken from the East Pediment, as well as the deities *Zeus*, *Hera*, *Hermes*, and *Hephaestos* or *Ares* from the east side of the Parthenon frieze. Burne-Jones made slight modifications to the ancient design in this study, where the figure remains seated, but is bent over in grief.

28. *Studies of a Seated Female Nude*, 1865–67 (illus. p. 17)

Red-brown chalk; 381 × 259 mm (sight)
Lit.: *Whitley*, p. 106
Purchased from Charles Fairfax Murray and presented by Subscribers, 1904 (1904P48)

This is one of six studies at BMAG (see B352–B354, B359–B360) that were all drawn from life, modelled by a tall girl, Mary Bartley, who also worked with Watts. The drawing may have been intended for the figure on the right in *The Lament*, or connected with the illustrations for *Cupid and Psyche*, which Burne-Jones was working on at this time.

29. *Working Drawing for Stained Glass: Moses, David, St John the Baptist and St Paul*, 1866 (illus. p. 45)

Brown-red chalk over pencil on two sheets of joined paper; 554 × 770 mm
Insc.: See catalogue entry for B908
Lit.: *Sewter*, II, pp. 80–81
Purchased from Charles Fairfax Murray and presented by Subscribers, 1904 (1904P217)

The inscription on the upper right of this drawing appears to refer to the destination of the stained glass window once it was executed by Morris & Co. Yet, such a window does not seem to have been executed in any of the locations in and around Glasgow for which Morris, Marshall, Faulkner & Co. supplied glass. The east window at Townhead Blochairn Church does contain figures of Moses, David, and SS John the Baptist and Paul, but they differ considerably from the figures that appear in this sketch. It is possible that this working composition was an early conception for the Townhead Blochairn scheme, but later altered.

This drawing was not catalogued by A. E. Whitley in 1939.

RIGHT: Composite drawing of a Stunner, c. 1861–63 (cat. 7)

FAR RIGHT: Composite drawing of a bewigged Figure, c. 1861–63 (cat. 6)

BELOW: Caricature: *The Sirens*, c. 1878–80 (cat. 50)

BELOW RIGHT: Caricature: Head of three Jews, 1877–80 (cat. 49)

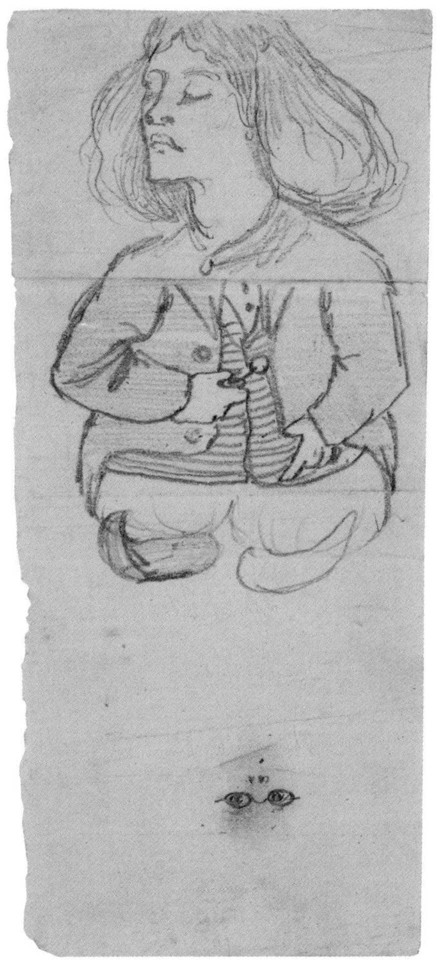

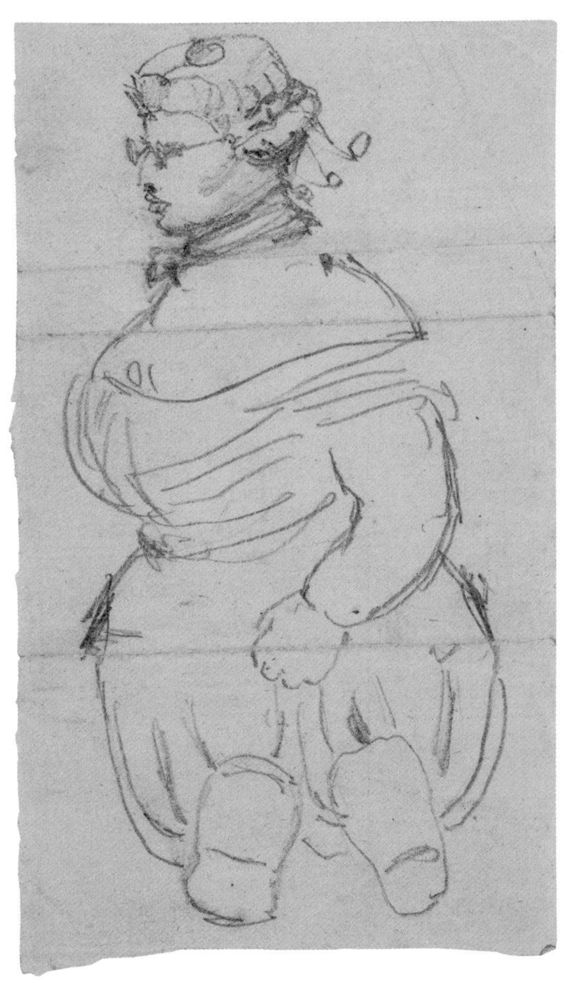

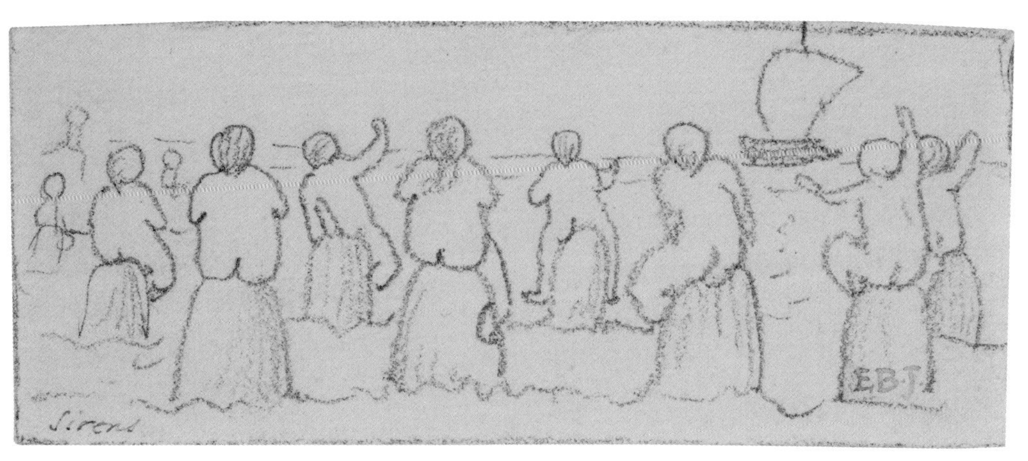

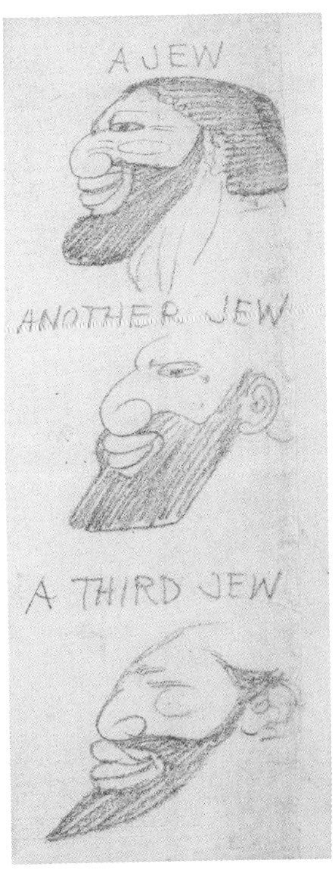

30. *Lucretia*, 1867 (illus. p. 42)

Watercolour, bodycolour and pastel with gold on paper laid on canvas; 1368 × 685 mm
Insc.: *.E.B.J. 1867 London/ Lucretia/ As when a wolfe findeth a lamb alone/ To whom shall she complaine or make mean*
Bequest of J. R. Holliday, 1927 (1931P61)

Burne-Jones's *Lucretia* is based on Part V of Chaucer's *Legend of Good Women*, where she is a married noblewoman raped by a prince of Rome, Tarquinius; ashamed, she commits suicide. Malcolm Bell makes no reference to any such painting in his *Record and Review* of 1892, so it is difficult to tell for what purpose this was executed. There is, however, an earlier cartoon executed in both stained glass and tile by Morris & Co. in 1864 (cat. 23), as well as an embroidered panel, *Lucretia, Hippolyte and Helen*, designed by Morris about the same time, embroidered by his wife Jane and her sister, Elizabeth Burden (finished 1888, Castle Howard, West Yorkshire).

It is very likely, however, that *Lucretia* was originally intended as a stained glass design of some kind, although not necessarily specifically meant to depict this figure. This seems probable, based on the blacked-out flowers that are painted over in the bottom of the picture, identical in composition to the flora on other stained glass cartoons of this period created by Burne-Jones. It was worked-up as an independent painting in 1867, and given as a wedding gift to Charles Augustus Howell that August, which Burne-Jones refers to in letters to George Howard (later 9th Earl of Carlisle), now in the Castle Howard Archives, West Yorkshire.

31. *Study of Drapery for 'Charity'*, 1867 (illus. p. 26)

Pencil; 390 × 282 mm
Insc.: *the top corner/ the bottom corner*
Lit.: *Whitley*, p. 92
Purchased from Charles Fairfax Murray and presented by Subscribers, 1904 (1904P156)

The Christian Cardinal Virtues of Hope (*Spes*), Faith (*Fides*) and Charity (*Caritas*) became the subject of a three-light window executed by Morris & Co. for the nave of Christ Church Cathedral, Oxford. Later versions of these virtues were redesigned for stained glass, then worked-up as independent watercolours. *Charity* compositionally remained the same for a painting worked on between 1867 and 1872, and now in the Collection of Andrew Lloyd Webber (B46).

This particular drawing focuses on the drapery for the main female figure, and is one of four for the Christ Church windows at BMAG (B47–B50). Also in the collection are two unrelated, earlier designs for another window by Morris & Co., representing *Charity standing on the figure of Envy* (B851–B852).

32. *Composition Study for 'Charity'*, 1867 (illus. p. 26)

Pencil; 367 × 210 mm (sight)
Lit./ Exh.: *Whitley*, p. 92; *Sheffield* (30)
Purchased from Charles Fairfax Murray and presented by Subscribers, 1904 (1904P155)

This full-length study belongs to a group of four drawings depicting *Charity*, intended for the Christ Church Cathedral, Oxford. The design was later worked-up as a watercolour of 1867–72 (see cat. 31).

33. *Maria Zambaco in traditional Greek Costume*, 1867–68 (illus. p. 41)

Black chalk and pencil; 561 × 388 mm
Lit./ Exh.: *Whitley*, p. 104; *Arts Council* (234)
Purchased from Charles Fairfax Murray and presented by Subscribers, 1904 (1904P216)

Maria Zambaco (née Cassavetti) was a medallist and sculptor of Greek descent, who was Burne-Jones's mistress around the time this drawing was produced. This may be an early design for his *Allegorical Portrait of Maria Zambaco*, produced in 1870 (now in the Clemens-Sels Museum, Neuss). There is a portrait by Watts of Zambaco, aged about five, in Greek costume (Private Collection), which may have been the inspiration for this study.

34. *Studies of female Drapery seen from the back*, 1867–69 (illus. p. 38)

Red-brown chalk; 379 × 270 mm
Lit.: *Whitley*, p. 116
Bequest of J. R. Holliday, 1927 (1927P552)

Burne-Jones made countless studies of female figures in drapery, many of which are in BMAG (B302–B334). The images in this particular study may have been intended for *The Passing of Venus*, an oil painting dating from about 1875 (Junior Common Room, Exeter College, Oxford).

35. *Study of a Man embracing a Tree*, 1868–69 (illus. p. 23)

Red-brown chalk; 295 × 156 mm
Lit.: *Whitley*, p. 107
Purchased from Charles Fairfax Murray and presented by Subscribers, 1904 (1904P120)

This male nude study probably originated from a sketchbook, along with another similar nude study (B505) and a draped study (B503). These may all be early conceptions of *Phyllis and Demophoön* (cat. 38) or an unrealised *Apollo and Daphne*.

36. *Stained Glass Design: Head Study of Maria Zambaco for St Mark the Evangelist*, 1869–71 (illus. p. 60 and frontispiece)

Pencil; 293 × 238 mm
Insc.: *E.B.J*/ to A C* [faint, EBJ's hand]
Lit.: *Whitley*, p. 104
Bequest of J. R. Holliday, 1927 (1927P455)

Most likely, this is the preparatory head study for the figure of St Mark the Evangelist executed in stained glass by Morris & Co. in 1874 for Jesus College Chapel, Cambridge (for a similar stained glass, see 1927M1016, dated 1883). This head study is in reverse from the 1873–74 stained glass cartoon of St Mark for which it was intended (cat. 43), but there are similar cases of reversal in Burne-Jones's output, especially in his illustration work.

It was not unusual for Burne-Jones to use female models for male subjects. Once he found a face that was ideal for a particular figure, he utilised it, regardless of gender. This happened with great frequency in the late 1860s and through to the mid-1870s, when he primarily used Maria Zambaco as his muse. The 'A C' in the inscription could refer to Aglaia Coronio, a patroness of Burne-Jones and correspondent of Morris, as well as Zambaco's first cousin.

37. *Small Composition Studies for 'Charity'*, 1870 (illus. p. 26)

Pencil with ink; 90 × 49 and 99 × 53 mm
Lit.: *Whitley*, p. 93
Bequest of J. R. Holliday, 1927 (1927P527 and 1927P528)

These small composition studies are most likely working designs by Burne-Jones used as a scheme for the arrangement of figures in a confined space. They were intended for the stained glass cartoon that was later worked-up as a watercolour of *Charity* or *Caritas*, from 1867–72 (cats 31, 32 and 61).

38. *Phyllis and Demophoön*, 1870 (illus. p. 22)

Bodycolour and watercolour with gold medium and gum arabic on composite layers of paper on canvas; 938 × 475 mm
Insc.: *E B J. 1870/* [label on reverse] *Dic mihi quid feci?/ Nisi non sapienter amavi* (Tell me what I have done?/ Except to unwisely fall in love with you)
Exh.: Old Water-Colour Society, 1870 (154); *New Gallery* (17); *Arts Council* (117); *Victorian Artist-Dreamer* (48); *Victorian Nude* (66)
Prov.: bought from the artist by Frederick Leyland; his sale, Christie's, 28 May 1892 (44); bought John Bibby
Presented by The John Feeney Charitable Trust, 1916 (1916P37)

The subject of this important work occurs in Chaucer's *Legend of Good Women*, though Burne-Jones also significantly cites Ovid's *Heroides* as the source for this painting. Phyllis, Queen of Thrace, fell in love with Demophoön, son of Theseus, after the Trojan War. Forced to return to his home in Athens, Demophoön departed, but promised to return to Phyllis in six months' time. When he failed to keep his word, Phyllis hanged herself and, pitied by the gods, was transformed into a barren almond tree. Demophoön, however, eventually returned to Thrace and, hearing of Phyllis' fate, embraced the tree, which suddenly blossomed. Burne-Jones depicts the moment of forgiveness in a slightly different manner than in literature, with Phyllis actually emerging from the tree to reconcile with her lover.

The faces of both Phyllis and Demophoön are modelled on Maria Zambaco, for which several studies exist (in Private Collections, as well as Tate, London). This was not an unusual practice for Burne-Jones (see above) and is less a fascination with androgyne figures, as some scholars suppose, than an obsession with the face of a particular model, which was characteristic of him throughout his career.

Supposedly because of Demophoön's nudity, a controversy erupted when the painting was displayed at the Old Water-Colour Society in the Summer Exhibition of 1870. Within two weeks of the exhibit's opening, Burne-Jones withdrew the picture due to these alleged complaints, and two works by other artists were chosen as replacements; it was the first instance in the Society's history of an artist withdrawing his work in the middle of exhibition. Two months later, Burne-Jones resigned from the Society, based on artistic integrity.

Burne-Jones later reworked the entire painting in oils, transforming both the bodies of Phyllis and Demophoön into an homage to Michelangelo's sculptural bodies. It was renamed *Tree of Forgiveness* (1882, Lady Lever Art Gallery, Port Sunlight), and reworked to feature Zambaco only as the face of Phyllis (see gouache study, National Museum of Wales, Cardiff).

39. *'The Days of Creation': Study of Hands and Globe for 'The Second Day'*, 1872 (illus. p. 20)

Pencil; 362 × 248 mm
Insc.: *E B-J/ 1872/ Studies for the Days of/ Creation/ II*
Lit./ Exh.: *Whitley*, p. 97; *Hong Kong* (17)
Bequest of J. R. Holliday, 1927 (1927P464)

The study is for the central angel holding the globe in the *Days of Creation: The Second Day* (1872–78, Fogg Art Museum, Harvard University; see also B257). Although all the central angels in the series of six panels hold globes (B256–B262), Burne-Jones has labelled this study with a 'II' indicating that this is for the *Second Day*, as well as depicting two different figural compositions for each of the two angels in the picture.

40. *Self-Caricature*, 1872–73

Pencil; 93 × 46 mm
Insc.: *E.B.J.**
Lit.: *Whitley*, p. 105
Bequest of J. R. Holliday, 1927 (1927P555)

Humour may not come immediately to mind alongside the seriousness of Burne-Jones's painting. Caricature, however, played an important part in his private life. He frequently ridiculed himself, particularly to family and friends, as described by Georgiana: 'There are hundreds of letters from Edward to his children still in existence. In these, from the first, he often jestingly assumed the character of an old man, and this led to him establishing a caricature likeness of himself which was as well known to his friends as a written signature' (*Memorials*, II, p. 15).

41. *The Masque of the Four Seasons,* 1873–75 (illus. p. 45)

Pencil with additional strips around four edges; 427 × 562 mm
Insc.: with verses of William Morris's poem *Lapse of the Year*
Exh: *Reality and Vision* (48); *Sheffield* (206)
Bequest of J. R. Holliday, 1927 (1927P538)

The Masque of the Four Seasons is derived from Morris's 1869 poem 'The Lapse of the Year', from his *Book of Verse* (1870, V&A). The verses, peculiar to each season, are written on scrolls beneath the stage on which the seasons progress in procession. Burne-Jones had already undertaken four gouaches of the seasons in 1869 (all now in a Private Collection; B473–B476), which also quote Morris's verses, but with each season in a separate panel. This drawing may have also been the inspiration for Walter Crane's own *Masque of the Four Seasons* of 1903–09 (Hessisches Landesmuseum, Darmstadt) and his substitution of a changing landscape for the classical interior.

Morris's poem on four separate scrolls reads as follows:

Spring: *Spring am I too soft of heart/ Much to speak ere I depart/ Ask the Summertide to prove/ The abundance of my love*

Summer: *Summer looked for long am I/ Much shall change or ere I die/ Prithee take it not amiss/ Though I weary thee with bliss*

Autumn: *Laden Autumn here I stand/ Worn of heart and weak of hand/ Nought but rest seems good to me/ Speak the word that sets me free*
Winter: *I am Winter that do keep/ Longing safe amidst of sleep/ Who shall say if I were dead/ What should be remembered*

42. *Pygmalion and the Image: Study of Pygmalion for 'The Soul Attains'*, 1873–75 (illus. p. 13)

With secondary figure sketch and faint outline of another figure
Pencil with brown crayon; 226 × 286 mm
Bequest of J. R. Holliday, 1927 (1927P476)

The model for this drawing has previously been identified as W. A. S. Benson. Benson certainly sat for Pygmalion, but only for the head, as described in *Memorials*. John Christian comments that, 'the model here does not look like him (nose too pointed, hair straight not curly), and I suspect the drawing was made from a professional model or even lay figure.'

43. *Stained Glass Design: St Mark the Evangelist*, 1873–74 (illus. p. 60)

Sepia wash and Indian ink with bodycolour over pencil on paper laid onto board; 1230 × 505 mm
Lit./ Exh.: *Whitley*, p. 143; *Sewter*, I, fig. 435; *Schoenherr*, p. 113; *Rome* (99)
Bequest of J. R. Holliday, 1927 (1927P423)

St Mark the Evangelist was designed for the south transept, west wall, of Jesus College Chapel, Cambridge, executed in stained glass by Morris & Co. in 1874. It was subsequently used for the west window of the Church of All Hallows, Allerton, Liverpool, in 1876, and later in the south transept chapel of St Paul's Church, Morton, Lincolnshire, in 1891. An independent stained glass panel was also executed in 1883, which is currently in BMAG (1927M1016).

The head of St Mark was taken from Maria Zambaco (cat. 36), which is in reverse from this cartoon, in three-quarter view to the right. Alterations such as this were often made by Burne-Jones in his decorative work.

44. *The Last Judgment*, 1874–80 (illus. p. 48)

Wax crayon, three panels; 3050 × 950, 3050 × 855, 3050 × 950 mm
Insc.: *E B J/ 1874*
Lit./ Exh.: Grosvenor Gallery, London, Winter 1881; *Victorian Artist-Dreamer* (71)
Prov.: First studio sale, Christie's, 16 July 1898 (lot 59)
Presented by Hon. William Kenrick and J. R. Holliday, 1898 (1898P19)

These three cartoons form the chancel east window of three lights at St Michael and St Mary Magdalene, Easthampstead, Berkshire, executed by Morris & Co. in 1876. It was crowned by a rose window of Christ in Majesty called *Dies Domini* (B264). *The Last Judgment* was drawn by Burne-Jones in 1874, but later returned to his studio, where several years later it was coloured in wax crayon, with the hues bearing little resemblance to the window. This was a common practice for studies and cartoons to be worked-up or coloured many years after its original composition (see *Study for 'The Garland Weavers'*, cat. 12).

Photographs of the finished cartoons appear in the *Morris & Company Windows Book: Photograph Album of Edward Burne-Jones Stained Glass Designs* (B527; nos 247, 203 and 248, respectively), taken before colouring.

45. *Sketchbook: Nudes and Drapery Studies for various subjects including 'Perseus'*, 1875 (illus. p. 23)

Pencil, twenty-two drawings in bound volume; 265 × 199 mm
Front cover: *III/ 47*; inside front cover: *July 1875*
Presented by Mrs Angela Thirkell, 1952 (1952P5)

This particular sketchbook contains the original compositional scheme for the *Court of Phineus*, a panel absent from the final Perseus Series. It is the penultimate scene, of great drama, intended to precede the *Baleful Head*, where Perseus uses the head of Medusa to turn Phineus, his mother's betrothed, and his courtiers to stone. Some of the most splendid male nudes for this series are to be found in this sketchbook, for example *Atlas turned to Stone, The Rock of Doom* and *Doom Fulfilled*. There are also a few nude figure studies for the *Romaunt of the Rose*. All the drawings are typical of Burne-Jones's use of a fine, but soft, pencil at this time, in which he set himself very high standards of finish.

46. *The Song of Solomon: 'Who is it that cometh out of the Wilderness?'*, 1875–76 (illus. p. 21)

Pencil; 350 × 203 mm
Insc.: *QVAE.EST.ISTA.QVAE.ASCENDIT.DE.DESERTO.DELICIIS.AFFLVENS.INNIXA. SVPER.DILECTVM.SVVM/ E B J*
Lit./ Exh.: *Whitley*, p. 98; *Harrison and Waters* (118); *Visions* (101); *Victorian Artist-Dreamer* (83)
Presented by Mrs George Frederick Watts, 1924 (1924P92)

This is the fifth and final illustration for an unrealised series of paintings, which bear little connection with *The Song of Solomon* stained glass cartoons of the early 1860s (cat. 14) other than subject matter. The title is taken from chapter 5, verse 6 of the biblical poem also known as the *Song of Songs* or *Canticles*. In 1902 New York publisher R. H. Russell reproduced the five designs, along with a reproduction of the watercolour *Sponsa de Libano/ Awake, O North Wind!* (1891, Lady Lever Art Gallery, Port Sunlight), to accompany the full text of *The Song of Solomon*.

Only one figure in this drawing is identifiable, the figure facing left on the far right; she is based on the profile of Maria Zambaco.

47. *Sketchbook: Nude, Draped and Cast Studies mostly for 'Perseus' Series*, 1875–79 (illus. p. 23)

Mostly pencil, with white bodycolour on blue ground, in bound sketchbook; twenty-one drawings; 272 × 194 mm
Insc.: *XII/ 50/ 52* [?]
Presented by Mrs Angela Thirkell, 1952 (1952P4)

Aside from the many highly finished designs for the Perseus Series, this sketchbook also contains two early studies for *Stella Vespertina* and *Stella Matutina* of the *Planets* Series (see B906 for the finished cartoon of *Mars*), later executed by Morris & Co. in stained glass for Angus Holden's Yorkshire home, Woodlands.

48. *Sketchbook: Alps, France, Birds and Dogs*, 1878 (illus. p. 80)

Mostly pencil with some crayon in Roberson & Co clothbound sketchbook; twenty-one drawings; 272 × 194 mm
Insc.: *32/ sketch/ book of Edward Burne-Jones/ drawings done in Switzerland in 1878/ bird copied from a Japanese screen**
Presented by Mrs Angela Thirkell, 1952 (1952P3)

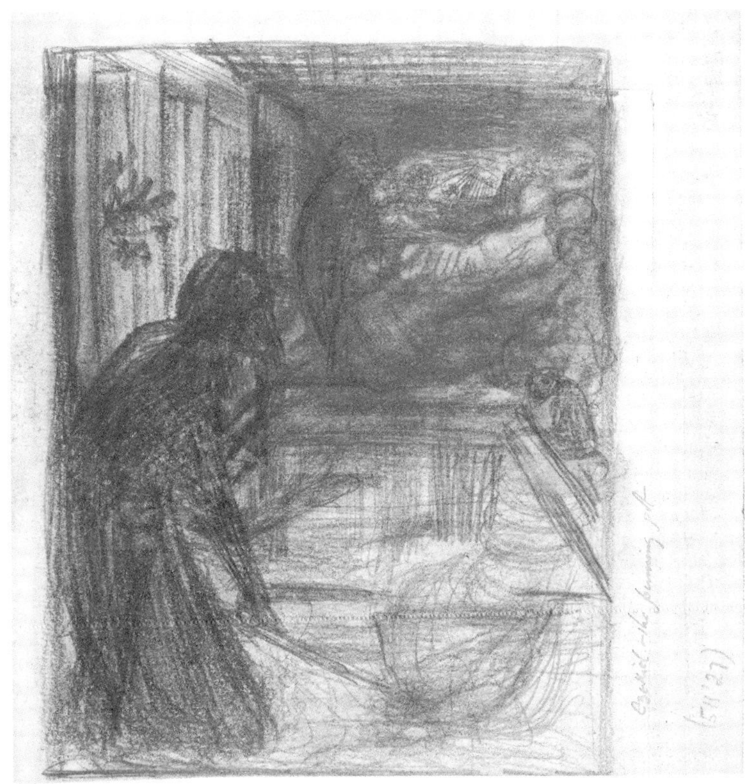

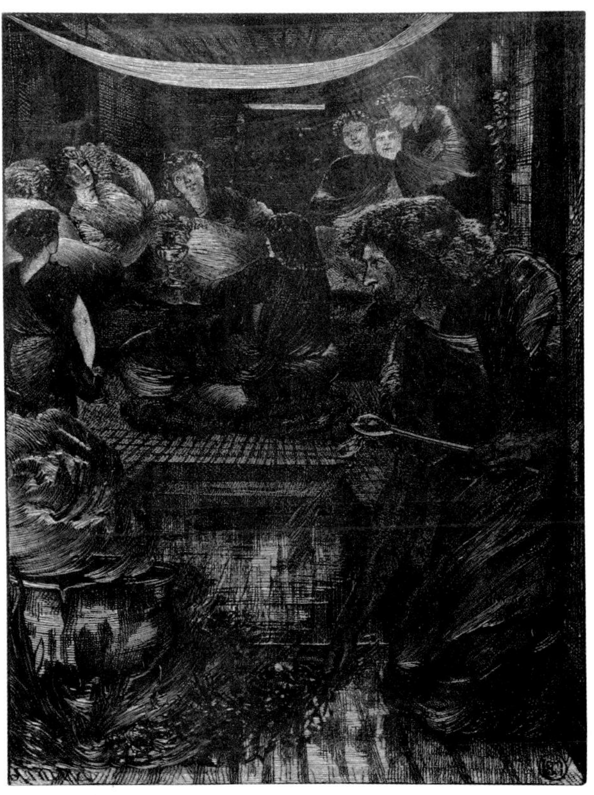

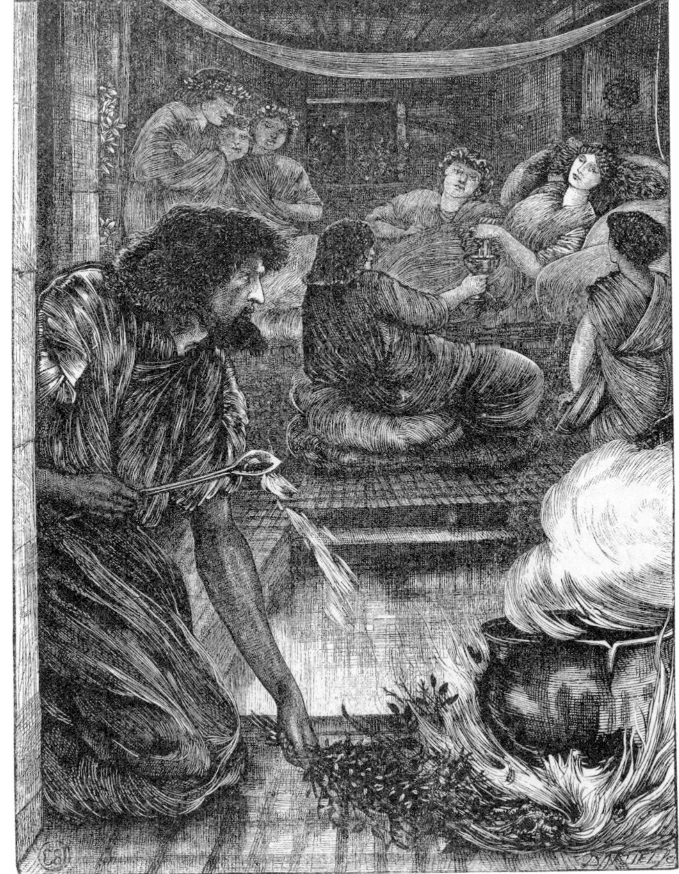

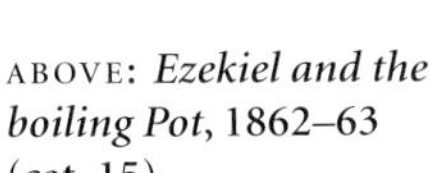

ABOVE: *Ezekiel and the boiling Pot*, 1862–63 (cat. 15)

ABOVE RIGHT: *Ezekiel and the boiling Pot*, c. 1863 (cat. 21)

RIGHT: *Dalziels' Bible Gallery: 'Ezekiel and the boiling Pot'*, pub. 1881 (cat. 52)

This complicated sketchbook of thirty-one loose pages (as a result of disintegrated binding), descended through the Burne-Jones family to Angela Thirkell, his granddaughter. She is almost certainly the author of the above inscription making the slightly misleading connection with Switzerland rather than the Haute-Savoie region of France, where Burne-Jones travelled in 1878. The reconstruction of the sketchbook by Stephen Wildman, and file correspondence with Dr William Hauptman of the Musée Cantonal des Beaux-Arts in Lausanne, suggest that the mountains were drawn in or around Chamonix, where Burne-Jones and his family took their holiday in August 1878. Georgiana Burne-Jones, in *Memorials,* describes a particular day when the family took a 'beautiful day's drive down through the mountains, by the river Arve, as far as Bonneville …'. The town of Annecy, as well as a mountainous view from Annecy Castle, also figure in this sketchbook. Burne-Jones seems to have also travelled further south on this holiday, as represented by a drawing of the tenth-century Abbaye de Montmajour, near Arles in Provence.

There may well be no immediate connection between this trip and the studies of transcribed and imagined birds taken from a Japanese screen, or indeed the dog studies and drawings of the Capitoline *Wolf* in the Palazzo dei Conservatori, Rome. Burne-Jones depicts this famous classical sculpture from a three-dimensional viewpoint, which implies that he actually saw it or an equivalent copy, rather than working from an illustration.

49. *Caricature: Head of three Jews*, 1877–80 (illus. p. 53)

Pencil; 323 × 122 mm
Insc.: *A Jew/ Another Jew/ A Third Jew*
Lit.: *Whitley*, p. 105
Bequest of J. R. Holliday, 1927 (1927P549)

BMAG has a small group of drawings (B35–B38) loosely labelled in the past as humorous, but specifically showing Burne-Jones stereotyping Jews. These private doodles lampoon bags of money, large noses, rubber lips and, here, the lack of individualisation among three Jews. While the message is clearly anti-Semitic, the drawings could be an expression of some kind of personal anger at a particular point in time. The tone of the humour is slightly different from the outright racial prejudice of contemporary cartoons found in the pages of *Punch*, and these were certainly not intended for any kind of public display. Indeed in *Memorials*, Georgiana Burne-Jones goes to some length to mention the Jewish neighbours to whom Burne-Jones owed 'much of the pleasure of his first years [in Birmingham]'. Later in life, Burne-Jones forged close friendships with the Jewish artist Simeon Solomon, as well as Sir George Lewis and his family, descended from the Sephardim.

50. *Caricature: The Sirens*, 1878–80 (illus. p. 53)

Pencil; 40 × 93 mm
Insc.: *Sirens*
Lit.: *Whitley*, p. 106
Bequest of J. R. Holliday, 1927 (1927P557)

The idea of 'a sort of Siren-land' of *femmes fatales* enticing men to their death occupied Burne-Jones over a thirty-year period. Caricature, for Burne-Jones, was probably a release from the intense process of painting, and here he transforms these dangerous, beautiful women into a thumbnail vision of rotund bottoms precariously balanced on rocks, calling out to a boat at sea. Fat ladies are one of the many themes that frequently figure in Burne-Jones's numerous caricatures.

51. *Caricature: Goblin Wrestler,* 1880–85

Pencil; 182 × 114 mm
Purchased from Sotheby's Belgravia, 25 March 1980 (1980P39)

This is one of two caricatures owned by BMAG showing the front and back (B40) of a goblin wrestler. Burne-Jones appears to have energised himself with such fantastical creatures, illustrating mythical monsters such as dragons, and also, for example, 'a struggle between a primeval baby and an extinct beast' (*Memorials*, II, p. 67).

52. *Dalziels' Bible Gallery*, pub. 1881 (illus. p. 57)

Bound volume of wood engravings, Old Testament subjects, on India paper; No 256 of 1000 copies; 430 × 360 mm
Lit./ Exh.: *Solomon* (30)
Presented by Wilfred Phillips, 1920 (1920P713.1)

The Brothers Dalziel were the leading wood-engravers in London, illustrating and publishing books for over fifty years until their receivership in 1893. The *Bible Gallery* project was originally intended to illustrate both the Old and the New Testaments in emulation of the German edition of *Bible in Pictures* by Julius Schnorr von Carolsfeld (Leipzig, 1852; English editions from 1855). The commissioned artists produced dozens of designs, nearly all complete in the 1860s, but the project was only published years later (London, Routledge, 1881), and then only as sixty-nine Old Testament engravings (seven of these as double pages). Unlike its German rival, the *Bible Gallery* proved a commercial disaster.

53. *King Cophetua and the Beggar Maid: Cartoon Study*, 1883

Bodycolour, watercolour, chalks, pastel with gum arabic and gold medium on paper mounted on stretcher; 2900 × 1390 mm
Lit./ Exh.: *Bell*, 1892 (60), *Victorian Artist-Dreamer* (113)
Prov.: William Graham (sold 1886)
Presented by Col. Rex Benson through the National Art Collections Fund, 1947 (1947P18)

The narrative of *King Cophetua and the Beggar Maid* derives from both a traditional Elizabethan ballad and Alfred Tennyson's poem 'The Beggar Maid', although the theme is also mentioned in a number of Shakespeare's plays. It tells of an African king who shunned women, but was forced to rethink his views upon seeing, and subsequently falling in love with, a beggar girl. Burne-Jones explored the idea of the transforming power of love with his earlier treatments of *Pygmalion and the Image* in the late 1860s and early 1870s. In the final panel, called *The Soul Attains*, Pygmalion kneels in front of his creation, similar here to Cophetua who, in awe of the maid's beauty, sits in submission below the beloved, now occupying his throne. This version of *King Cophetua* is a full-scale cartoon design, which measures the same size as the finished oil on canvas in Tate, London, and was almost certainly painted to obtain the full effect of the final image.

54. *King Cophetua and the Beggar Maid: Study of a Boy's Head*, c. 1883 (illus. p. 30)

Black chalk touched with white chalk on brown paper; 435 × 459 mm
Lit./ Exh.: *Whitley*, p. 100; *Sheffield* (155); *Rome* (66)
Purchased from Charles Fairfax Murray and presented by Subscribers, 1904 (1904P221)

This is a study for the boy on the left, singing in the background of *King Cophetua and the Beggar Maid.* It is one of five drawings at BMAG for this painting (B447–B451), demonstrating Burne-Jones's meticulous attention to detail, such as the crown and legs, as well as a full nude study for the seated king. It shows his use of the chalk medium to work in broad areas of form and colour, which is in marked contrast with his early 1860s pencil study of a boy (cat. 5).

55. *The Star of Bethlehem: Study for the Angel's Head*, 1886–90 (illus. p. 19)

Red and white chalk on brown paper; 375 × 290 mm
Insc.: *E B J 1890*
Bequest of J. R. Holliday, 1927, accessioned in 1931 (1931P62)

Compositionally, this head study is very similar to that in the earlier gouache version of *The Star of Bethlehem*, dated 1887–88 and now in the Collection of Andrew Lloyd Webber. Burne-Jones may have intended to repeat the figural and facial composition of that angel when he began the large watercolour for Birmingham Corporation (cat. 56), but opted instead to alter the position of the neck.

56. *The Star of Bethlehem*, 1887, 1888–91 (illus. p. 19)

Watercolour and bodycolour with scraping on ten sheets of J. Whatman Turkey Mill Kent paper dated 1882 or 1883 on stretcher; 2560 × 3868 mm (sight)
Insc.: *E B J 18/ 90*
Lit./ Exh.: New Gallery, London, 1891 (63); *Birmingham* 1891 (183); *Victorian Artist-Dreamer* (141)
Commissioned by the Corporation of Birmingham, 1887 (1891P75)

Burne-Jones was approached by the Corporation of Birmingham in 1887 to paint a major work for the new municipal Museum and Art Gallery. He chose the subject of the Adoration of the Magi, and titled it *The Star of Bethlehem*, a design he had already been working on for Morris & Co. in tapestry. Several tapestries of this subject were made, currently located in: Exeter College, Oxford (the original), National Gallery of South Australia; Castle Museum, Norwich; Eton College Chapel; State Hermitage Museum, St Petersburg; and Manchester Metropolitan University, among others.

There are dozens of preliminary sketches and studies associated with this painting, in private and public collections across the world. A sampling includes: a preliminary compositional sketch dated c. 1887 in the Cincinnati Art Museum, Ohio; a study for the angel's head (cat. 55) along with a study for Balthazar are in the BMAG (B1096); Lord Lloyd Webber is in possession of finished studies for the Virgin, Joseph, Melchior, Gaspar, as well as the early gouache version of *The Star of Bethlehem*; another study for Joseph is in the London Borough of Hammersmith and Fulham Public Libraries, Cecil French Bequest; and a rough study of the Virgin is in Tate, London.

The scale of *The Star of Bethlehem* has ensured that it has moved very infrequently since its arrival in BMAG in 1891, and as a result remains in good condition. Burne-Jones's views on how to frame such a large work are recorded in a letter to William Kenrick:

> It isn't a wide frame, for a wide frame would dwarf the picture; I find little pictures are good in vast frames but big ones frame themselves. About all this I have used my best judgment, but the sooner I order the frame the better, for I want its horrible new glare to tone a little. And glad I shall be … for it to be in Birmingham, and gladder if they are content. (*Memorials*, II, pp. 214–15)

57. *Sketchbook: Byzantine and Romanesque Decoration*, c. 1887–94 (illus. p. 13)

Pencil with some watercolour and coloured pencils in bound Roberson & Co. sketchbook; 109 pages; 279 × 227 mm
Insc.: see catalogue entry for B693
Presented by Mrs Angela Thirkell, 1952 (1952P6)

Many of these designs were intended for the *Holy Grail* tapestries (see BMAG: 1907M129–131, 1947M52–53 and 1980M60), the mosaics for St Paul's, the American Episcopal church in Rome (1886–90), or for the unfinished masterpiece *The Last Sleep of Arthur in Avalon* (oil, 1881–98, Museo de Arte, Ponce, Puerto Rico).

58. *Edward Burne-Jones Painting 'The Star of Bethlehem'*, 27 July 1890

By Barbara Leighton, later Sotheby (1870–1952)
Platinum print, printed by Frederick Hollyer; 340 × 260 mm
Presented by Lady Leighton, 1891 (1989P26)

Georgiana Burne-Jones, in *Memorials*, describes the garden-studio at The Grange, Fulham, in 1891 as becoming, 'A frequent background against which I see Edward, busy upon work of a larger scale than the Grange painting-room would hold. *The Star of Bethlehem*, finished early in 1891, was succeeded by *Avalon* and *The Car of Love*'.

Recent conservation inspection of this tapestry-scale painting has revealed the precision with which ten sheets of high-quality Whatman paper are abutted to create a seamless surface for painting, as well as the extensive amount of scraping applied to light-filled and lightened areas. Burne-Jones no doubt made use of assistants to help him in this construction.

This photograph appears to have been presented to mark the presentation of the finished watercolour received by the Museum and Art Gallery in 1891. Notes in the National Portrait Gallery refer to Barbara Leighton as the daughter of Baldwyn Leighton and Eleanor Leicester. She married Alfred Francis Sotheby in September 1909, and later exhibited as a portraitist rather than a photographer, notably at the Royal Society of Portrait Painters, where her subjects included Gertrude Jekyll.

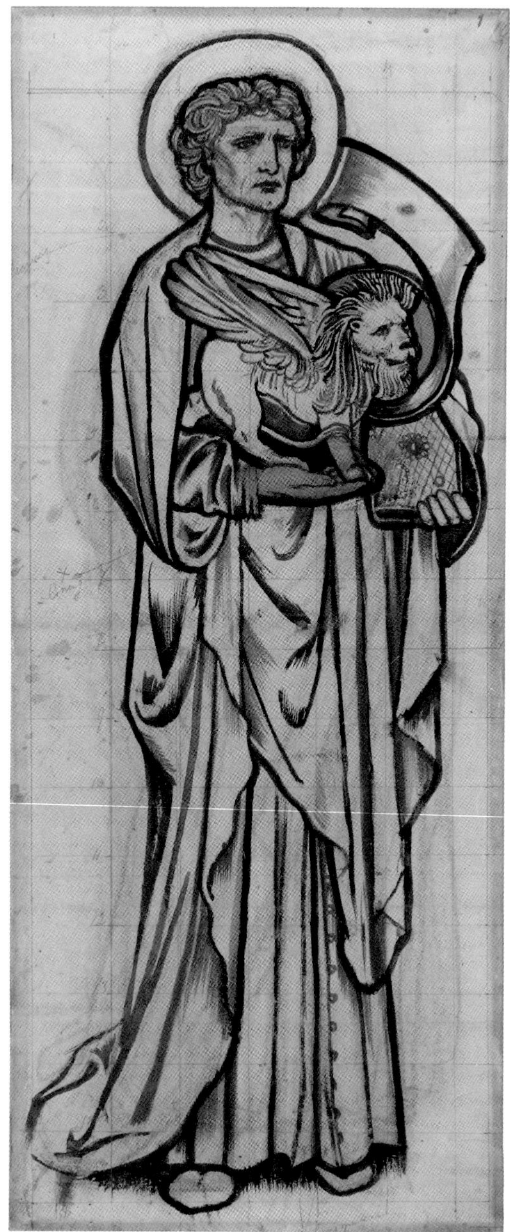

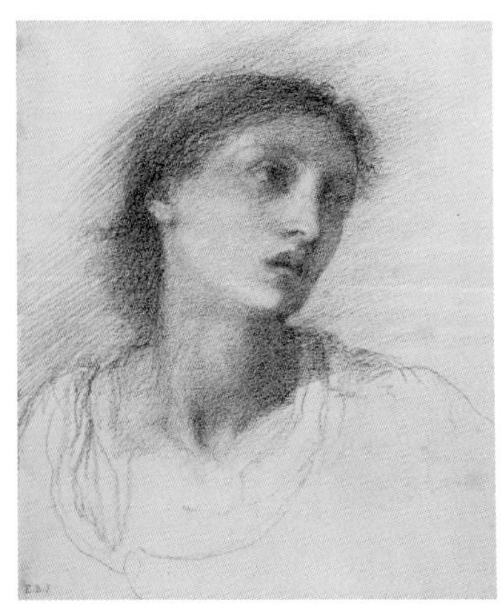

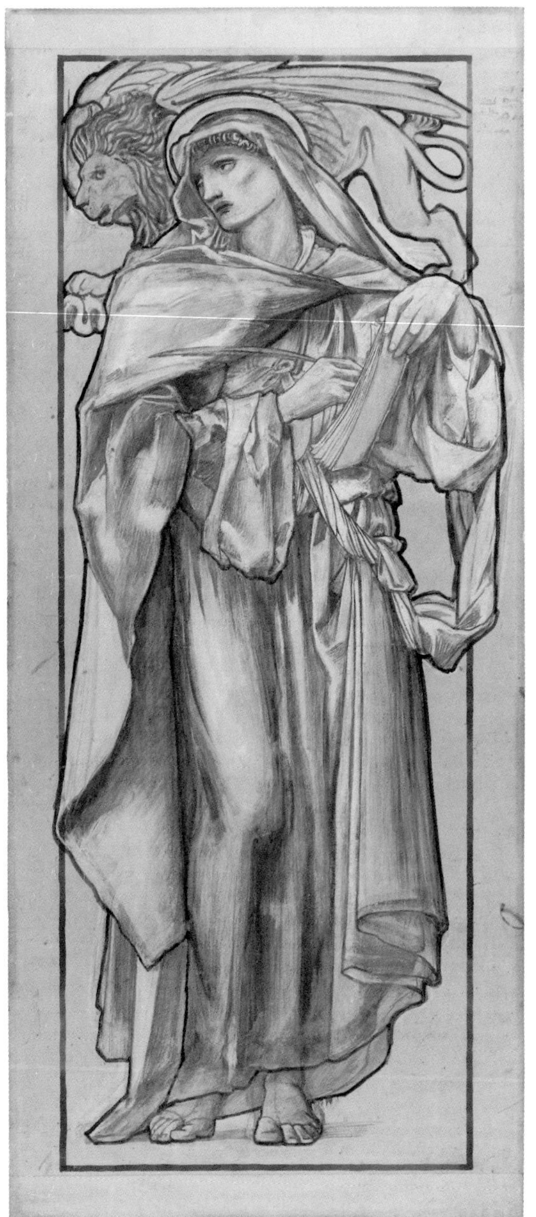

ABOVE LEFT: Stained Glass Design: *St Mark the Evangelist*, 1863–64 (cat. 22)

ABOVE: Stained Glass Design: Head Study of Maria Zambaco for *St Mark the Evangelist*, 1869–71 (cat. 36)

LEFT: Stained Glass Design: *St Mark the Evangelist*, 1873–74 (cat. 43)

59. *Head Study for 'The Sirens'*, 1895 (illus. p. 41)

Pencil; 449 × 331 mm
Insc.: *E B-J/ 1895/ for the picture of The Sirens*
Exh: *Rome* (80); *Visions* (117); *Victorian Artist-Dreamer* (158)
Presented by Arthur S. Dixon, 1898 (1898P45)

Three large-scale versions of *The Sirens* are extant, but all are unfinished: the large oil on canvas (1870–75) is currently in the John and Mable Ringling Museum of Art, Sarasota, Florida; a watercolour and gouache version (1871–98) is in a Private Collection (see Sotheby's, 3 November 1993, lot 201); and a large pastel version (1872–90), previously owned by Philip Burne-Jones, also remains in a Private Collection (see *Burne-Jones et l'influence des préraphaélites*, Hartnoll & Eyre, catalogue of exhibition at the Galerie du Luxembourg, Paris, 1972 [17]). There is also a full-scale compositional study in coloured chalks, dated c. 1870, in the Collection of Virginia Surtees (exhibited at Piccadilly Gallery, London, 1971 [11]).

Dozens of head studies executed by Burne-Jones for *The Sirens* are now in various private and public locations, including the Fine Arts Gallery of San Diego, California, and the Fogg Art Museum, Harvard University. A study for the ship is in the National Gallery of South Africa, Cape Town.

60. *The Works of Geoffrey Chaucer Now Newly Imprinted*, pub. 1896 (illus. p. 43)

First edition, one of 48 copies in full white tooled pigskin leather, with 87 designs by Edward Burne-Jones, engraved on wood by W. H. Hooper, printed in Chaucer type and published by Kelmscott Press, Hammersmith, London; with decorative designs and lettering by William Morris; 338 × 297 mm
Presented by Col and Mrs Howard Wilkinson in memory of Norman Wilkinson, 1934 (1934P675)

The public response to the publishing of the *Kelmscott Chaucer* included a debate on the respective roles of those involved in producing the publication, as seen in R. Catterson Smith's letter to the editor of the *Daily Chronicle*:

> Sir – It is not with the intention of denying/ me credit for the help I gave in the illustrations/ that William Morris did not place my name at the end of the 'Chaucer'. But (as he told me at the/ time to avoid making a long and perhaps mis-/ leading statement at the end of the book. As it/ is, the statement is of the briefest, and you will/ notice that he has not mentioned his own share in/ designing and drawing the borders and capital/ letters – which was a pretty huge piece of work./ Now as to the amount of credit to be given to/ me I only claim to have made myself as complete/ a tool for Burne-Jones as I could. Fingers, eyes and sympathy I brought, But Sir Edward was re/ sponsible for every line and dot in the eighty/ 'Chaucer' drawings which I did under his guid-/ ance. I worked at his elbow for months, often spending whole days seeking out a simple/ and expressive treatment of a passage, and in many/ cases doing drawings over and over again, until/ he was satisfied that the treatment or convention (he used to call it shorthand) expressed him/ The final touches were given when the drawing had/ been printed on the rough 'Chaucer' paper (the India-proof was never looked at). So that I do not hesitate to say the drawings that the public got are more absolutely Burne-/ Jones than if he had done them with his own/ hand – Yours faithfully/ R. Catterson Smith/ 11 Blenheim – Road, Bedford Park, W, Nov 18 [1896]

61. *Charity/ Caritas*, pub. 1900 (illus. p. 26)

Photogravure; 352 × 484 (i.), 670 × 510 mm (p.)
No. 38 of 91 photogravures, taken from Burne-Jones's watercolour *Charity* (1867–72, Collection of Andrew Lloyd Webber) and published by The Berlin Photographic Company, 133 New Bond Street, London
Purchased in 1900 (1900P57)

BMAG owns one of 200 folio copies endorsed with the signature of Philip Burne-Jones, below the line: 'The Best Edition of the Work of Edward Burne-Jones'. The question of the photographer Frederick Hollyer's involvement in this project remains, but seems to be negated by his general dislike of the photogravure process as well as the publisher's printed statement,

> We take this opportunity of expressing our gratitude to the various owners by whose courtesy we have been enabled to obtain reproductions from the original pictures belonging to them. Further acknowledgements are due to the following: Whitworth Wallis Esq, FSA, Director of the Museum and Art Gallery, Birmingham; L. Lindsay Esq, FSA; Messrs Henry Graves and Co. and Messers Thomas Agnew and Sons as well as to Mr Fairfax Murray who kindly allowed the photographs to be taken at the Grange, the house in which Sir Edward lived for many years.

62. *The Flower Book: Star of Bethlehem*, pub. 1905 (illus. p. 19)

Colour facsimile on Arches paper; 160 mm roundel, 330 × 250 mm (p)
Insc.: *STAR OF BETHLEHEM/* [with the following script]: *xx Star of Bethlehem/ The Angel leads the Wise Men by its light*
Purchased from K. G. Brooks, 1953 (1953P5.20)

The floral 'Star of Bethlehem' is actually the flowering part of the Prussian asparagus (*Ornithogalum umbellatum*). Burne-Jones probably titled his 1891 watercolour masterpiece after this plant, as it appears directly below the angel in the bottom centre of the picture (cat. 56). Burne-Jones was busy at work on his private allegorical representations of folkloric botanical names, now known as *The Flower Book,* when he received the commission from the Birmingham Corporation for the watercolour. As a painting, *The Star of Bethlehem* is more than just another Adoration of the Magi scene: it is the visualisation of the very flower that is represented within it.

The Flower Book version of the *Star of Bethlehem* theme is compositionally very different. Perhaps most notably, it includes an angel based on Uriel for the mosaics Burne-Jones designed for St Paul's, the American Episcopal church in Rome (1882–84, cartoon, Private Collection).

Catalogue

Edward Burne-Jones: Catalogue of Drawings, Watercolours, Prints and Archive Material at Birmingham Museums and Art Gallery

Introductory Note

The following catalogue sets out to provide a comprehensive listing of works on paper by Edward Burne-Jones, identified by the capital B number sequence and accompanying accession number. The collection was principally acquired by Birmingham Museum and Art Gallery (now Birmingham Museums and Art Gallery) from the artist and collector Charles Fairfax Murray and presented by Subscribers in May 1903 to be accessioned in 1904, or bequeathed by the solicitor James Richardson Holliday in 1927. In addition to these, an early engraved proof set of the *Cupid and Psyche* Series was presented by Mrs William Harris in 1913, and four sketchbooks donated by Mrs Angela Thirkell in 1952. Each of the photogravures after paintings by Burne-Jones, published by the Berlin Photographic Company in 1900, has been listed individually under its title. It has been decided not to include Richard Bridges's version of *Eros and Psyche,* published by The Gregynog Press in 1935 (1935P610), which is illustrated with drawings based on those produced by Burne-Jones.

The following works on paper have been arranged alphabetically by title. Within this format there are group headings that may cross reference to more than one grouping. These include: Chaucer; Cupid and Psyche; Female: Drapery; Female: Head; Female: Nude; Male: Drapery; Male: Nude; Pygmalion and the Image; Sketchbook; Stained Glass Design; Embroidery Design; and Tile Design. The dating of Burne-Jones's work remains a continuous concern, which in some cases is difficult to consign to a particular year or range of years. Burne-Jones is also known to have sometimes misdated drawings when preparing them for an exhibition, often long after they were executed. The compilers have attempted to be as accurate as possible, incorporating the findings of recent research.

The result is very much a reference listing that, because of space, is limited to the briefest of entries. It should be seen and used alongside both A. E. Whitley's *Catalogue of Drawings*, published in 1939, and a new Burne-Jones resource website, located at http://www.bmag.org.uk, which provides full information on, for example, the locations for stained-glass cartoons.

Measurements are given in millimetres, height before width. The inclusion of an asterisk refers to an inscription that is not in the artist's hand. Unless stated otherwise, drawings are typically on cream wove paper, identified in a number of instances as bearing the J. Whatman watermark. The term *sketch* has been used to denote a drawing that is clearly in process as opposed to a more realized *study*. Abbreviations are as follows:

B. bequeathed
i. image
Insc. inscribed
P. purchased
p. paper

ELISA KORB AND TESSA SIDEY

B1 *The Adoration of the Kings Triptych: Study of Head for Infant Christ*, 1861
Pencil; 134 × 110 mm
Insc.: *E.B.J.**
1927P559

B2 *Altar of Hymen*, pub. 1900
Photogravure; 240 × 170 (i.), 670 × 510 mm (p.)
See B583 and B584
P.: 1900 (1900P108)

B3 *Amy Gaskell Bonham*, pub. 1900
Photogravure; 340 × 185 (i.), 670 × 510 mm (p.)
P.: 1900 (1900P98)

B4 *Angel of the Martyrs (with Violin)*, pub. 1900
Photogravure; 460 × 160 (i.), 670 × 510 mm (p.)
P.: 1900 (1900P87)

B5 *The Annunciation: Study for the Virgin*, c.1859
Pencil; 313 × 135 mm
1927P586

B6 *The Annunciation*, 1857–61
Watercolour and bodycolour with gum arabic on two sheets of paper; 524 × 374 mm
Insc.: *E B J 1861*
1927P441

B7 *The Annunciation*, pub. 1900
Photogravure; 515 × 215 (i.), 670 × 510 mm (p.)
P.: 1900 (1900P94)

B8 *Astrologia: Profile Study of Augusta Jones*, 1865
Red chalk over pencil; 483 × 350 mm
1904P202

B9 *Aurora*, pub. 1900
Photogravure; 505 × 210 (i.), 670 × 510 mm (p.)
P.: 1900 (1900P101)

B10 *The Backgammon Players*, 1861–62
Watercolour and bodycolour on paper, laid down on canvas; 222 × 350 mm
Insc verso: *E. Burne Jones, 62 St Russell Street, Bloomsbury*
1923P146

B11 *The Backgammon Players*, pub. 1900
Photogravure; 143 × 233 (i.), 670 × 510 mm (p.)
P.: 1900 (1900P26)

B12 *The Bath of Venus*, pub. 1900
Photogravure; 400 × 140 (i.), 670 × 510 mm (p.)
P.: 1900 (1900P79)

B13 *The Bath of Venus: Study of Attendant Maidens*, c. 1873
Pencil; 577 × 256 mm
1927P448

B14 *The Beguiling of Merlin*, pub. 1900
Photogravure; 490 × 290 (i.), 670 × 510 mm (p.)
P.: 1900 (1900P66)

B15 *The Blessed Damozel: Study of Drapery*, c. 1859
Pencil; 336 × 204 mm
1904P37

The Briar Rose Series

B16 *The Briar Rose Series: Study for 'The Garden Court'*, 1889
Bodycolour and chalk on paper laid onto prepared board; 890 × 590 mm
Insc.: *E B.J/ 1889/ BRIAR RO/ SE*; reverse: *1/ 6 Studies for the Picture called The Garden Court/ in the series of the Sleeping Palace/ E Burne-Jones/ sketch for the picture of Sleeping Beauty/ Fine Art Society/ 168*
B.: Miss K. E. Lewis, 1961 (1961P50.1)

B17 *The Briar Rose Series: Study for 'The Garden Court'*, 1889
Bodycolour and chalk on paper laid onto prepared board; 890 × 590 mm
Insc.: *E B J/ 1889/ BRIAR ROSE*; reverse: *II/ Sketch for figure in picture of Sleeping Beauty/ Fine Art Society/ Foord & Dickinson/ Carvers & Gilders/ 120 Wardour St. W/ drawings Mounted, Pictures Cleaned & Restored*
B.: Miss K. E. Lewis, 1961 (1961P50.2)

B18 *The Briar Rose Series: Study for 'The Garden Court'*, 1889
Bodycolour and chalk on paper laid onto prepared board; 588 × 890 mm
Insc.: *E B.J 1889/ BRIAR ROSE*; reverse: *170/ Foord & Dickinson/ Carvers & Gilders/ 120 Wardour St. W/ Drawings Mounted, Pictures Cleaned & Restored*
B.: Miss K. E. Lewis, 1961 (1961P50.3)

B19 *The Briar Rose Series: Study for 'The Garden Court'*, 1889
Bodycolour and chalk on paper laid onto prepared board; 890 × 590 mm
Insc.: *E B-J/ 1889/ BRIAR ROSE*; reverse: *171/ Fine Art Society/ New Bond St*
B.: Miss K. E. Lewis, 1961 (1961P50.4)

B20 *The Briar Rose Series: Study for 'The Garden Court'*, 1889
Bodycolour and chalk on paper laid onto prepared board; 590 × 890 mm
Insc.: *E B.J/ 1889/ BRIAR ROSE/ GARDEN COURT*; reverse: *172/ Foord & Dickinson/ Carvers & Gilders/ 120 Wardour St. W/ Drawings Mounted, Pictures Cleaned & Restored*
B.: Miss K. E. Lewis, 1961 (1961P50.5)

B21 *The Briar Rose Series: Study for 'The Garden Court'*, 1889
Bodycolour and chalk on paper laid onto prepared board; 588 × 892 mm
Insc.: *E B.J for BRIAR ROSE 1889*; reverse: *173/ Foord & Dickinson/ carvers & Gilders/ 120 Wardour St. W./ Drawings Mounted, Pictures Cleaned & Restored*
B.: Miss K. E. Lewis, 1961 (1961P50.6)

B22 *The Briar Rose Series: Study of a sleeping Maiden for 'The Garden Court'*, 1882–85
Autotype of a black crayon drawing on grey toned paper; 212 × 237 mm
Insc.: *E B J*
1970P140

B23 *The Briar Rose Series: The Knight enters the Briar Wood (I)*, pub. 1900
Photogravure; 257 × 287 (i.), 670 × 510 mm (p.)
P.: 1900 (1900P27)

B24 *The Briar Rose Series: The Council Chamber (II)*, pub. 1900
Photogravure; 226 × 503 (i.), 670 × 510 mm (p.)
P.: 1900 (1900P28)

B25 *The Briar Rose Series: The Rose Bower/ The Sleeping Beauty (III)*, pub. 1900
Photogravure; 230 × 435 (i.), 670 × 510 mm (p.)
P.: 1900 (1900P29)

B26 *Burne-Jones's list of his own designs, drawings and pictures dating from 1856 and his accounts with the firm of Morris & Co., 1874–1900*
by J. R. Holliday (1840–1927), from original in Fitzwilliam Museum, Cambridge
Bequest of J. R. Holliday, 1927 (2006.1447)

The Car of Love (Love's Wayfaring)

B27 *The Car of Love (Love's Wayfaring): Study of Maria Zambaco*, 1875
Pencil; 158 × 139 mm
Insc.: *E B.J1875*
Presented anonymously, 1898 (1898P49)

B28 *The Car of Love (Love's Wayfaring): Study of a Man's Head*, 1876
Pencil; 158 × 138 mm
Insc.: *E B.J1876/ head for Love's Wayfaring.*
Presented anonymously, 1898 (1898P47)

B29 *The Car of Love (Love's Wayfaring): Study of Margaret Drummond*, 1880
Pencil; 184 × 140 mm
Insc.: *E B.J18/ 80*
Presented anonymously, 1898 (1898P48)

Caricature

B30 *Caricature: Composite Drawing: Bewigged Head* , c. 1861–63
verso: *Probably William Morris* thought to be by Ford Madox Brown and William Morris with Edward Burne-Jones and Dante Gabriel Rossetti
Pencil; 136 × 79 mm
P.: Sotheby's Belgravia 25 March 1980 (1980P38)

B31 *Caricature: Composite Drawing: A Stunner*, c. 1861–63
verso: *Girl with Ringlets* thought to be by Dante Gabriel Rossetti and Edward Burne-Jones with William Morris and Ford Madox Brown
Pencil; 212 × 90 mm
P.: Sotheby's Belgravia, 25 March 1980 (1980P37)

B32 *Caricature: William Morris as an ancient Poet*, c. 1870–73
Pencil on paper; 125 × 79 mm
Insc.: *WM* [E B J's hand]/ *E B J.**
1927P554

B33 *Caricature: Self-Portrait*, c. 1872–73
Pencil; 93 × 46 mm
Insc.: *E B.J.**
1927P555

B34 *Caricature: Study of Seated Figure*, 1873
Pencil; 119 × 77 mm
Insc.: *E B.J 1873 Done for me in Florence*
1927P556

B35 *Caricature: Line of Heads*, c. 1877–80
Pencil; 140 × 251 mm
1927P548

B36 *Caricature: Heads of Three Jews*, c. 1877–80
Pencil; 324 × 122 mm
Insc.: *A Jew/ Another Jew/ A Third Jew*
1927P549

B37 *Caricature: A Good and a Bad Jew*, c. 1877–80
Pencil; 152 × 251 mm
Insc.: *A Good Jew/ A Bad Jew*
1927P550

B38 *Caricature: Hands with 30 Pieces of Silver*, c. 1877–80
Pencil on cream-toned paper; 193 × 165 mm
Insc.: *xxx pieces of silver*
1927P551

B39 *Caricature: Goblin Wrestler*, c. 1880–85
Pencil; 182 × 114 mm
P.: Sotheby's Belgravia, 25 March 1980 (1980P39)

B40 *Caricature: Goblin Wrestler from behind*, c. 1880–85
Pencil on paper; 182 × 112 mm
P.: Sotheby's Belgravia, 25 March 1980 (1980P40)

B41 *Caricature: Unpainted Masterpieces (Self-Portrait)*, c. 1891–95
Pen and ink over pencil on notepaper; 176 × 107 mm
Insc.: *Unpainted Masterpieces*
P.: Sotheby's Belgravia, 25 March 1980 (1980P128)

Le Chant d'Amour

B42 *Le Chant d'Amour: Three Studies of Cupid*, c. 1864
Pencil and red chalk; 242 × 390 mm
1904P225

B43 *Le Chant d'Amour: Study for the Knight*, 1864–66
Sepia wash and white bodycolour, on brown paper, laid down; 168 × 183 (i.), 216 × 209 mm (p.)
1904P226

B44 *Le Chant d'Amour*, pub. 1896
Etching printed in sepia by Robert Macbeth Walker (1848–1910); published by the Fine Art Society, London; 390 × 531 (i.), 496 × 635mm (p.)
Insc.: *E.B.J.*
Found uninventoried in 1978 (1978P866)

B45 *Le Chant d'Amour*, pub. 1900
Photogravure; 352 × 484 (i.), 670 × 510 mm (p.)
P.: 1900 (1900P55)

Charity/Caritas

B46 *Charity/Caritas*, pub. 1900
Photogravure; 352 × 484 (i.), 670 × 510 mm (p.)
P.: 1900 (1900P57)

B47 *Charity/Caritas: Drapery Study*, c. 1867
Pencil, laid down on card; 390 × 282 mm
Insc.: *the top corner/ the bottom corner*
1904P156

B48 *Charity/Caritas: Figure Study*, c. 1867
Pencil; 367 × 210 mm (sight)
1904P155

B49 *Charity/Caritas: Study*, c. 1870
Pencil with ink; 90 × 49 mm
1927P527

B50 *Charity/Caritas: Study*, c. 1870
Pen and ink over pencil; 99 × 53 mm
1927P528

Chaucer

B51 *Chaucer's Dream of Good Women*, pub. 1900
Photogravure; 192 × 260 (i.), 670 × 510 mm (p.)
P.: 1900 (1900P24)

B52 *Chaucer's 'Legend of Good Women': Constance*, 1863
Pencil on buff paper; 152 × 152 (i.), 185 × 186 mm (p.)
Insc.: *Constance*
1904P526

B53 *Chaucer's 'Legend of Good Women': Cressida*, 1863
Pencil on buff paper; 152 × 152 (i.), 188 × 188 mm (p.)
1904P527

B54 *Chaucer's 'Legend of Good Women': Dorigen*, 1863
Pencil on buff paper; 153 × 151 (i.), 187 × 185 mm (p.)
Insc.: *Dorigen*
1904P525

B55 *Chaucer's 'Legend of Good Women': Griselda*, 1863–64
Pencil on buff paper; 152 × 152 (i.), 183 × 183 mm (p.)
Insc.: *Griselda*
1904P524

B56 *Chaucer's 'Legend of Good Women': Sketch Design for Needlework*, 1863
Pencil; 266 × 362 mm; sketch continues on reverse

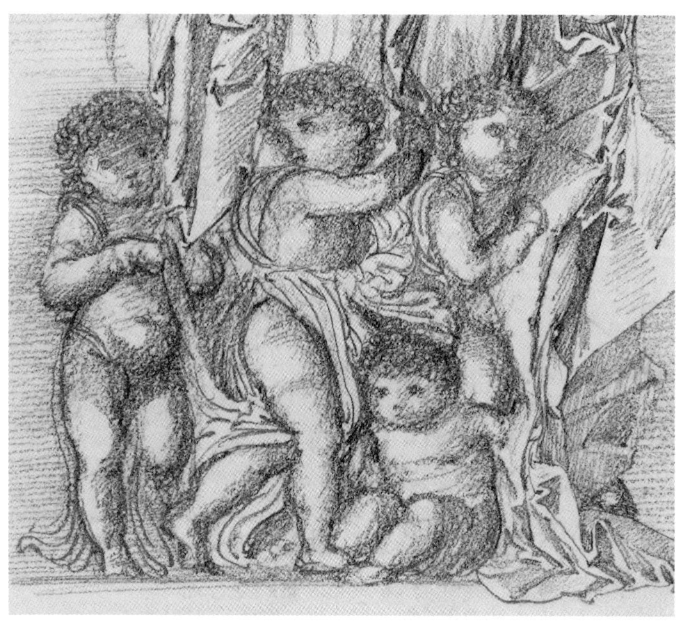

B48 (cat. 32), detail

Insc.: extensive technical notes
1904P13

B57 *Chaucer's 'Legend of Good Women': Chaucer Asleep*, 1864
Pencil; 434 × 433 (i.), 460 × 462 mm (p.)
Insc.: *all this space covered with stone/ red* [on shield]*/ perhaps this poppy may be red/ Imago/ all this carefully drawn as the stones have been*
1904P517

B58 *Chaucer's 'Legend of Good Women': Thisbe and Philomela*, 1864
Pencil; 406 × 407 (i.), 465 × 485 mm (p.)
1904P518

B59 *Chaucer's 'Legend of Good Women': Phyllis and Hypermnestra*, 1864
Pen and ink, sepia wash over pencil; 435 × 439 mm
Insc.: *SP 13092*
1904P519

B60 *Chaucer's 'Legend of Good Women': Amor and Alcestis*, 1864
Pencil, pen and sepia wash; 465 × 490 mm
Insc.: *Imago Amoris/ let nimbus quite* [cut off]*/ Imago Alcestis Martyris/ in black letters* [cut]*/ lining/ lining/ lining/ lining*
1904P520

B61 *Chaucer's 'Legend of Good Women': Hypsiphile and Medea*, 1864
Sepia ink and wash over pencil; 425 × 453 (i.), 464 × 492 mm (p.)
Insc.: *Imago Hypsip Martyris/ Imago Me Veneficae Martyris/ + purp*
1904P521

B62 *Chaucer's 'Legend of Good Women': Dido and Cleopatra*, 1864
Sepia ink and wash over pencil on two sheets of toned paper, strips around edges; 435 × 460 (i.), 465 × 492 mm (p.)
Insc.: *let all the flowers fall at the ground/ lining/ lining/ Imago* [C] *leopatrae* [sic] *Martyris/ Imago Didonis M(artyris)/ R/ R/ Why* [illegible] *on both sides chalk*
1904P522

B63 *Chaucer's 'Legend of Good Women': Ariadne and Lucretia*, 1864
Pencil and sepia wash on brown washed paper; 423 × 447 (i.), 465 × 489 mm (p.)
Insc.: *drawing? from/ buildings up/ Ard?/ N 3/ W/ Imago Ariadnes Mart/ Imago Lucretiae Mart/ lining/ lining/ SP12?*
1904P523

B64 *Chaucer's 'Legend of Good Women': Drapery Study of Hypermnestra*, 1863–64
Pencil; 329 × 148 mm
1904P14

B65 *Chaucer's 'Legend of Good Women': Drapery Study for Figure of Lucretia*, 1863–64
Pencil; 358 × 170 mm
1904P15

B66 *Chaucer's 'Legend of Good Women': Drapery Studies for Figure of Philomela*, 1863–64
Pencil; 327 × 276 mm
1904P16

B67 *Chaucer's 'Legend of Good Women': Drapery Study for Figure of Phyllis*, 1863–64
Pencil; 358 × 119 mm
1904P17

B68 *Chaucer's 'Man of Laws' Tale': Design*, 1862–64
Brown wash over pencil, with scratching out; 500 × 256 mm
1904P34

B69 *Chaucer's 'Man of Laws' Tale': Design*, 1862–64
Pencil; 350 × 209 mm
1904P35

B70 *The Works of Geoffrey Chaucer Now Newly Imprinted*, pub. 1896
With 87 woodcut illustrations by Burne-Jones on vellum, bound in full white tooled pigskin;
338 × 297 mm (overall size)
Published by Kelmscott Press; edition of 48
Presented by Col and Mrs Howard Wilkinson in memory of Norman Wilkinson, 1934
(1934P675)

Cinderella

B71 *Cinderella: Drapery Study*, 1862–63
Pencil over brown-red chalk; 297 × 145 mm
1904P104

B72 *Cinderella: Study*, 1862–63
Pencil on Whatman paper watermarked *1862*; 398 × 214 mm
1927P584

B73 *Cinderella: Study*, 1862–63
Pencil on Whatman paper; 408 × 214 mm
1927P585

B74 *Composition Design: Man and Woman facing each other, surrounded by six Figures*, c. 1865
possibly related to *Cupid and Psyche* Series: *Psyche at the Gate of Olympus*
Pencil; 65 × 125 mm
1927P567

Cupid and Psyche

B75 *Cupid and Psyche: Volume of 86 Illustrations for 'The Earthly Paradise'*, 1865
Mostly pencil, laid down in vellum album; 409 × 307 mm
Insc.: list of subjects written by William Morris
Prov.: Charles Fairfax Murray
1927P648

B76 *Cupid and Psyche: Two Studies of 'Venus on the Margin of the Sea' and 'Psyche at the Bath'*, 1865
Pencil; 104 × 162 (i.), 108 × 166 mm (p.)
1927P648.1

B77 *Cupid and Psyche: Study for 'Venus on the Margin of the Sea'*, 1865
Pen and ink; 104 × 79 (i.), 107 × 80 mm (p.)
1927P648.2

B78 *Cupid and Psyche: Study for 'Psyche at the Bath'*, 1865
Pen and ink; 102 × 75 mm
1927P648.3

B79 *Cupid and Psyche: Sketch for 'The reading of Apollo's Oracle to Psyche and her Father'*, 1865
Pencil; 109 × 159 mm
1927P648.4

B80 *Cupid and Psyche: Sketch for 'The reading of Apollo's Oracle to Psyche and her Father'*, 1865
Pencil; 105 × 159 mm
1927P648.5

B81 *Cupid and Psyche: Study for 'The reading of Apollo's Oracle to Psyche and her Father'*, 1865
Pencil; 101 × 157 mm
1927P648.6

B82 *Cupid and Psyche: Sketches for 'The reading of Apollo's Oracle to Psyche', and 'Venus setting Psyche the Task of separating the Heap of Grain and Seed'*, 1865
Pencil; 170 × 127 mm
1927P648.7

B83 *Cupid and Psyche: Study for 'The Procession of Psyche led to the Monster'*, 1865
Pencil; 104 × 162 (i.), 127 × 183 mm (p.)
1927P648.8

B84 *Cupid and Psyche: Sketch for 'The Procession of Psyche led to the Monster'*, 1865
Pencil; 103 × 314 (i.), 109 × 321 mm (p.)
1927P648.9

B85 *Cupid and Psyche: Study for 'The Procession of Psyche led to the Monster'*, 1865
Pencil; 104 × 313 (i.), 128 × 342 mm (p.)
1927P648.10

B86 *Cupid and Psyche: Sketch for 'The Procession of Psyche led to the Monster'*, 1865
Pencil; 104 × 314 (i.), 107 × 317 mm (p.)
1927P648.11

B87 *Cupid and Psyche: Three Sketches for 'Psyche entering Cupid's Palace'*, 1865
Pencil; 103 × 158 (i.), 125 × 184 mm (p.)
1927P648.12

B88 *Cupid and Psyche: Three Sketches of Psyche in Cupid's Palace*, 1865
Pencil; 104 × 157 (i.), 147 × 179 mm (p.)
1927P648.13

B89 *Cupid and Psyche: Sketches of Psyche at her Bath, and Hands*, 1865
Pencil; 105 × 150 mm
1927P648.14

B90 *Cupid and Psyche: Sketch of Psyche, Nude, holding Drapery*, 1865
Pencil touched with red chalk; 183 × 109 mm
1927P648.15

B91 *Cupid and Psyche: Sketch of Psyche*, 1865
Pencil; 113 × 70 mm
1927P648.16

B92 *Cupid and Psyche: Two Sketches of Psyche in Cupid's Palace*, 1865
Pencil; 117 × 163 mm
1927P648.17

B93 *Cupid and Psyche: Sketch of Psyche feasting in Cupid's Palace*, 1865
Pencil; 108 × 242 mm
1927P648.18

B94 *Cupid and Psyche: Two slight Sketches of Musicians*, 1865
Pencil; 114 × 164 mm
1927P648.19

B95 *Cupid and Psyche: Sketch of Cupid flying with Psyche waiting*, 1865
Pencil; 111 × 167 mm
1927P648.20

B96 *Cupid and Psyche: Sketch of Cupid flying with Psyche waiting*, 1865
Pencil; 107 × 83 mm
1927P648.21

B97 *Cupid and Psyche: Sketch of Psyche, seated, awaiting Cupid*, 1865
Pencil; 107 × 81 mm
1927P648.22

B98 *Cupid and Psyche: Rough Sketches of Cupid and Psyche flying*, 1865
Pencil (left hand drawing on secondary sheet, laid down);
110 × 169 mm
1927P648.23

B99 *Cupid and Psyche: Rough Sketch of Cupid flying through the Air*, 1865
Pencil; 107 × 82 mm
1927P648.24

B100 *Cupid and Psyche: Sketch of Psyche, seated, awaiting Cupid*, 1865
Pencil; 106 × 82 mm
1927P648.25

B101 *Cupid and Psyche: Five Studies of the Head and Figure of Psyche reclining*, 1865
Pencil; 239 × 177 mm
1927P648.26

B102 *Cupid and Psyche: Two Sketches of Psyche and her Sisters*, 1865
Pencil; 108 × 163 mm
1927P648.27

B103 *Cupid and Psyche: Two Sketches of Psyche and her Sisters*, 1865
Pencil; 107 × 160 mm
1927P648.28

B104 *Cupid and Psyche: Rough Sketch for 'Psyche gazing at Cupid sleeping'*, 1865
Pencil; 105 × 157 mm
1927P648.29

B105 *Cupid and Psyche: Study for 'Psyche gazing at Cupid sleeping'*, 1865
Pencil; 105 × 161 mm
1927P648.30

B106 *Cupid and Psyche: Three Sketches for 'Psyche gazing at Cupid sleeping'*, 1865
Pencil; 184 × 185 mm
1927P648.31

B107 *Cupid and Psyche: Sketch for 'Psyche gazing at Cupid sleeping'*, 1865
Pencil; 108 × 162 mm
1927P648.32

B108 *Cupid and Psyche: Three Sketches for 'Psyche abandoned by Cupid'*, 1865
Pencil; 108 × 235 mm
1927P648.33

B109 *Cupid and Psyche: Sketch for ' Psyche outside her Sister's House'*, 1865
Pencil; 106 × 84 mm
1927P648.34

B110 *Cupid and Psyche: Slight Sketch for 'Psyche outside her Sister's House'*, 1865
Pencil; 105 × 81 mm
1927P648.35

B111 *Cupid and Psyche: Two Sketches for 'Psyche and her Sister', and 'Pan and Psyche'*, 1865
Pencil; 116 × 170 mm
1927P648.36

B112 *Cupid and Psyche: Two Sketches for 'Psyche at the Shrine of Ceres'*, 1865
Pencil; 129 × 158 mm
1927P648.37

B113 *Cupid and Psyche: Three Sketches for 'Psyche at the Shrine of Juno or Ceres'*, 1865
Pencil; 127 × 197 mm
1927P648.38

B114 *Cupid and Psyche: Three Sketches for 'Psyche at the Shrine of Juno or Ceres'*, 1865
Pencil; 87 × 126 mm
1927P648.39

B115 *Cupid and Psyche: Two Sketches for 'Psyche at the Shrine of Juno or Ceres'*, 1865
Pencil; 110 × 157 mm
1927P648.40

B116 *Cupid and Psyche: Sketch for 'Venus and her Handmaidens'*, 1865
Pencil; 106 × 158 mm
1927P648.41

B117 *Cupid and Psyche: Sketch for 'Venus and her Handmaidens'*, 1865
Pencil; 106 × 159 mm
1927P648.42

B118 *Cupid and Psyche: Sketch for 'Venus and her Handmaidens'*, 1865
Pencil; 107 × 162 mm
1927P648.43

B119 *Cupid and Psyche: Study for 'Psyche brought into the Presence of Venus'*, 1865
Pencil; 107 × 162 mm
1927P648.44

B120 *Cupid and Psyche: Two Sketches for 'Psyche Brought into the Presence of Venus'*, 1865
verso: *Sketch for 'Psyche helped by Voice from the Reeds'*
Pencil heightened with red chalk (recto and verso); 237 × 192 mm
1927P648.45

B121 *Cupid and Psyche: Two Sketches for 'Psyche brought into the Presence of Venus'*, 1865
Pencil; 234 × 188 mm
1927P648.46

B122 *Cupid and Psyche: Sketch for 'Psyche brought into the Presence of Venus'*, 1865
Pencil with touches of sepia chalk; 124 × 123 mm
1927P648.47

B123 *Cupid and Psyche: Rough Sketch for 'Psyche brought into the Presence of Venus'*, 1865
Pencil; 62 × 95 mm
1927P648.48

B124 *Cupid and Psyche: Sketch for 'Venus setting Psyche the Task of separating the Heap of Grain and Seed'*, 1865
Pencil; 104 × 79 mm
1927P648.49

B125 *Cupid and Psyche: Sketch of 'Venus setting Psyche the Task of separating the Heap of Grain and Sand'*, 1865
Pencil; 103 × 154 mm
1927P648.50

B126 *Cupid and Psyche: Study for 'Venus setting Psyche the Task of separating the Heap of Grain and Sand'*, 1865
Pencil; 107 × 164 mm
1927P648.51

B127 *Cupid and Psyche: Sketch for 'Psyche and Syrinx'*, 1865
Pencil; 105 × 77 mm
1927P648.52

B128 *Cupid and Psyche: Two Studies for 'Psyche wading across the Stream'*, 1865
Pencil; 110 × 166 mm
1927P648.53

B129 *Cupid and Psyche: Sketch for 'Venus making Psyche go to the Black Mountain'*, 1865
Pencil; 110 × 82 mm
1927P648.54

B130 *Cupid and Psyche: Sketch for 'Jupiter's Eagle bearing Water from the Black Mountain'*, 1865
Pencil; 107 × 81 mm
1927P648.55

B131 *Cupid and Psyche: Sketch for 'Jupiter's Eagle giving Water to Psyche'*, 1865
Pencil; 109 × 155 mm
1927P648.56

B132 *Cupid and Psyche: Sketches for 'Psyche and the Dead Queen at the Tower'*, 1865
Pencil; 110 × 159 mm
1927P648.57

B133 *Cupid and Psyche: Sketch of Psyche and Charon*, 1865
Pencil and black chalk; 109 × 164 mm
1927P648.58

B134 *Cupid and Psyche: Sketch of Psyche and Charon*, 1865
Pencil and black chalk; 108 × 162 mm
1927P648.59

B135 *Cupid and Psyche: Sketch of Psyche and Charon*, 1865
Pencil and black chalk; 107 × 162 mm
1927P648.60

B136 *Cupid and Psyche: Sketch of Psyche and Charon*, 1865
Pencil; 110 × 163 mm
1927P648.61

B137 *Cupid and Psyche: Two Sketches for 'Charon rowing Psyche across the Styx'*, 1865
Pencil and black chalk; 228 × 162 mm
1927P648.62

B138 *Cupid and Psyche: Sketch for 'Psyche seeing her dead Father as Charon rows'*, 1865
Pencil and black chalk; 108 × 162 mm
1927P648.63

B139 *Cupid and Psyche: Sketch for 'Charon rowing Psyche across the Styx'*, 1865
Pencil and black chalk; 122 × 161 mm
1927P648.64

B140 *Cupid and Psyche: Sketch for 'Psyche at the Gates of Hades'*, 1865
Pencil; 105 × 161 mm
1927P648.65

B141 *Cupid and Psyche: Four Sketches of Psyche feeding Cerberus*, 1865
Pencil; 211 × 316 mm
1927P648.66

B142 *Cupid and Psyche: Four Sketches of Cerberus and Psyche*, 1865
Pencil; 212 × 317 mm
1927P648.67

B143 *Cupid and Psyche: Sketch for 'Psyche receiving the Casket from Proserpine'*, 1865
Pencil; 108 × 158 mm
1927P648.68

B144 *Cupid and Psyche: Sketch for 'Psyche receiving the Casket from Proserpine'*, 1865
Pencil; 109 × 167 mm
1927P648.69

B145 *Cupid and Psyche: Sketch for 'Psyche receiving the Casket from Proserpine'*, 1865
Pencil; 107 × 158 mm
1927P648.70

B146 *Cupid and Psyche: Study for 'Psyche receiving the Casket from Proserpine'*, 1865
Pencil; 109 × 161 mm
1927P648.71

B147 *Cupid and Psyche: Sketch for 'Psyche receiving the Casket from Proserpine'*, 1865
Pencil; 111 × 163 mm
1927P648.72

B148 *Cupid and Psyche: Four Sketches of Psyche in the Underworld*, 1865
Pencil; 227 × 214 mm
1927P648.73

B149 *Cupid and Psyche: Sketches of Psyche, Proserpine and Cerberus*, 1865
Pencil; 107 × 221 mm
1927P648.74

B150 *Cupid and Psyche: Sketch for 'Psyche unconscious after opening the Casket'*, 1865
Pencil; 107 × 162 mm
1927P648.75

B151 *Cupid and Psyche: Sketch for 'Cupid delivering Psyche'*, 1865
Pencil; 107 × 157 mm
1927P648.76

B152 *Cupid and Psyche: Sketch for 'Cupid delivering Psyche'*, 1865
Pencil; 105 × 159 mm
1927P648.77

B153 *Cupid and Psyche: Sketch for 'Cupid delivering Psyche'*, 1865
Pencil; 107 × 130 mm
Insc.: *Sketch for/ Painting*
1927P648.78

B154 *Cupid and Psyche: Sketch for 'Cupid giving back the Casket to Psyche'*, 1865
Pencil; 112 × 165 mm
1927P648.79

B155 *Cupid and Psyche: Study for 'Cupid giving back the Casket to Psyche'*, 1865
Pencil; 110 × 83 mm
1927P648.80

B156 *Cupid and Psyche: Two Sketches for 'Psyche on Olympus offered the Cup of Immortality'*, 1865
Pencil; 208 × 320 mm
Insc. upper left to right: *Juno/ Vesta/ Minerva/ Venus/ Mars/ Ceres, Diana*
1927P648.81

B157 *Cupid and Psyche: Sketch for 'Psyche on Olympus offered the Cup of Immortality'*, 1865
Pencil; 104 × 318 mm
1927P648.82

B158 *Cupid and Psyche: Four rough Sketches of Psyche on Olympus*, 1865–66
Pencil; 233 × 159 mm
1927P648.83

B159 *Cupid and Psyche: Sketch for 'Psyche on Olympus being offered the Cup of Immortality'*, 1865
Pencil; 158 × 318 mm
1927P648.84

B160 *Cupid and Psyche: Sketch for 'Psyche at the Gate of Olympus being offered the Cup of Immortality'*, 1865
Pencil; 161 × 320 mm
1927P648.85

B161 *Cupid and Psyche: Sketch for 'Psyche at the Gate of Olympus being offered the Cup of Immortality'*, 1865
Pencil; 161 × 314 mm
1927P648.86
See B74

B162 *Cupid and Psyche: Study of Psyche for 'Psyche awaiting Cupid'*, 1865
Pencil on tracing paper (for engraving); 105 × 79 mm
1927P601

B163 *Cupid and Psyche: Cupid flying to his Palace by Night*, 1865
Pencil on tracing paper; 107 × 85 mm
1927P602

B164 *Cupid and Psyche: Study of Psyche and Venus's Attendants*, 1865
Pencil on tracing paper (for engraving); 105 × 162 mm
1927P603

B165 *Cupid and Psyche: Three Studies of Psyche and Venus's Attendants*, 1865
Pencil on tracing paper (for engraving); 121 × 170 mm
1927P604

B166 *Cupid and Psyche: Two Studies of Psyche and Venus's Attendants*, 1865
Pencil on tracing paper (for engraving); 118 × 174 mm
1927P605

B167 *Cupid and Psyche: Study for 'Psyche wading through Water with the Golden Fleece'*, 1865
Pencil on tracing paper (for engraving); 109 × 82 mm
1927P606

B168 *Cupid and Psyche: Study of Psyche*, 1865
Pencil on tracing paper (for engraving); 109 × 83 mm
1927P607

B169 *Cupid and Psyche: Study of Two Figures*, 1865
Pencil on tracing paper (for engraving); 110 × 82 mm
1927P608

B170 *Cupid and Psyche: Cupid's Palace Musicians*, 1865
Pencil on tracing paper (for engraving); 118 × 82 mm
1927P609

B171 *Cupid and Psyche: Study of Psyche and Ceres*, 1865
Pencil on tracing paper (for engraving); 140 × 173 mm
1927P610

B172 *Cupid and Psyche: Study for 'Cupid and Psyche before the Throne of Juno'*, 1865
Pencil on tracing paper (for engraving); 140 × 173 mm
1927P611

B173 *Cupid and Psyche: Psyche in the presence of Venus*, 1865
Pencil heightened with white bodycolour on woodblock; 109 × 159 (i.), 110 × 167 mm (p.)
Insc.: BLOCK
1927P646

B174 *Cupid and Psyche: Psyche saved by the dead Queen*, 1865
Pencil on woodblock; 103 × 81(i.), 109 × 83 mm (p.)
1927P647

B175 *Cupid and Psyche: Venus on the Margin of the Sea*, 1866–67
Wood engraving, printed in black; 105 × 79 (i.), 467 × 327 mm (p.)
1913P155

B176 *Cupid and Psyche: Psyche at the Bath*, 1866–67
Wood engraving, printed in black; 103 × 78 (i.), 461 × 324 mm (p.)
1913P156

B177 *Cupid and Psyche: Venus dispatching Cupid to punish Psyche*, 1866–67
Wood engraving, printed in black; 113 × 82 (i.), 473 × 325 mm (p.)
1913P157

B178 *Cupid and Psyche: The reading of Apollo's Oracle to Psyche and the King, her Father*, 1866–67
Wood engraving, printed in black; 106 × 160 (i.), 470 × 318 mm (p.)
1913P158

B179 *Cupid and Psyche: Cupid finding Psyche asleep in the Garden*, 1866–67
Wood engraving, printed in black; 112 × 82 (i.), 467 × 324 mm (p.)
1913P159

B180 *Cupid and Psyche: Procession of Musicians and Torchbearers accompanying Psyche to the Mountain, where she is to be abandoned to the Monster*, 1866–67
Wood engraving, printed in black; 106 × 160 (i.), 468 × 330 mm (p.)
1913P160

B181 *Cupid and Psyche: The King and Handmaidens accompanying Psyche to the Mountain, where she is to be abandoned to the Monster*, 1866–67
Wood engraving, printed in black; 105 × 158 (i.), 471 × 310 mm (p.)
1913P161

B182 *Cupid and Psyche: Zephyrus bearing Psyche to Cupid's Valley*, 1866–67
Wood engraving, printed in black; 108 × 78 (i.), 470 × 330 mm (p.)
1913P162

B183 *Cupid and Psyche: Psyche entering the Garden of Cupid's Palace*, 1866–67
Wood engraving, printed in black; 105 × 51 (i.), 469 × 330 mm (p.)
1913P163

B184 *Cupid and Psyche: Psyche in Cupid's Garden*, 1866–67
Wood engraving, printed in black; 104 × 59 (i.), 471 × 330 mm (p.)
1913P164

B185 *Cupid and Psyche: Psyche walking through Cupid's Palace*, 1866–67
Wood engraving, printed in black; 105 × 53 (i.), 322 × 47 mm (p.)
1913P165

B186 *Cupid and Psyche: Psyche at Table spread with Food*, 1866–67
Wood engraving, printed in black; 106 × 56 (i.), 466 × 325 mm (p.)
1913P166

B187 *Cupid and Psyche: Psyche sits down to eat*, 1866–67
Wood engraving, printed in black; 106 × 81 (i.), 469 × 315 mm (p.)
1913P167

B188 *Cupid and Psyche: The Choir of unseen Folk singing to Psyche*, 1866–67
Wood engraving, printed in black; 106 × 82 (i.), 472 × 318 mm (p.)
1913P168

B189 *Cupid and Psyche: Psyche entering the Bath in the Palace*, 1866–67
Wood engraving, printed in black; 104 × 56 (i.), 469 × 323 mm (p.)
1913P169

B190 *Cupid and Psyche: Psyche entering the Bedroom*, 1866–67
Wood engraving, printed in black; 106 × 55 (i.), 470 × 320 mm (p.)
1913P170

B191 *Cupid and Psyche: Psyche disrobing*, 1866–67
Wood engraving, printed in black; 110 × 82 (i.), 470 × 321 mm (p.)
1913P171

B192 *Cupid and Psyche: Psyche conducts her Sisters through Cupid's Palace*, 1866–67
Wood engraving, printed in black; 104 × 80 (i.), 470 × 325 mm (p.)
1913P172

B193 *Cupid and Psyche: Cupid flying through the Night*, 1866–67
Wood engraving, printed in black; 110 × 80 (i.), 470 × 325 mm (p.)
1913 P173

B194 *Cupid and Psyche: Psyche's Sisters bidding her farewell, after their second Visit to the Palace*, 1866–67
Wood engraving, printed in black; 106 × 82 (i.), 466 × 317 mm (p.)
1913P174

B195 *Cupid and Psyche: Psyche, lighting the Lamp, discovers Cupid*, 1866–67
Wood engraving, printed in black; 106 × 160 (i.), 470 × 330 mm (p.)
1913P175

B196 *Cupid and Psyche: Psyche is abandoned by Cupid*, 1866–67
Wood engraving, printed in black; 469 × 326 mm
1913P176

B197 *Cupid and Psyche: Psyche at the Palace Door watching Cupid's Flight*, 1866–67
Wood engraving, printed in black; 104 × 79 (i.), 470 × 325 mm (p.)
1913P177

B198 *Cupid and Psyche: Psyche, seeking Death, about to leap into the Stream*, 1866–67
Wood engraving, printed in black; 108 × 82 (i.), 470 × 325 mm (p.)
1913P178

B199 *Cupid and Psyche: Psyche outside her first Sister's House*, 1866–67
Wood engraving, printed in black; 105 × 81 (i.), 470 × 315 mm (p.)
1913P179

B200 *Cupid and Psyche: Psyche outside her second Sister's House*, 1866–67
Wood engraving, printed in black; 105 × 81 (i.), 470 × 315 mm (p.)
1913P180

B201 *Cupid and Psyche: Psyche's Sister flinging herself into Cupid's Valley*, 1866–67
Wood engraving, printed in black; 107 × 83 (i.), 470 × 324 mm (p.)
1913P181

B202 *Cupid and Psyche: Psyche at the Shrine of Ceres*, 1866–67
Wood engraving, printed in black; 106 × 82 (i.), 469 × 320 mm (p.)
1913P182

B203 *Cupid and Psyche: Psyche at the Shrine of Juno*, 1866–67
Wood engraving, printed in black; 108 × 81 (i.), 470 × 321 mm (p.)
1913P183

B204 *Cupid and Psyche: Venus and her Handmaidens*, 1866–67
Wood engraving, printed in black; 110 × 159 (i.), 470 × 320 mm (p.)
1913P184

B205 *Cupid and Psyche: Venus sets Psyche the Task of separating the Heaps of Grain and Seed*, 1866–67
Wood engraving, printed in black; 108 × 160 (i.), 468 × 324 mm (p.)
1913P185

B206 *Cupid and Psyche: Psyche is set the Task of collecting the Golden Fleece from Venus's Flocks and is helped by a Voice from the Reeds*, 1866–67
Wood engraving, printed in black; 106 × 83 (i.), 469 × 328 mm (p.)
1913P186

B207 *Cupid and Psyche: Psyche wading across the Stream, her Dress held up, filled with the Golden Fleece*, 1866–67
Wood engraving, printed in black; 110 × 82 (i.), 469 × 320 mm (p.)
1913P187

B208 *Cupid and Psyche: Psyche sent by Venus to the Black Mountain to fill an Ewer at the Fountain guarded by Dragons and is aided by Jove's Eagle*, 1866–67
Wood engraving, printed in black; 106 × 160 (i.), 470 × 325 mm (p.)
1913P188

B209 *Cupid and Psyche: Psyche, sent by Venus with a Casket to Proserpine, determines to fling herself from a Tower, but is restrained and assisted by the Voice of a Dead Queen*, 1866–67
Wood engraving, printed in black; 108 × 83 (i.), 469 × 310mm (p.)
1913P189

B210 *Cupid and Psyche: Psyche's Descent into Hades*, 1866–67
Wood engraving, printed in black; 105 × 82 (i.), 470 × 327 mm (p.)
1913P190

B211 *Cupid and Psyche: Psyche reaches the Shadowy Meads*, 1866–67
Wood engraving, printed in black; 106 × 82 (i.), 470 × 325 mm (p.)
1913P191

B212 *Cupid and Psyche: Psyche, disregarding their Call for Help, passes safely by the shadowy Man trying to load an Ass and three old Women weaving*, 1866–67
Wood engraving, printed in black; 106 × 160 (i.), 465 × 329 mm (p.)
1913P192

B213 *Cupid and Psyche: Psyche giving the Coin to the Ferryman of the Styx*, 1866–67
Wood engraving, printed in black; 108 × 158 (i.), 467 × 317 mm (p.)
1913P193

B214 *Cupid and Psyche: The dead Man rising from the Water as Psyche is ferried across the Styx*, 1866–67
Wood engraving, printed in black; 109 × 159 (i.), 469 × 317 mm (p.)
1913P194

B215 *Cupid and Psyche: Psyche throwing the Honey-Cakes to Cerberus*, 1866–67
Wood engraving, printed in black; 105 × 160 (i.), 470 × 325 mm (p.)
1913P195

B216 *Cupid and Psyche: Psyche, opening the Magic Casket, is overcome by Sleep, and Cupid flies to her once more*, 1866–67
Wood engraving, printed in black; 105 × 153 (i.), 468 × 316 mm (p.)
1913P196

B217 *Cupid and Psyche: Psyche, at the Gate of Olympus, is offered the Cup of Immortality*, 1866–67
Wood engraving, printed in black; 164 × 158 (i.), 469 × 328 mm (p.)
1913P197

B218 *Cupid and Psyche: Psyche, now Immortal, is led by the Gods and Goddesses into Olympus*, 1866–67
Wood engraving, printed in black; 163 × 157 (i.), 468 × 319 mm (p.)
1913P198

B219 *Cupid and Psyche: Nude Study for Psyche*, 1865–66
Pencil on cream paper; 179 × 90 mm
Insc.: *Story of Cupid & Psyche/ Psyche/* E.B.J.*
1927P526

B220 *Cupid and Psyche: Nude Study for Psyche*, 1865–66
Red chalk on cream-toned paper; 482 × 241mm
1904P194

B221 *Cupid and Psyche: Nude Study for Psyche*, 1864–65
Pencil, charcoal, and yellow chalk; 324 × 132 mm
1904P124

B222 *Cupid and Psyche: Two Nude Studies of Women*, 1865–67
Red chalk; 357 × 260 mm
1904P10

B223 *Cupid and Psyche: Study for the Palace Green Mural of 'Cupid finding Psyche'*, 1872
Sepia, watercolour, bodycolour over pencil; 152 × 158 mm
1922P199

B224 *Cupid and Psyche: Study for the Palace Green Mural of 'The King and Mourners'*, 1872
Watercolour and bodycolour over pencil; 152 × 412 mm
1922P200

B225 *Cupid and Psyche: Study for the Palace Green Mural of 'Zephyrus bearing Psyche'*, 1872
Watercolour and bodycolour; 152 × 165 mm
1922P201

B226 *Cupid and Psyche: Study for the Palace Green Mural of 'Psyche's Sisters visiting her at Cupid's House'*, 1872
Watercolour, bodycolour and scraping; 152 × 340 mm
1922P202

B227 *Cupid and Psyche: Study for Palace Green Mural of 'Psyche holding the Lamp'*, 1872
Watercolour, bodycolour over pencil; 152 × 412 mm
1922P203

B228 *Cupid and Psyche: Study for Palace Green Mural of 'Psyche gazing in despair at Cupid'*, 1872
Watercolour and bodycolour over pencil; 152 × 32 mm
1922P204

B229 *Cupid and Psyche: Study for Palace Green Mural of 'Cupid flying away from Psyche'*, 1872
Watercolour, bodycolour over pencil; 152 × 32 mm
1922P205

B230 *Cupid and Psyche: Study for Palace Green Mural of 'Psyche at the Shrines of Juno or Ceres'*, 1872
Watercolour, bodycolour, over pencil; 152 × 158 mm
1922P206

B231 *Cupid and Psyche: Study for Palace Green Mural of 'Venus setting Psyche the Task'*, 1872
Bodycolour and watercolour; 152 × 260 mm
1922P207

B232 *Cupid and Psyche: Study for Palace Green Mural of 'Psyche giving the Coin'*, 1872
Watercolour, bodycolour, over pencil; 152 × 343 mm
1922P208

B233 *Cupid and Psyche: Study for the Palace Green Mural of 'Psyche receiving the Casket'*, 1872
Watercolour, bodycolour and scraping; 152 × 241 mm
1922P209

B234 *Cupid delivering Psyche*, pub. 1900
Photogravure; 265 × 320 (i.), 670 × 510 mm (p.)
P.: 1900 (1900P36)

B235 *Cupid delivering Psyche: Drapery Study for Psyche*, 1865–66
Black and white chalk on brown paper; 316 × 265 mm
1904P199

B236 *Cupid delivering Psyche: Drapery Study for Psyche*, 1865–66
Black and white chalks on brown paper; 287 × 247 mm
1904P200

B237 *Cupid delivering Psyche: Drapery Study for Psyche*, 1865–66
Black and white chalks on brown paper; 297 × 176 mm
1904P198

B238 *Cupid delivering Psyche: Drapery Study for Psyche*, 1865–66
Black and white chalk on brown paper; 302 × 208 mm
1904P197

B239 *Cupid delivering Psyche: Study of Flying Drapery*, 1865–66
Pencil and brown wash; 201 × 258 mm
1904P201

B240 *Cupid delivering Psyche: Study of Psyche*, 1865–66
Black and white chalks on brown paper, laid down; 353 × 281 mm
1904P222

B241 *Cupid delivering Psyche: Study of Maria Zambaco for the Head of Psyche*, 1867
Pencil on paper; 252 × 169 mm
Insc.: *E B J. 1867*
1927P451

B242 *Cupid finding Psyche*, pub. 1900
Photogravure; 278 × 192 (i.), 670 × 510 mm (p.)
P.: 1900 (1900P34)

Danaë

B243 *Danaë: Drapery Study for Figure of Danaë*, 1863
Pencil and charcoal on cream-toned paper (torn diagonally), laid down on second sheet; 423 × 267 mm
1904P220

B244 *Danaë and the Brazen Tower*, pub. 1900
Photogravure; 495 × 245 (i.), 670 × 510 mm (p.)
P.: 1900 (1900P83)

B245 *Study of dancing Girl*, c. 1890
Pencil; 401 × 227 mm
1927P443

B246 *Study of dancing Girl*, c. 1890
Pencil and coloured chalks; 400 × 232 mm
1927P444

B247 *Study of dancing Girl*, c. 1890
Pencil; 402 × 225 mm
1927P445

B248 *Day: Study for Figure*, 1867–70
Pencil over red-brown chalk; 228 × 182 mm
1904P96

The Days of Creation

B249 *The Days of Creation: Light And Darkness (Dalziels' Bible Gallery)*, 1863
Watercolour, gold and bodycolour over pencil on white paper; 62 × 134 mm
Lit.: *Dalziel*, pp. 164, 166
Prov.: bought from the artist by George and Edward Dalziel, 1863; Edward Dalziel's sale, Christie's, 19 June 1886 (6); purchased Edward Clifford 19 gns; J. R. Holliday
1927P465

B250 *The Days of Creation: The Waters (Dalziels' Bible Gallery)*, 1863
Watercolour and bodycolour with gold; 62 × 134 mm
1927P466 (See B249)

B251 *The Days of Creation: Earth (Dalziels' Bible Gallery)*, 1863
Watercolour and bodycolour with gold; 62 × 134 mm
1927P467 (See B249)

B252 *The Days of Creation: Sky (Dalziels' Bible Gallery)*, 1863
Watercolour and bodycolour with gold; 62 × 134 mm
1927P468 (See B249)

B253 *The Days of Creation: Animal Life (Dalziels' Bible Gallery)*, 1863
Watercolour and bodycolour with gold; 62 × 134 mm
1927P469 (See B249)

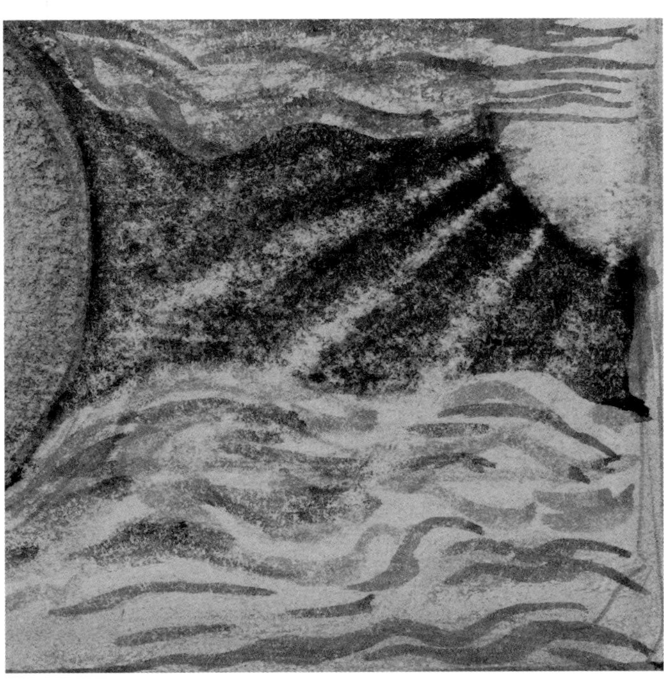

B250 (cat. 16), detail

B254 *The Days of Creation: Adam and Eve (Dalziels' Bible Gallery)*, 1862–63
Watercolour, bodycolour and gold scraping over pencil; 62 × 134 mm
1927P470 (See B249)

B255 *The Days of Creation: Angels Ringing Bells (Dalziels' Bible Gallery)*, 1863
Watercolour, bodycolour and gold scraping over pencil; 62 × 134 mm
1927P471 (See B249)

B256 *The Days of Creation: The First Day*, pub. 1900
Photogravure; 396 × 136 (i.), 670 × 510 mm (p.)
P.: 1900 (1900P41)

B257 *The Days of Creation: The Second Day*, pub. 1900
Photogravure; 396 × 136 (i.), 670 × 510 mm (p.)
P.: 1900 (1900P42)

B258 *The Days of Creation: Study of Hands and Globe for 'The Second Day'*, 1872
Pencil on off-white paper; 362 × 248 mm
Insc.: *E B.J/ 1872/ Studies for the/ DAYS OF/ CREATION/ II*
1927P464

B259 *The Days of Creation: The Third Day*, pub. 1900
Photogravure; 396 × 136 (i.), 670 × 510 mm (p.)
P.: 1900 (1900P43)

B260 *The Days of Creation: The Fourth Day*, pub. 1900
Photogravure; 396 × 136 (i.), 670 × 510 mm (p.)
P.: 1900 (1900P44)

B261 *The Days of Creation: The Fifth Day*, pub. 1900
Photogravure; 396 × 136 (i.), 670 × 510 mm (p.)
P.: 1900 (1900P45)

B262 *The Days of Creation: The Sixth Day*, pub. 1900
Photogravure; 396 × 136 (i.), 670 × 510 mm (p.)
P.: 1900 (1900P46)

B263 *The Depths of the Sea*, pub. 1900
Photogravure; 515 × 195 (i.), 670 × 510 mm (p.)
P.: 1900 (1900P99)

B264 *Dies Domini*, pub. 1900
Photogravure; 353 × 359 (i.), 670 × 510 mm (p.)
P.: 1900 (1900P75)

B265 *Dorigen of Bretaigne*, pub. 1900
Photogravure; 240 × 135 (i.), 670 × 510 mm (p.)
P.: 1900 (1900P23)

B266 *Dorothy Drew*, pub. 1900
Photogravure; 260 × 135 (i.), 670 × 510 mm (p.)
P.:1900 (1900P102)

B267 *The Dream of Sir Lancelot at the Chapel of the San Graal*, pub. 1900
Photogravure; 330 × 400 (i.), 510 × 670 mm (p.)
P.: 1900 (1900P107)

B268 *Edward Burne-Jones*, pub. 1900
Photogravure after the portrait by Philip Burne-Jones; 300 × 210 (i.), 670 × 510 mm (p.)
P.: 1900 (1900P109)

B269 *Embroidery Design: Saints Cecilia and Dorothea*, 1861
Indian ink, with watercolour over chalk and crayon on 2 sheets; 1455 × 1340 mm (sight)
Presented by Charles Fairfax Murray, 1898 (1898P50)

See *Chaucer* section for other embroidery designs

B270 *The Entombment: Study for a Design in Bronze Relief*, 1875–77
Pencil on blue paper; 117 × 235 (i.), 123 × 241 mm (p.)
Insc.: *Entombment/* E.B.J.*
1927P566

Eros and Psyche, see Introductory Note

B271 *The Evening Star*, pub. 1900
Photogravure; 260 × 182 (i.), 670 × 510 mm (p.)
P.: 1900 (1900P48)

B272 *The Evening Star: Studies of the Figure's right Arm*, 1869–70
Black, red and white chalk over pencil on thickly textured buff paper, laid down on card; 300 × 240 mm
Insc.: *168;* 1904P141

Ezekiel and the Boiling Pot

B273 *Ezekiel and the Boiling Pot (Dalziels' Bible Gallery)*, 1862–63
Pencil with chalk; 182 × 140 (i.), 190 × 179 mm (p.)
Insc.: *Ezekiel & the boiling pot**
1927P511 (See B1058)

B274 *Ezekiel and the Boiling Pot*, 1863
Wood engraving on India paper, no. 68 in *Dalziels' Bible Gallery*, pub. 1881; 178 × 133 mm
1920P713.1.68

B275 *Ezekiel and the Boiling Pot*, 1863
Wood engraving on India paper, no. 68 in *Dalziels' Bible Gallery*, pub. 1881; 178 × 133 mm
1920P713.2.68

B276 *Ezekiel and the Boiling Pot*, 1863
Woodblock, engraved; 176 × 133 mm
Insc.: *Ezekiel/ 918/ 24 × 10/ 533/ Dalziel/ J N Hart No 44* (label)
Acquired through the executors of J. N. Hart in or shortly after 1965 (2006.1040.68)

B277 *Fair Rosamund and Queen Eleanor*, 1862–63
Pen and ink, watercolour and bodycolour; 341 × 435 mm
1927P568

B278 *Fair Rosamund: Drapery Studies of Sleeve*, 1862–63
Pencil on cream-toned paper-card; 140 × 149 mm
Insc.: E.B.J.*
1927P562

B279 *The Fairy Family: A Series of Ballads & Metrical Tales Illustrating the Fairy Family of Europe*, pub. 1857
By Archibald Maclaren (1819–1884)
Bound volume with frontispiece, title-page and tailpiece engravings from pen-and-ink drawings by Burne-Jones; 185 × 130 mm (overall size)
1927P1616

B280 *The Fall of Lucifer*, pub. 1900
Photogravure; 530 × 255 (i.), 670 × 510 mm (p.)
P.: 1900 (1900P93)

The Fates

B281 *The Fates: Composition Sketch*, 1865
Pencil; 287 × 240 mm
Insc.: *Fates/* E.B.J.*
1927P482

B282 *The Fates: Composition Sketch*, 1865
Pencil; 266 × 139 mm
Insc.: *Fates/* E.B.J.*
1927P483

B283 *The Fates: Composition Study*, 1865
Brown wash, heightened with white chalk on two sheets of brown paper; 318 × 178 mm
1904P1

B284 *The Fates (or The Hours): Drapery Study*, 1865
Pencil and brown chalk; 250 × 136 mm
1904P208 (See *The Hours*)

B285 *The Fates: Nude Study of the Lovers*, 1865
Brown chalk on cream-toned paper; 359 × 244 mm
1904P4

B286 *The Fates: Rough Sketches of the Lovers and seated Figure*, 1865–66
Pencil; 287 × 240 mm
Insc.: *Fates/* E.B.J./ E.B.J./ *Fates**
1927P481

B287 *The Fates: Sketches of the Lovers*, 1865–66
verso: *Sketches of the Lovers* (formerly joined with 1927P480.2)
Black and white chalk and pencil on brown paper; 350 × 272 mm
Insc.: *Fates* E.B.J./ *Fates**
1927P480.1

B288 *The Fates: Sketches of the Lovers and seated Figure*, 1865–66
verso: *Sketches of the Lovers* (formerly joined with 1927P480.1)
Black chalk and pencil with touches of white highlight on brown paper; 353 × 275 mm
Insc.: *Fates/* E.B.J.*
1927P480.2

B289 *The Fates: Study for the Figure of Clotho*, 1865
Black chalk on paper; 533 × 340 mm
1904P6

B290 *The Fates: Study of classical Drapery*, 1865
Pencil and red chalk; 375 × 274 mm
1904P7

B291 *The Fates: Study of seated Female Figure with Book*, 1865
Brown chalk and pencil; 226 × 206 mm
1904P210

B292 *The Fates(?): Three Studies of female Lover*, 1865
Black chalk on grey paper; 403 × 523 mm
1904P8

B293 *The Fates: Study of the Lovers*, 1865
Red-brown chalk; 403 × 240 mm
1904P2

B294 *The Fates: Study of the male Lover*, 1865
Red chalk; 171 × 127 mm
1904P5

B295 *The Fates: Three Studies for one of the Lovers*, 1865
Black and white chalks on brown paper, laid down on second sheet; 510 × 441 (i.), 570 × 485 mm (p.)
1904P231

B296 *The Fates: Two nude Studies of the Lovers*, 1865
Brown chalk on paper; 290 × 355 mm
1904P3
See *The Hours* B435

The Feast of Peleus

B297 *The Feast of Peleus*, pub. 1900
Photogravure; 175 × 520 (i.), 510 × 670 mm (p.)
1900P80

B298 *The Feast of Peleus: Study for Venus, Minerva and Juno*, c. 1872
Pencil, laid down; 150 × 240 mm
1904P214

B299 *The Feast of Peleus: Studies for Clotho, Juno, Ceres, Atropos and Minerva*, 1872–73
verso: *Pygmalion and the Image: The Godhead Fires – Two Studies for the Hands and Arms of Venus and Galatea*
Pencil; 365 × 255mm
1927P472

B300 *The Feast of Peleus: Composition Sketch with list of associated Names*, 1872–73
verso: various unidentified sketches
Pencil; 178 × 256 mm
Insc.: *Feast of Peleus/* E.B.J.*
1927P473

B301 *The Feast of Peleus: Slight composition Sketch*, 1872–75
Pencil; 179 × 257 mm
Insc.: *Feast of Peleus/* E.B.J.*
1927P474

Female: Drapery Studies

B302 *Female: Drapery Study of a reclining Figure*, 1860–62
Pencil; 157 × 267 mm
1904P100

B303 *Female: Drapery Study*, 1862–64
Red-brown chalk and pencil; 346 × 165 mm
1904P113

B304 *Female: Drapery Studies for female Saints*, c. 1864
Pencil with red chalk; 270 × 366 mm
1927P569

B305 *Female: Drapery Study (Full-Length)*, c. 1864
Brown chalk over pencil; 310 × 174 mm
1904P115

B306 *Female: Drapery Study*, c. 1864
Pencil with red chalk; 301 × 169 mm
1904P109

B307 *Female: Drapery Sketch of a seated Figure*, 1864–66
White, red and black chalk on brown paper; 272 × 305 mm (i.)
1904P44

B308 *Female: Drapery Sketch*, 1864–66
White chalk on brown paper, flesh tinted red, with black chalk; 305 × 205 mm (sight)
1904P45

B309 *Female: Drapery Sketch*, 1864–66
White chalk on brown paper; 312 × 202 mm
1904P46

B310 *Female: Drapery Study*, c. 1864
Pencil and red-brown chalk; 357 × 190 mm
1904P112

B311 *Female: Drapery Study*, c. 1864
Pencil and chalk on cream-toned paper; 308 × 176 mm
1904P108

B312 *Female: Drapery Study*, c. 1864
Pencil and red-brown chalk; 330 × 153 mm
1904P111

B313 *Female: Drapery Study*, c. 1864
Pencil with red-brown chalk; 326 × 160 mm
1904P110

B314 *Female: Drapery Study*, c. 1864
Pencil on cream-toned paper; 360 × 207 mm
1927P456

B315 *Female: Drapery Study*, c. 1864
Red chalk on cream-toned paper, laid down; 264 × 128 mm
1904P101

B316 *Female: Drapery Study*, c. 1864
Red-brown chalk on cream-toned paper; 330 × 128 mm
1904P117

B317 *Female: Drapery Study of standing female Figure*, 1864–65
Black and white chalk on brown paper; 260 × 120 mm
1904P125

B318 *Female: Drapery Studies for female Saints*, c. 1865
Pencil and red chalk; 361 × 404 mm
1927P570

B319 *Female: Drapery Study (background figure for St Theophilus and the Angel?)*, c. 1865
Pencil with red-brown chalk; 309 × 178 mm
1904P116

B320 *Female: Drapery Study of a seated Woman (The Hours?)*, c. 1865
Pencil over red-brown chalk; 226 × 182 mm
1904P99

B321 *Female: Drapery Study of a seated Figure*, 1865–66
White chalk on brown paper, with red chalk; 240 × 165 mm (sight)
1904P43

B322 *Female: Drapery (Two Studies on one Sheet)*, c. 1865
Pencil with red and black chalk; 273 × 195 mm
1904P106

B323 *Female: Drapery Study of two female Figures*, 1865–66
White chalk with touches of pencil and red chalk on brown paper; 345 × 233 mm
1904P122

B324 *Female: Drapery Study for full-length female Figure*, 1865–66
Pencil over red-brown chalk; 342 × 140 mm
1904P107

B325 *Female: Drapery Study for lower half of Figure*, 1865–66
verso: another drawing of same subject
Black and white chalks on brown paper; 337 × 158 mm
1904P11

B326 *Female: Drapery Study of a reclining Figure*, 1865–66
Red chalk on Dutch laid paper; 153 × 199 mm
1904P56

B327 *Female: Drapery Study of a young woman playing a musical Instrument*, 1865–66
Pencil and black chalk on light grey paper; 395 × 300 mm
1904P219

B328 *Female: Drapery Study of flying Drapery*, 1865–66
Pencil and red-brown chalk; 269 × 160 (i.), 305 × 199 mm (p.)
1904P196

B329 *Female: Drapery Study of flying Drapery*, 1865–66
Black and white chalks; 410 × 214 mm
1904P195

B330 *Female: Drapery Study of two seated Figures*, 1865–66
White chalk on brown paper, the flesh slightly tinted with red, background in black chalk; 334 × 375 mm
1904P42

B331 *Female: Drapery Study of two standing Figures*, 1865–68
White and red chalk on brown paper; 276 × 255 mm
1904P47

B332 *Female: Thirteen Drapery Studies*, 1865–68
White chalk on brown paper; 345 × 505 mm
Presented by T. Williams, 1935 (1935P529)

B333 *Female: Drapery Studies*, 1867–69
Red-brown chalk; 379 × 270 mm
1927P552

B334 *Female: Drapery Study alongside Study of Hands with Branches*, 1873–75
Pencil; 271 × 157 mm
1927P450

Female: Head Studies

B335 *Female: Head Study of Augusta Jones*, 1864–65
Red chalk and pencil; 180 × 233 mm
1904P54

B336 *Female: Head Study from an Italian Model*, 1864–66
Red chalk over pencil; 241 × 206 mm
1904P20

B337 *Female: Head Study (from an Italian Model?)*, 1864–66
Pencil; 245 × 198 mm
1904P19

B338 *Female: Head Study of a Woman, looking right*, c. 1865
Red chalk over pencil; 182 × 137 mm
1904P18

B339 *Female: Head Study of a Girl (Three Studies)*, c. 1865
Pencil; 278 × 220 mm
1904P55

B340 *Female: Head Study of Agnes MacDonald*, c. 1865
Pencil and charcoal, 272 × 227 mm
1904P23

Female: Nude Studies

B341 *Female: Nude Study of Figure holding a Harp, facing left*, c. 1864
Red-brown chalk with pencil; 310 × 175 mm
1927P571

B342 *Female: Nude Study of Figure holding a Harp, facing right*, c. 1864
Red-brown chalk with pencil; 280 × 108 mm
1927P572

B343 *Female: Nude Study of Figure with musical Instrument*, c. 1864
Pencil and brown chalk; 284 × 95 mm
1927P576

B344 *Female: Nude Study of a Figure with Hands behind Back*, c. 1864
Brown chalk and pencil; 340 × 97 mm
1927P580

B345 *Female: Nude Study of a Figure with Hands behind Back*, c. 1864
Brown chalk; 306 × 108 mm
1927P579

B346 *Female: Nude Study of Figure with Hands behind Back*, c. 1864
Brown chalk with touches of pencil on cream-toned paper; 287 × 115 mm
1927P581

B347 *Female: Nude Study*, c. 1864
Brown chalk; 286 × 100 mm
1927P582

B348 *Female: Nude Study*, c. 1864
Brown chalk; 301 × 99 mm
1927P583

B349 *Female: Nude Study*, c. 1864
Red-brown chalk and pencil; 353 × 166 mm
1904P114

B350 *Female: Nude Study of a female Figure holding Drapery*, c. 1864
Brown chalk; 313 × 115 mm
1927P577

B351 *Female: Nude Study of a female Figure holding Drapery*, 1864–65
Brown chalk; 326 × 109 mm
1927P578

B352 *Female: Nude seated Figure*, 1864–65
Red chalk; 98 × 110 mm
1904P51

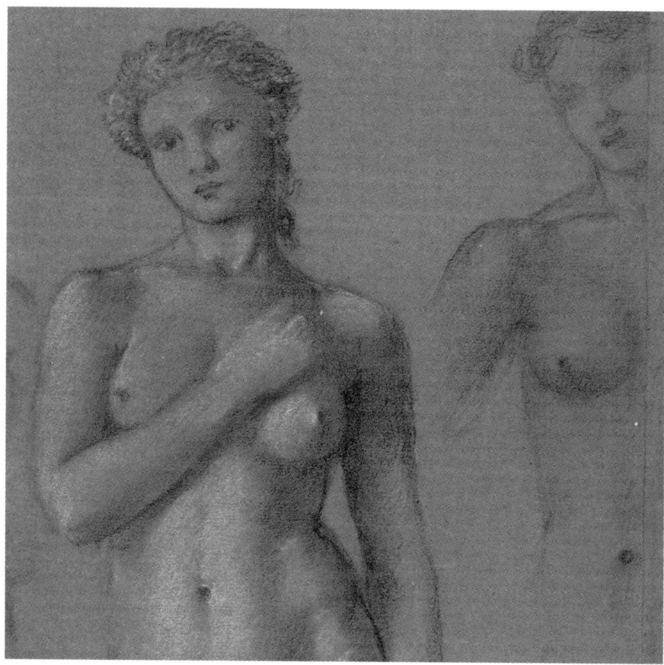

B358 (cat. 25), detail

B353 *Female: Nude seated Figure*, 1864–65
Red chalk; 132 × 164 mm
1904P53

B354 *Female: Nude Study of a seated Figure*, 1864–65
Red chalk; 99 × 112 mm
1904P52

B355 *Female: Nude Study*, 1864–65
Light brown-green chalk; 119 × 74 mm
1904P229

B356 *Female: Nude Study*, 1864–65
Black and white chalk on brown paper; 365 × 162 mm
1904P126

B357 *Female: Nude Study*, 1864–66
Pencil on grey paper; 228 × 167 mm
1904P127

B358 *Female: Nude (Three Studies)*, 1865–66
Black and white chalks on brown paper with attached strips on side edges; 510 × 331 mm
1904P9

B359 *Female: Nude (Three Studies of a seated Girl)*, 1865–67
Brown chalk; 312 × 263 mm
1904P49

B360 *Female: Nude (Five Studies)*, 1865–67
Brown chalk; 330 × 267 mm
1904P50

B361 *Female: Nude (Five Studies of a seated Girl)*, 1865–67
Brown chalk; 381 × 259 mm (sight)
1904P48

B362 *Female: Nude Study of Head and Shoulders, and seated Nude*, 1865–67
Black and white chalks on brown paper, laid on second sheet of brown paper; 192 × 200 (i.), 202 × 215 mm (p., sight)
1904P228

B363 *Female: Nude Study of a female Figure holding musical Instrument*, 1865–67
Brown chalk and pencil; 306 × 111 mm
1927P575

B364 *Female: Nude Study of a female Figure holding Violin*, 1865–67
Brown chalk and pencil; 281 × 128 mm
1927P574

B365 *Female: Nude Study of figure seen from the back, holding Violin and Bow*, 1865–67
Red-brown chalk and pencil; 291 × 112 mm
1927P573

B366 *Female: Study of seated Girl in contemporary Dress, reading*, 1860–62
Pencil; 252 × 204 mm
1927P558

B367 *Female: Sketch of Musician*, 1864–65
Pencil; 165 × 121 mm
1904P215

B368 *Study of two seated Figures*, 1865–67
White chalk on brown paper; 261 × 244 mm
Insc.: E.B.J.*
1927P587

B369 *Faith/ Fides*, pub. 1900
Photogravure; 455 × 162 (i.), 670 × 510 mm (p.)
P.: 1900 (1900P72)

B370 *Flamma Vestalis*, pub. 1900
Photogravure; 520 × 190 (i.), 670 × 510 mm (p.)
P.: 1900 (1900P104)

The Flower Book

B371 *The Flower Book*, pub. 1905
Thirty-eight facsimiles on laid Michallet paper, inscribed with title and second sheet with Letter press by Lady Burne-Jones and individual descriptions of scenes by Graily Hewitt; unnumbered volume from an edition of 300. Printed by Henri Piazza after watercolours by Burne-Jones (from 1882) for the Fine Art Society.
Bound in box in full sealskin; 330 × 252 mm (p., slight variations), 451 × 343 mm (box)
Accompanying folio with text by Georgiana Burne-Jones, followed by index of 38 titles and Burne-Jones's hand-written long-list of proposed flowers and their visual interpretation
Purchased from K. G. Brooks, 1953 (1953P5)

B372 *The Flower Book: Love in a Mist*, pub. 1905
Colour facsimile; 167 × 167 mm (i.)
1953P5.1

B373 *The Flower Book: Golden Thread*, pub. 1905
Colour facsimile; 161 × 168 mm (i.)
1953P5.2

B374 *The Flower Book: Jacob's Ladder*, pub. 1905
Colour facsimile; 152 × 154 mm (i.)
1953P5.3

B375 *The Flower Book: Traveller's Joy*, pub. 1905
Colour facsimile; 155 × 160 mm (i.)
1953P5.4

B376 *The Flower Book: Rose of Heaven*, pub. 1905
Colour facsimile; 57 × 160 mm
1953P5.5

B377 *The Flower Book: Flower of God*, pub. 1905
Colour facsimile; 159 × 161 mm (i.)
1953P5.6

B378 *The Flower Book: Golden Cup*, pub. 1905
Colour facsimile; 159 × 163 mm (i.)
1953P5.7

B379 *The Flower Book: Adder's Tongue*, pub. 1905
Colour facsimile; 161 × 163 mm (i.)
1953P5.8

B380 *The Flower Book: Golden Gate*, pub. 1905
Colour facsimile; 158 × 160 mm (i.)
1953P5.9

B381 *The Flower Book: Venus' Looking Glass*, pub. 1905
Colour facsimile; 160 × 158 mm (i.)
1953P5.10

B382 *The Flower Book: Key of Spring*, pub. 1905
Colour facsimile; 168 × 170 mm (i.)
1953P5.11

B383 *The Flower Book: Ladder of Heaven*, pub. 1905
Colour facsimile; 163 × 165 mm (i.)
1953P5.12

B384 *The Flower Book: Comes He Not?*, pub. 1905
Colour facsimile; 158 × 160 mm (i.)
1953P5.13

B385 *The Flower Book: Love in a Tangle*, pub. 1905
Colour facsimile; 167 × 166 mm (i.)
1953P5.14

B386 *The Flower Book: Witch's Tree*, pub. 1905
Colour facsimile; 168 × 169 mm
1953P5.15

B387 *The Flower Book: Grave of the Sea*, pub. 1905
Colour facsimile; 165 × 170 mm (i.)
1953P5.16

B388 *The Flower Book: Golden Greeting*, pub. 1905
Colour facsimile; 165 × 167 mm (i.)
1953P5.17

B389 *The Flower Book: Golden Shower*, pub. 1905
Colour facsimile; 162 × 165 mm (i.)
1953P5.18

B390 *The Flower Book: Flame Heath*, pub. 1905
Colour facsimile; 161 × 162 mm (i.)
1953P5.19

B391 *The Flower Book: Star of Bethlehem*, pub. 1905
Colour facsimile; 160 mm (circular)
1953P5.20

B392 *The Flower Book: Morning Glories*, pub. 1905
Colour facsimile; 163 × 162 mm (i.)
1953P5.21

B393 *The Flower Book: With the Wind*, pub. 1905
Colour facsimile; 155 × 156 mm
1953P5.22

B394 *The Flower Book: Wake, Dearest*, pub. 1905
Colour facsimile; 155 × 158 mm
1953P5.23

B395 *The Flower Book: Wall Tryst*, pub. 1905
Colour facsimile; 155 × 158 mm
1953P5.24

B396 *The Flower Book: Helen's Tears*, pub. 1905
Colour facsimile; 165 × 168 mm (i.)
1953P5.25

B397 *The Flower Book: Marvel of the World*, pub. 1905
Colour facsimile; 160 × 163 mm (i.)
1953P5.26

B398 *The Flower Book: Black Archangel*, pub. 1905
Colour facsimile; 163 × 166 mm (i.)
1953P5.27

B399 *The Flower Book: Arbor Tristis*, pub. 1905
Colour facsimile; 160 × 160 mm (i.)
1953P5.28

B400 *The Flower Book: Scattered Starwort*, pub. 1905
Colour facsimile; 164 × 165 mm (i.)
1953P5.29

B401 *The Flower Book: Saturn's Loathing*, pub. 1905
Colour facsimile; 152 × 150 mm (i.)
1953P5.30

B402 *The Flower Book: Welcome to the House*, pub. 1905
Colour facsimile; 157 × 161 mm (i.)
1953P5.31

B403 *The Flower Book: Honour's Prize*, pub. 1905
Colour facsimile; 158 × 162 mm (i.)
1953P5.32

B404 *The Flower Book: Most Bitter Moonseed*, pub. 1905
Colour facsimile; 157 × 160 mm (i.)
1953P5.33

B405 *The Flower Book: White Garden*, pub. 1905
Colour facsimile; 150 × 157 mm (i.)
1953P5.34

B406 *The Flower Book: Meadow Sweet*, pub. 1905
Colour facsimile; 162 × 163 mm (i.)
1953P5.35

B407 *The Flower Book: False Mercury*, pub. 1905
Colour facsimile; 157 × 159 mm (i.)
1953P5.36

B408 *The Flower Book: Fire Tree*, pub. 1905
Colour facsimile; 160 × 165 mm (i.)
1953P5.37

B409 *The Flower Book: Day and Night*, pub. 1905
Colour facsimile; 158 × 160 mm (i.)
1953P5.38

B410 *The Garden of Pan*, pub. 1900
Photogravure; 375 × 460 (i.), 510 × 670 mm (p.)
1900P105

B411 *The Garden of the Hesperides*, pub. 1900
Photogravure; 246 × 200 (i.), 510 × 670 mm (p.)
1900P54

B412 *Georgiana Burne-Jones, née MacDonald (1840–1920)*, 1863
Bodycolour on paper laid onto board; 345 × 260 mm
Insc.: G.M.J./ *Ætat: suae: xxii/ pinxit* E.B.J./ AD MDCCCLXIII
Presented by Colin MacInnes, 1956 (1956P3)

B413 *Gertrude Lewis*, pub. 1900
Photogravure; 280 × 185 (i.), 670 × 510 mm (p.)
1900P103

B414 *The Golden Stairs*, pub. 1900
Photogravure; 525 × 225 (i.), 670 × 510 mm (p.)
1900P73

Green Summer

B415 *Green Summer: Drapery Study for the central Figure*, 1863–64
Red chalk and pencil; 250 × 183 mm
1904P191

B416 *Green Summer: Study of a Girl*, 1863–64
Red chalk and pencil; 220 × 303 (i.), 245 × 320 mm (p.)
1904P192

B417 *Green Summer: Study of Back of seated Girl*, 1863–64
Red chalk over pencil; 205 × 261 mm
1904P193

B418 *The Heart of the Rose*, pub. 1900
Photogravure; 300 × 420 (i.), 510 × 670 mm (p.)
P.: 1900 (1900P86)

The Hill of Venus

B419 *The Hill of Venus: Walter at the Hill of Venus*, 1866
Pencil on tracing paper; 104 × 157 (i.), 115 × 167 mm (p.)
1927P633

B420 *The Hill of Venus: Walter at the Hill of Venus*, 1866
Pencil on tracing paper; 103 × 158 (i.), 120 × 175 mm (p.)
1927P634

B421 *The Hill of Venus: Lovers on the Hill of Venus*, 1866
Pencil on tracing paper; 102 × 159 (i.), 117 × 174 mm (p.)
1927P635

B422 *The Hill of Venus: Lovers on the Hill of Venus*, 1866
Pencil on tracing paper; 100 × 156 (i.), 114 × 170 mm (p.)
1927P636

B423 *The Hill of Venus: Walter at the Hill of Venus*, 1866
Pencil on tracing paper; 100 × 153 (i.), 110 × 164 mm (p.)
1927P637

B424 *The Hill of Venus: Walter joining the Pilgrimage to Rome*, 1866
Pencil on tracing paper; 113 × 169 mm
1927P638

B425 *The Hill of Venus: Walter and the Pilgrims in Rome*, 1866
Pencil on tracing paper; 106 × 162 (i.), 118 × 174 mm (p.)
1927P639

B426 *The Hill of Venus: Walter and the Pope*, 1866
Pencil on tracing paper; 107 × 159 (i.), 120 × 170 mm (p.)
1927P640

B427 *The Hill of Venus: The Pope's Bedroom*, 1866
Pencil on tracing paper; 109 × 161 (i.), 118 × 173 mm (p.)
1927P641

B428 *The Hill of Venus: Walter pulling back a Curtain*, 1866
Pencil on tracing paper; 124 × 157 (i.), 135 × 168 mm (p.)
1927P642

B429 *The Hill of Venus: Walter meeting a Group of fair Women*, 1866
Pencil on tracing paper; 103 × 157 (i.), 117 × 170 mm (p.)
1927P643

B430 *The Hill of Venus: Walter, dressed in Rags, meets a Group of Knights*, 1865–66
Pencil on tracing paper; 104 × 162 (i.), 118 × 172 mm (p.)
1927P644

B431 *The Hill of Venus: Walter, dressed in Rags, meets a Group of Knights*, 1865–66
Pencil on tracing paper; 100 × 156 (i.), 132 × 185 mm (p.)
1927P645

B432 *The Hill of Venus: Nude Study of one of the Reapers for 'Reapers Appealing to Venus'*, 1866
Red-brown chalk; 283 × 233 mm
1904P97

B433 *Hope/ Spes*, pub. 1900
Photogravure; 462 × 160 (i.), 670 × 510 mm (p.)
P.: 1900 (1900P20)

B434 *Studies of a Horse*, 1862–63
Pencil; 218 × 264 mm
verso: head of a horse and saddle bag?
Insc.: E.B.J.*
1927P563

The Hours

B435 *The Hours*, pub. 1900
Photogravure; 213 × 513 (i.), 510 × 670 mm (p.)
1900P56

B436 *The Hours: Study*, 1864–66
Red-brown chalk with touch of pencil; 262 × 247 mm
1904P140

B437 *The Hours: Study*, 1864–66
Brown-red chalk; 280 × 176 mm
1904P139

B438 *The Hours: Study for Drapery*, 1864–66
Brown chalk; 310 × 187 (i.), 316 × 185 mm (p.)
1904P223

B439 *The Hours: Three female nude Studies*, 1864–66
Brown chalk and pencil; 293 × 260 (i.), 298 × 260 mm (p.)
1904P212

B440 *The Hours: Drapery Study*, 1865
Pencil with brown chalk, laid down; 251 × 135 mm
Insc.: E.B.J.*
1904P209

B441 *The Hours (or The Fates): Studies of Drapery and Feet*, 1865
Pencil; 257 × 182 (i.), 266 × 187 mm (p.)
1904P211
See *The Fates* B284

B442 *An Idyll*, 1862
Watercolour and bodycolour with gum arabic, scraping on paper stretched on canvas; 295 × 277 (i.), 532 × 515 mm (frame)
Insc.: E B J/ *1862*
Presented by Mrs George Frederic Watts, 1924 (1924P91)

B443 *An Idyll: Study*, 1862
Charcoal over pencil; 221 × 329 mm
1904P36

B444 *Jane Morris: Head Study*, 1863–64
Red chalk over pencil; 513 × 562 mm
1904P24

King Cophetua and the Beggar Maid

B445 *King Cophetua and the Beggar Maid*, pub. 1900
Photogravure; 510 × 230 (i.), 670 × 510 mm (p.)
1900P97

B446 *King Cophetua and the Beggar Maid: Full-Scale Cartoon for the Oil Painting*, c. 1883
Pastel, watercolour, bodycolour with gum arabic; 2900 × 1390 mm
Presented by Col Rex Benson through the National Art Collections Fund, 1947 (1947P18)

B447 *King Cophetua and the Beggar Maid: Nude Study for Cophetua*, c. 1883
Black and white chalks on brown laid paper; 609 × 457 mm
1904P230

B448 *King Cophetua and the Beggar Maid: Study for Cophetua*, c. 1883
Pencil; 272 × 181 mm
1972P74

B449 *King Cophetua and the Beggar Maid: Studies for Cophetua*, c. 1883
Pencil on laid paper; 304 × 188 mm
1972P73

B450 *King Cophetua and the Beggar Maid: Study of Cophetua's Legs*, c. 1883
Black chalk on laid paper; 305 × 199mm
1972P75

B451 *King Cophetua and the Beggar Maid: Study of a Boy's Head*, c. 1883
Black chalk touched with white on brown paper; 435 × 459 mm
1904P221

King Mark and La Belle Iseult

B452 *King Mark and La Belle Iseult*, 1862
Watercolour, bodycolour and gum arabic; 585 × 555 mm
1912P28

B453 *King Mark and La Belle Iseult: Study for the Head of Iseult*, 1862
Pencil; 98 × 78 mm
Insc.: *Iseult & King Mark/* E.B.J.*
1927P477

B454 *King Mark and La Belle Iseult: Study For the Head of Iseult*, 1862
Pencil; 163 × 138 mm
1927P478

B455 *King Mark and La Belle Iseult: Three Studies for the left Hand of Iseult*, 1862
Pencil; 62 × 166 mm
Insc.: *Iseult & King Mark/* E.B.J.*
1927P479

B456 *King René's Honeymoon: Sculpture*, 1861
Pen, Indian ink and wash over coloured chalk and pencil; 550 × 342 mm (sight)
1904P528

B457 *King Sigurd the Crusader – A Norse Saga*, pub. 1862
Wood engraving, engraved by Dalziel Brothers for *Good Words*, 1862, pp. 247–9; 154 × 115 mm
1978P548.2

Ladies and Animals Sideboard

B458 *Ladies and Animals Sideboard ('Good and Bad Animals'): Study of a Lady feeding Goldfish*, 1860
Pen and sepia wash over pencil; 79 × 68 mm
Presented by W. M. Keeley, 1971 (1971P274)

B459 *Ladies and Animals Sideboard ('Good and Bad Animals'): Study of a Lady feeding Parrots*, 1860
Pen and sepia wash over pencil; 92 × 84 mm
Presented by W. M. Keeley, 1971 (1971P273)

B460 *Ladies and Animals Sideboard ('Good and Bad Animals'): Study of a Lady feeding Pigs*, 1860
Pen and sepia wash over pencil; 76 × 75 mm
Presented by W. M. Keeley, 1971 (1971P272)

B461 *Ladies and Animals Sideboard ('Good and Bad Animals'): Study of a Lady frightened by a Newt*, 1860
Pen and sepia wash over pencil; 110 × 85 mm
Presented by W. M. Keeley, 1971 (1971P275)

B462 *Ladies and Animals Sideboard ('Good and Bad Animals'): Study of a Lady pursued by Bees*, 1860
Pen and sepia ink wash over pencil; 110 × 83 mm
Presented by W. M. Keeley, 1971 (1971P271)

The Lament

B463 *The Lament: Study for the right-hand figure*, 1865–66
Pencil and brown chalk; 300 × 210 mm
1904P207

B464 *The Lament: Study for the right-hand Figure*, 1865–66
Pencil; 227 × 247 mm
1904P204

B465 *The Lament: Studies of Hands*, 1865–66
Pencil and sepia wash on laid paper; 113 × 94 mm
Insc.: E.B.J./*'The Lament'**
1927P475

B466 *Study of two female Heads: The Lament(?)*, 1865–66
Red-brown and black chalks over pencil; 345 × 295 mm
1904P188

B467 *The Lament: Two nude female Studies for the right-hand Figure*, 1865–66
Brown chalk; 348 × 233 mm
1904P206

B468 *The Lament: Two Studies for the right-hand Figure*, 1865–66
Pencil with red chalk laid onto card; 271 × 415 mm
1904P203

B469 *The Lament: Two Studies of Drapery for the right-hand Figure*, 1865–66
Pencil with red-brown chalk; 282 × 327 mm
1904P205

Landscape

B470 *Landscape: Study*, 1863
Watercolour and bodycolour with gum arabic; 257 × 448 mm
Presented by Mrs Angela Thirkell, 1954 (1954P61)

B471 *Landscape: Study*, 1863
Watercolour and bodycolour with scraping on paper; 214 × 490 mm
Presented by Mrs Angela Thirkell, 1954 (1954P60)

B472 *Landscape: Study*, 1863
Watercolour and bodycolour with ink on paper; 245 × 451 mm
Presented by Mrs Angela Thirkell, 1954 (1954P62)

The Lapse of the Year

B473 *The Lapse of the Year: Spring*, pub. 1900
Photogravure; 290 × 110 (i.), 670 × 510 mm (p.)
P.: 1900 (1900P49)

B474 *The Lapse of the Year: Summer*, pub. 1900
Photogravure; 290 × 108 (i.), 670 × 510 mm (p.)
P.: 1900 (1900PP50)

B475 *The Lapse of the Year: Autumn*, pub. 1900
Photogravure; 290 × 108 (i.), 670 × 510 mm (p.)
P.: 1900 (1900P51)

B476 *The Lapse of the Year: Winter*, pub. 1900
Photogravure; 290 × 105 (i.), 670 × 510 mm (p.)
P.: 1900 (1900P52)

B477 *Laus Veneris*, pub. 1900
Photogravure, 335 × 515 (i.), 510 × 670 mm (p.)
P.: 1900 (1900P82)

Letters

B478 *Letter: Edward Burne-Jones to Mrs Leslie Stephen (née Julia Jackson)*
Undated, from The Grange, West Kensington; three sides of a folded sheet; 156 × 98 mm
P.: Sotheby's, London, 22 July 1980 (Charleston papers, lot 212), 1980P129

B479 *Letter: Edward Burne-Jones to Mrs Leslie Stephen (née Julia Jackson)*
Undated, from The Grange, West Kensington; one side of a torn sheet; 156 × 98 mm
P.: Sotheby's, London; 22 July 1980 (Charleston papers, lot 212), 1980P130

B480 *Love among the Ruins*, pub. 1900
Photogravure; 340 × 515 (i.), 510 × 670 mm (p.)
P.: 1900 (1900P70)

B481 *Love disguised as Reason*, pub. 1900
Photogravure; 393 × 193 (i.), 670 × 510 mm (p.)
P.: 1900 (1900P31)

B482 *Love disguised as Reason: Study for the Figure of Love*, 1870
Pencil and black chalk on paper; 476 × 184 (i.), 479 × 186 mm (p.)
Insc. verso: *1st sketch for 'Love disguised as Reason'**
1927P529

Love is Enough

B483 *Love is Enough: Initial Letter 'L' entwined with Laurel Leaves*, 1866–67
Wood engraving, printed in black; 40 × 40 (i.), 493 × 315 mm (p.)
1913P199

B484 *Love is Enough: Initial Letter 'L' entwined with Laurel Leaves*, 1872
Wood engraving, printed in black on laid Michallet paper; 39 × 39 (i.), 492 × 315 mm (p.)
1913P200

B485 *Love is Enough: upright Border or Sidepiece with four Putti*, 1872
Wood engraving, printed in black; 139 × 35 (i.), 495 × 316 mm (p.)
1913P201

B486 *Love is Enough: upright Border or Sidepiece with Foliage entwined around a Pole*, 1872
Wood engraving, printed in black; 137 × 34 (i.), 495 × 325 mm (p.)
1913P202

B487 *Love is Enough: upright Border or Sidepiece with entwined Foliage and Flowers*, 1872
Wood engraving, printed in black; 135 × 33 (i.), 492 × 325 mm (p.)
1913P203

B488 *Love is Enough: upright Border and Sidepiece with entwined Foliage and Flowers*, 1866–67
Wood engraving, printed in black; 135 × 32 (i.), 495 × 327 mm (p.)
1913P204

B489 *Love is Enough: upright Border or Sidepiece, with Roses and Vines with Bunches of Grapes entwined around a Pole*, 1872
Wood engraving, printed in black; 135 × 32 (i.), 494 × 327 mm (p.)
1913P205

B490 *Love is Enough: narrow Band of Ornament with Flowers and Foliage*, 1872
Wood engraving, printed in black; 136 × 20 (i.), 487 × 323 mm (p.)
1913P206

B491 *Love is Enough: narrow Band of Ornament Foliage*, 1872
Wood engraving, printed in black; 171 × 23 (i.), 487 × 323 mm (p.)
1913P207

B492 *Love is Enough: narrow Band of Ornament with Apples and Foliage*, 1872
Wood engraving, printed in black, 169 × 22 (i.), 495 × 309 mm (p.)
1913P208

B493 *Love leading the Pilgrim: Study of Bird (Finches and Sparrows)*, c. 1877–97
Coloured chalks on brown paper, laid onto thin card; 302 × 200 mm
1927P457

B494 *Love leading the Pilgrim: Study of Birds (Crows, Kingfishers and Sparrows?)*, c. 1877–97
Coloured chalks on brown paper; 303 × 200 mm
1927P458

B495 *Lucretia*, 1867
Watercolour, bodycolour and pastel, with gold, on paper laid on canvas; 1368 × 685 mm
Insc.: *E.B.J. 1867 London/ Lucretia/ As when a wolfe findeth a lamb alone/ To whom shall she complaine or make moan.*
Bequest of J. R. Holliday, 1927 (1931P61)

B496 *Luna*, pub. 1900
Photogravure; 260 × 184 (i.), 670 × 510 mm (p.)
P.: 1900 (1900P53)

Male Studies

B497 *Male: Drapery Study of seated Figure*, 1860–63
Pencil on Whatman paper, watermarked; 253 × 179 mm
1927P588

B498 *Male: Drapery Study of a young Man*, 1861–64
Pencil; 233 × 82 mm
1904P103

B499 *Male: Drapery Study for Stained Glass in Lyndhurst Church, Hampshire*, 1862–63
Pencil; 324 × 165 mm
Insc.: *Study for Lyndhurst/ window/ E.B.J.**
1927P545

B500 *Male: Drapery Study for a Saint*, 1864–65
Pencil on Whatman paper, watermarked 1864; 339 × 144 mm
1927P546

B501 *Male: Two Drapery Studies*, 1865–66
Black and white chalk on brown paper, laid down; 262 × 254 mm (sight)
1904P118

B502 *Male: Drapery Studies of Bishop's Vestments*, 1865–67
Brown and blue chalks; 303 × 241 mm
1904P157

B503 *Male: Drapery Study of Man embracing Tree*, 1868–69
Pencil and red-brown chalk; 315 × 190 mm
1904P119

B504 *Male: Nude Study of Man holding Shaft of Spear*, c. 1866
White and black chalk on brown paper, laid down; 305 × 155 mm
1904P123

B505 *Male: Nude: Study of Man embracing Tree*, 1868–69
Red-brown chalk over touches of pencil on cream-toned paper; 317 × 189 mm
1904P121

B506 *Male: Nude Study of Man embracing Tree*, 1868–69
Red-brown chalk; 295 × 156 mm
1904P120

B507 *Male: Nude (St Michael/ St George[?])*, 1869–72
Black and white crayon on brown paper, laid down on grey paper; 318 × 152 mm
1904P149

B508 *Male Portrait*, c. 1865 *possibly related to background figures in 'The Princess draws the Lot' (St George Series)*
Red and black chalk touched with pencil, on paper; 356 × 234 mm
Insc.: *E.B.J.**
1927P564

B509 *Male: Study of southern Italian Peasant Boy*, 1860–62
Watercolour and bodycolour, with pencil annotations, on brown paper; 235 × 116 mm
Insc.: *leather/( )/ flannel/ leather*
1904P38

B510 *Male: Study of southern Italian Peasant Boy*, 1860–62
Watercolour and bodycolour, over pencil, on brown paper; 223 × 108 mm
1904P39

B511 *Margaret Burne-Jones*, pub. 1900
Photogravure; 332 × 238 (i.), 670 × 510 mm (p.)
P.: 1900 (1900P95)

Maria Zambaco

B512 *Maria Zambaco: Profile Study*, 1866
Brown chalk, with pencil; 314 × 205 mm
1904P22

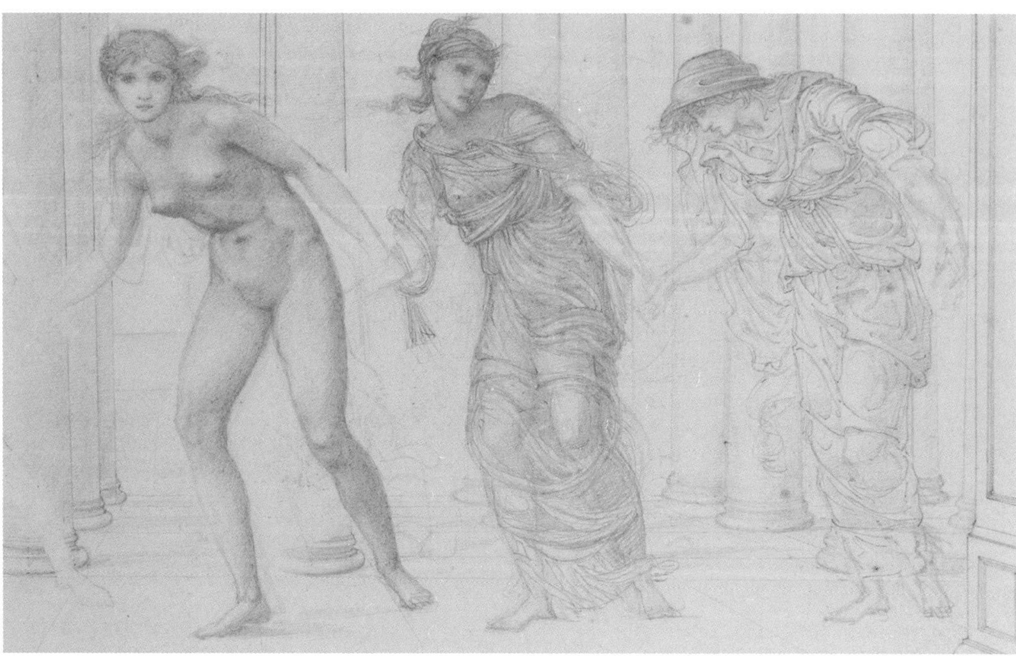

B519 (cat. 41), detail

B513 *Maria Zambaco in traditional Greek Costume*, 1867–68
Black chalk and pencil on thick wove paper; 561 × 388 mm
1904P216

B514 *Maria Zambaco: Study*, 1873
attrib. to Edward Burne-Jones
Pencil; 249 × 172 mm
Insc.: *Maria, Paris**
1904P21

The Masque of Cupid

B515 *The Masque of Cupid: Final Portion, Part I*, c. 1872
Pencil on tracing paper, laid down; 364 × 342 mm
Insc.: *be bold/ Pigritia/ mutabilitas/ be bold/ Tristitia/ Profusio/ Tracundia/ be not too bold/ rixa*
1927P460

B516 *The Masque of Cupid: Final Portion, Part II*, c. 1872
Pencil on tracing paper; 356 × 394 mm
Insc.: *be bold/ Exitium/ Metus/ be bold/ infirmitas/ penuria/ be not too bold/ luxuria*
1927P459

B517 *The Masque of Cupid: First Portion*, c. 1872
Woodblock with pencil drawing on white bodycolour base; 147 × 216 mm
Insc.: *be not too bold/ Imaginato/ concupiscentia/ Periculum/ Dubitatio/ be bold/ Timor/ Spes/ suspicio/ dissimulatio/ be bold/ Furor/ Dolor*
1927P461

B518 *The Masque of Cupid: Second Portion*, c. 1872
Pencil heightened with white bodycolour on woodblock; 146 × 216 mm
Insc.: *be not too bold/ saevilia/ crudelitas/ infamia/ be bold/ CUPIDO/ Pudor/ be bold/ penitentia*
1927P462

B519 *The Masque of the Four Seasons*, 1873–75
Pencil, with additional strips around four edges; 427 × 562 mm
1927P538

B520 *The Merciful Knight*, 1863
Watercolour with bodycolour; 1014 × 586 (i.), 1585 × 1265 mm (frame)
Insc.: *EDWARD:BURNE.JONES.1863.* with inscription on frame
Purchased from The Middlemore Trustees, 1973 (1973P84)

B521 *The Merciful Knight*, pub. 1900
Photogravure; 355 × 240 (i.), 670 × 510 mm (p.)
1900P30

B522 *The Mill* (proof), pub. 1899
By Emile Sulpis (1856–1943) after an oil painting in the Victoria & Albert Museum, London, by Edward Burne-Jones
Etching with white bodycolour and pencil on vellum, laid down; 246 × 535 (i.), 377 × 629 mm (p.)
Insc.: *make all the background stronger and more( )as in photograph/ note carefully where lights shine on the water or buildings/ note high lights on water/ E B J./ 1870*
1923P7

B523 *The Mill*, pub. 1900
Photogravure; 240 × 514 (i.), 670 × 510 mm (p.)
P.: 1900 (1900P68)

B524 *The Mirror of Venus*, pub. 1900
Photogravure; 310 × 515 (i.), 510 × 670 mm (p.)
P.:1900 (1900P78)

B525 *The Mirror of Venus: Study of kneeling female Attendant*, 1865–66
Red-brown chalk; 258 × 147 mm
1904P98

B526 *The Morning of the Resurrection*, pub. 1900
Photogravure; 235 × 420 (i.), 510 × 670 mm (p.)
P.: 1900 (1900P106)

Morris & Company Windows Book

B527 *Morris & Company Windows Book: Photograph Album of Edward Burne-Jones Stained Glass Designs*, 1900–10
Photographs by Frederick Hollyer, in leather-bound volume; 385 × 315 mm
Insc.: *Morris & Company,/ London W1/ This Book Must Not be taken From The Show Room*
Presented anonymously, 1940 (1940P604.1)

B528 *Morris & Company Windows Book: Photograph Album of mostly Edward Burne-Jones and John Henry Dearle Stained Glass Designs*, 1900–10
Photographs by Frederick Hollyer, in leather-bound volume; 385 × 323 mm
Insc.: *Morris & Company,/ London W1/ This Book Must Not Be taken From The Show Room*
Presented anonymously, 1940 (1940P604.2)

B529 *Morris & Company Windows Book: Photographic Album of completed Stained Glass Windows*, 1900–10
Photographs by Frederick Hollyer, in leather-bound volume; 385 × 322 mm
Insc.: *Windows/ Morris & Company,/ London W1/ This Book Must Not Be taken From The Show Room*
Presented anonymously, 1940 (1940P604.3)

B530 *Morris & Company Revised Index of Stained Glass Cartoons by Edward Burne-Jones, Ford Madox Brown, Dante Gabriel Rossetti, William Morris, Philip Webb, Simeon Solomon, Arthur Hughes etc.*, 1900–10
Pen and ink with pencil annotations and small photo inserts and pen and ink drawings; 325 × 218 mm
Insc.: front cover, *Revised/ Glass Cartoon Index*; inside, *Morris and Company/ 449 Oxford Street London W*
Presented anonymously, 1940 (1940.604.4)

B531 *Morris & Company Windows Book: Photograph Album of Stained Glass Designs by Dante Gabriel Rossetti, Ford Madox Brown, William Morris, Edward Burne-Jones, Simeon Solomon and Philip Webb*, 1900–10
Photographs by Frederick Hollyer, in leather-bound volume; 381 × 323 mm
Insc.: *Morris & Company,/ 449 Oxford Street,/ London, W/ This book Must Not Be Taken From The Showroom*
Presented anonymously, 1940 (1940P604.5)

B532 *Mortuary Design: Gravestone and Plot* (attrib. Burne-Jones), 1887–98
Pencil on heavy cream paper; 355 × 251 mm
Insc.: *Rottingdean Church East – suggested arrangement of stone and supports/ about 6 ft 6 ins over/ slab/ narrow space for flowers on each side/ cobbles/ slats/ supporting stones at ends/ earth/ section/ paving**
Found unaccessioned in 1978 (1978P533.1)

B533 *Mural Design: The Wedding Procession of Sir Degrevaunt*, 1860
Pencil on blue paper, squared for transfer; 289 × 288 mm
1927P452

The Muses leaving the dying Poet

B534 *The Muses leaving the dying Poet: Study of Figures*, c. 1866
Sepia wash heightened with white chalk on brown paper, sized; 523 × 357 mm
1927P517

B535 *The Muses leaving the dying Poet: Composition Study*, c. 1866
Sepia wash heightened with white chalk on brown felt paper; 520 × 354 mm
1927P518

B536 *The Muses leaving the dying Poet: Composition Study*, c. 1866
Sepia wash heightened with white chalk on brown felt paper, with another sepia sketch on reverse; 338 × 285 mm
Insc. verso: *Muses leaving dying poet/ Edward Burne-Jones**
1927P519

B537 *The Muses leaving the dying Poet: Three Sketches*, c. 1866
Pencil; 276 × 195 mm
Insc.: *Muses leaving dying poet/ E.B.J.**
1927P520

B538 *The Muses leaving the dying Poet: Composition Sketch*, c. 1866
Pencil; 256 × 172 mm
Insc.: *Muses leaving dying poet./ E.B.J.**
1927P521

B539 *The Muses leaving the dying Poet: Composition Sketch*, c. 1866
Pencil touched with brown chalk on cream paper; 182 × 163 mm
Insc.: *Muses and dying/ Poet/ E.B.J.**
1927P522

B540 *The Muses leaving the dying Poet: Composition Sketch*, c. 1866
Pencil; 156 × 109 mm
1927P523

B541 *Music*, pub. 1900
Photogravure; 260 × 168 (i.), 670 × 510 mm (p.)
1900P22

B542 *The Nativity: Composition Sketch*, 1863
for central panel of watercolour triptych, now at Lady Margaret Hall, Oxford
Pencil; 362 × 347 mm
1927P591

B543 *Needlework Design: Deer by a Fountain*, 1875–88
Watercolour and gouache on paper, mounted on linen; 530 × 1848 mm
Insc.: *SI DIEV LE VEVLT/ SANS DIEV NE PEVX*
1962P2

B544 *Needlework Design: Study for Poesis/ Poetry*, 1873–75
Pencil; 342 × 237 mm
Insc.: *POESIA*
1904P190

B545 *Study of Three Ostrich Feathers*, 1865–67
Black and white chalk on brown paper; 380 × 269 mm
1904P93 (See B1054)

B546 *Pan and Psyche*, pub. 1900
Photogravure; 232 × 208 (i.), 670 × 510 mm (p.)
P.: 1900 (1900P35)

B547 *Paris and Helen: Study for Paris*, 1860–62
Pencil; 283 × 165 mm
1927P453

B548 *Parnassus*, c. 1871–80
Bodycolour, heightened with gold; 142 × 227 mm
Insc.: *E B J*
Presented by Sir John Holder, 1912 (1912P36)

The Passing of Venus

B549 *The Passing of Venus: Study of a seated Woman*, 1877
Pencil touched with white on green paper; 153 × 232 mm
Insc.: *E B J 1877/ The Passing of Venus*
Presented by Rt Hon. William Kenrick, 1911 (1911P64)

B550 *The Passing of Venus: Study of a seated Woman*, 1877
Pencil on green paper; 199 × 171 mm
Insc.: *The Passing of Venus/ E B J/ 1877*
Presented by Rt Hon. William Kenrick, 1911 (1911P65)

B551 *The Passing of Venus: Study of a seated Woman*, 1877
Pencil with touches of white bodycolour on green paper; 158 × 209 mm
Insc.: *The Passing of Venus/ E B-J/ 1877*
Presented by Rt Hon. William Kenrick, 1911 (1911P66)

The Perseus Series

B552 *The Perseus Series: Study of Perseus in Armour for 'The Finding of Medusa'*, 1881
Watercolour, bodycolour and chalk on brown paper; 385 × 264 mm
Insc.: *E B.J 1881/ Study of armour/ for the fourth/ picture in the/ series of/ PERSEUS*
Presented anonymously, 1898 (1898P46)

B553 *The Perseus Series: Study of Wings for 'The Death of Medusa'*, 1881
Pencil on paper; 364 × 247 mm
Insc.: *E.B.J./ 1881/ WINGS FOR/ GORGONS/ IN PERSEUS*
1927P447

B554 *The Perseus Series: Perseus and the Nereids*, pub. 1900
Photogravure; 473 × 393 (i.), 670 × 510 mm (p.)
P.: 1900 (1900P88)

B555 *The Perseus Series: Perseus and the Graiae*, pub. 1900
Photogravure; 412 × 556 (i.), 510 × 670 mm (p.)
P.: 1900 (1900P89)

B556 *The Perseus Series: The Rock of Doom*, pub. 1900
Photogravure; 464 × 388 (i.), 670 × 510 mm (p.)
P.: 1900 (1900P90)

B557 *The Perseus Series: The Doom Fulfilled*, pub. 1900
Photogravure; 455 × 410 (i.), 670 × 510 mm (p.)
P.: 1900 (1900P91)

B558 *The Perseus Series: The Baleful Head*, pub. 1900
Photogravure; 470 × 395 (i.), 670 × 510 mm (p.)
P.: 1900 (1900P92)
See *Sketchbooks*

B559 *Philip Comyns Carr*, pub. 1900
Photogravure; 260 × 175 (i.), 670 × 510 mm (p.)
P.: 1900 (1900P100)

Phyllis and Demophoön

B560 *Phyllis and Demophoön*, 1870
Bodycolour and watercolour with gold medium and gum arabic on composite layers of paper on canvas; 915 × 458 mm
Insc.: *E B J./ 1870*
Presented by The John Feeney Charitable Trust, 1916 (1916P37)

B561 *Phyllis and Demophoön*, pub. 1900
Photogravure; 359 × 179 (i.), 670 × 510 mm (p.)
P.: 1900 (1900P21)

B562 *The Pilgrim at the Gate of Idleness*, pub. 1900
Photogravure; 305 × 425 (i.), 510 × 670 mm (p.)
P.: 1900 (1900P85)

B563 *The Pilgrim in the Garden of Idleness: Study of nine Figures*, c. 1874
Watercolour with bodycolour; 1450 × 305 mm
Presented by Donald and Ralph Hope in memory of their brother Arthur Hope, 1918 (1918P25)

B564 *The Prioress's Tale*, pub. 1900
Photogravure; 400 × 245 (i.), 670 × 510 mm (p.)
P.: 1900 (1900P76)

Pygmalion and the Image

B565 *Pygmalion and the Image: Study for 'Pygmalion in his Workshop' (The Heart Desires)*, 1867
Pencil on tracing paper; 118 × 89 mm
1927P612

B566 *Pygmalion and the Image: Study for 'Pygmalion fashioning the Image'*, 1867
Pencil on tracing paper;
102 × 78 (i.), 121 × 90 mm (p.)
1927P613

B567 *Pygmalion and the Image: Study for 'Pygmalion contemplating the Image' (The Hand Refrains)*, 1867
Pencil on tracing paper;
117 × 89 mm
1927P614

B568 *Pygmalion and the Image: Study for 'Pygmalion playing the Organ'*, 1867
Pencil on tracing paper; 104 × 80 (i.), 120 × 89 mm (p.)
1927P615

B569 *Pygmalion and the Image: Study for 'Pygmalion playing the Organ'*, 1867
Pencil on tracing paper; 106 × 80 (i.), 125 × 95 mm (p.)
1927P616

B570 *Pygmalion and the Image: Study for 'Pygmalion gazing at the Image'*, 1867
Pencil on tracing paper; 127 × 78 (i.), 141 × 92 mm (p.)
1927P617

B571 *Pygmalion and the Image: Study for 'Pygmalion praying'*, 1867
Pencil on tracing paper; 121 × 79 (i.), 140 × 88 mm (p.)
1927P618

B572 *Pygmalion and the Image: Study for 'Pygmalion offering Incense to Venus'*, 1867
Pencil on tracing paper; 108 × 78 (i.), 118 × 90 mm (p.)
1927P619

B573 *Pygmalion and the Image: Study for 'Venus bringing the Image to Life' (The Godhead Fires)*, 1867
Pencil on tracing paper;
148 × 98 mm
1927P620

B574 *Pygmalion and the Image: Study for 'Pygmalion returns to his House'*, 1867
Pencil on tracing paper; 103 × 79 (i.), 113 × 87 mm (p.)
1927P621

B575 *Pygmalion and the Image: Two Sketches for Pygmalion*, 1867
Pencil on tracing paper;
113 × 85 mm
1927P622

B576 *Pygmalion and the Image: Sketch for 'Pygmalion seeing the Image come to Life'*, 1867
Pencil on tracing paper;
117 × 86 mm
1927P623

B577 *Pygmalion and the Image: Sketch for 'Pygmalion seeing the Image come to Life'*, 1867
Pencil on tracing paper;
114 × 84 mm
1927P624

B578 *Pygmalion and the Image: Sketch for 'Pygmalion seeing the Image come to Life'*, 1867
Pencil on tracing paper;
110 × 84 mm
1927P625

B579 *Pygmalion and the Image: Sketch for 'Pygmalion seeing the Image come to Life',* 1867
Pencil on tracing paper;
115 × 85 mm
1927P626

B580 *Pygmalion and the Image: Sketch for 'Pygmalion seeing the Image come to Life'*, 1867
Pencil on tracing paper; 111 × 83 mm
1927P627

B581 *Pygmalion and the Image: Sketch for 'Pygmalion seeing the Image come to Life'*, 1867
Pencil on tracing paper;
108 × 81 mm
1927P628

B582 *Pygmalion and the Image: Three Sketches for 'Pygmalion praying' and 'Pygmalion entering his House'*, 1867
Pencil on tracing paper; 121 × 87 (i.), 136 × 103 mm (p.)
1927P629

B583 *Pygmalion and the Image: Study for 'Pygmalion and Galatea at the Altar of Hymen'*, 1867
Pencil on tracing paper; 111 × 79 (i.), 121 × 88 mm (p.)
1927P630

B584 *Pygmalion and the Image: Sketch for 'Pygmalion and Galatea at the Altar of Hymen'*, 1867
Pencil on tracing paper; 114 × 81 (i.), 119 × 87 mm (p.)
1927P631
See B2

B585 *Pygmalion and the Image: Study for 'Pygmalion and Galatea offering Incense'*, 1867
Pencil on tracing paper;
114 × 80 mm
1927P632

B586 *Pygmalion and the Image: The Heart Desires*, pub. 1900
Photogravure; 285 × 220 (i.), 670 × 510 mm (p.)
P.: 1900 (1900P37)

B587 *Pygmalion and the Image: The Hand Refrains*, pub. 1900
Photogravure; 288 × 220 (i.), 670 × 510 mm (p.)
P.: 1900 (1900P38)

B588 *Pygmalion and the Image: The Godhead Fires*, pub. 1900
Photogravure; 186 × 220 (i.), 510 × 670 mm (p.)
P.: 1900 (1900P39)

B589 *Pygmalion and the Image: Study of Maria Zambaco for the Head of Venus in 'The Godhead Fires'*, 1870
Pencil; 186 × 168 mm
Insc.: *E B.J 1870/ STUDY FOR VENUS IN SERIES OF/ PYGMALION*
1924P60

B590 *Pygmalion and the Image: Study of Maria Zambaco for the Head of Galatea in 'The Godhead Fires'*, 1870
Pencil; 173 × 198 mm
Insc.: *E B.J 1870/ STUDY FOR GALATEA/ IN THE SERIES OF/ PYGMALION*
1924P61

B591 *Pygmalion and the Image: The Soul Attains*, pub. 1900
Photogravure; 280 × 220 (i.), 670 × 510 mm (p.)
P.: 1900 (1900P40)

B592 *Pygmalion and the Image: Study of Pygmalion for 'The Soul Attains'*, c. 1875
Pencil with brown crayon;
226 × 286 mm
1927P476

B593 *The Rape of Proserpine*, 1883
Pencil with some red chalk;
199 × 321 mm
Insc.: *E B J*
1927P446

The Ring Given to Venus

B594 *The Ring Given to Venus*, c. 1867
Copper plate, etched;
128 × 170 mm
1927P1030

B595 *The Ring Given to Venus*, c. 1867
Series of ten etching proofs printed in black and sepia;
112 × 160 (i.), 260 × 321 mm (p.)
1927P1031. 1–10

B596 *The Ring Given to Venus: Study of Laurence and Venus*, c. 1867
Pencil on tracing paper;
117 × 166 mm
1927P612.1

B597 *The Rose Garden: Study of Georgiana Burne-Jones*, 1862
Red chalk on cream-toned paper;
223 × 148 mm
1904P57

B598 *The Rose Garden: Study*, 1862
Red chalk and pencil;
249 × 159 mm
1904P58

B599 *A Sea Nymph*, pub. 1900
Photogravure; 300 × 300 (i.), 670 × 510 mm (p.)
1900P81

B600 *Sibylla Delphica*, pub. 1900
Photogravure; 460 × 182 (i.), 670 × 510 mm (p.)
1900P74

B601 *The Sirens: Caricature Sketch*, 1878–80
Pencil on cream-toned paper;
40 × 93 mm
Insc.: *Sirens/ E B.J.**
1927P557

B602 *The Sirens: Female Head Study*, 1895
Pencil; 449 × 331 mm
Insc.: *E B-J/ 1895/ for the picture of The Sirens.*
Presented by Arthur S. Dixon, 1898 (1898P45)

Sketchbooks

B603 *Sketchbook: Nudes and Drapery Studies for various subjects including 'The Perseus Series'*, 1875
Pencil; twenty two drawings in bound volume; 265 × 199 mm
Insc.: front cover, *III/ 47*; inside cover, *July 1875*
1952P5

B604 *Sketchbook: Study of Perseus for 'The Baleful Head'*, 1875
Pencil; 254 × 183 mm
Insc.: *Study for the figure/ of Perseus in 'The/ Baleful Head'*
1952P5.1

B605 *Sketchbook: Study of Perseus for 'The Baleful Head'*, 1875
Pencil; 255 × 183 mm
Insc.: *Study for Perseus/ in 'The Baleful Head'*
1952P5.2

B606 *Sketchbook: Study of Perseus in 'The Baleful Head'*, 1875
Pencil; 255 × 183 mm
Insc.: *Study for Perseus/ in The Baleful Head.*
1952P5.3

B607 *Sketchbook: Study of Atlas in 'Atlas turned to Stone'*, 1875
Pencil; 255 × 183 mm
Insc.: *Study for Atlas in/ Perseus Series*
1952P5.4

B608 *Sketchbook: Study of Perseus in 'Perseus slaying the Sea-Monster'*, 1875
Pencil; 255 × 183 mm
Insc.: *Study for Perseus/ slaying the Sea-Monster*
1952P5.5

B609 *Sketchbook: Study of Figure in 'The Court of Phineus'*, 1875
Pencil; 255 × 183 mm
Insc.: *Study for figure in Court of/ Phineus–Perseus Series*
1952P5.6

B610 *Sketchbook: Study of Mirth in 'The Pilgrim in the Garden of Idleness'*, 1875–79
Pencil; 255 × 183 mm
Insc.: *'Mirth' – for Romaunt of the Rose.*
1952P5.7

B611 *Sketchbook: Studies of Figures for 'The Court of Phineus'*, 1875
Pencil; 255 × 183 mm
Insc.: *Figures in Court of Phineus/ Perseus Series*
1952P5.8

B612 *Sketchbook: Nude Studies for 'Perseus slaying Sea-Monster'*, 1875
Pencil; 255 × 183 mm
Insc.: *Perseus Slaying Sea-Monster*
1952P5.9

B613 *Sketchbook: Study for 'Perseus slaying Sea-Monster' or 'The Doom Fulfilled'*, 1875
Pencil; 255 × 183 mm
Insc.: *Perseus Slaying Sea Monster*
1952P5.10

B614 *Sketchbook: Study of Drapery for 'The Romaunt of the Rose'*, 1875
Pencil; 265 × 199 mm
Insc.: *Study for Drapery/ Romaunt of the Rose*
1952P5.11

B615 *Sketchbook: Studies of Drapery for 'The Romaunt of the Rose'*, 1875
Pencil; 265 × 199 mm
Insc.: *Romaunt of the Rose*
1952P5.12

B616 *Sketchbook: Studies of Andromeda for 'The Rock of Doom'*, 1875
Pencil; 255 × 183 mm
Insc.: *Andromeda*
1952P5.13

B617 *Sketchbook: Studies of Andromeda for 'The Rock of Doom'*, 1875
Pencil; 255 × 183 mm
Insc.: *Andromeda*
1952P5.14

B618 *Sketchbook: Study of Andromeda for 'The Rock of Doom'*, 1875
Pencil; 255 × 183 mm
Insc.: *Andromeda*
1952P5.15

B619 *Sketchbook: Study for Cupid's Hunting Fields*, 1875
Pencil; 255 × 183 mm
Insc.: *Cupid – in/ Cupid's Hunting Ground*
1952P5.16

B620 *Sketchbook: Head Studies of Medusa and Perseus*, 1875
Pencil; 255 × 183 mm
1952P5.17

B621 *Sketchbook: Study for the Head of Perseus*, 1875
Pencil; 255 × 183 mm
1952P5.18

B622 *Sketchbook: Studies of Figures for 'The Court of Phineus'*, 1875
Pencil; 255 × 183 mm
Insc.: *Figures in Court of Phineus/ Perseus Series*
1952P5.19

B623 *Sketchbook: Study of Perseus for 'The Court of Phineus'*, 1875
Pencil; 255 × 183 mm
1952P5.20

B624 *Sketchbook: Studies of Figures for 'The Court of Phineus'*, 1875
Pencil; 255 × 183 mm
Insc.: *figures Court of Phineus/ Perseus Series*
1952P5.21

B625 *Sketchbook: Studies for Perseus*, 1875
Pencil; 255 × 183 mm
Insc.: *Perseus* –
1952P5.22

B626 *Sketchbook: Alps, France, Birds and Dogs*, 1878
Mostly pencil with some crayon in Roberson & Co. cloth-bound sketchbook; forty-four sketches over sixty-three pages; overall size: 132 × 90 mm
Insc. : front, *32*; inside front page, *sketch/ book of Edward Burne-Jones/ drawings done in Switzerland in 1878/ birds copied from a Japanese screen*
1952P3

B627 *Sketchbook: Range of Mountains*, 1878
Pencil; 87 × 125 mm
1952P3.1

B628 *Sketchbook: Range of Mountains*, 1878
Pencil; 87 × 125 mm
Insc.: *from the castle at Annecy*
1952P3.2

B629 *Sketchbook: Range of Mountains*, 1878
Pencil; 125 × 87 mm
1952P3.3

B630 *Sketchbook: Range of Mountains*, 1878
Pencil, over two pages; 125 × 171 mm
1952P3.4

B631 *Sketchbook: Range of Mountains*, 1878
Pencil, over two pages; 125 × 171 mm
1952P3.5

B632 *Sketchbook: Medieval Street and Courtyard, Annecy*, 1878
Pencil over two pages; 125 × 171 mm
Insc.: *Annecy*
1952P3.6

B633 *Sketchbook: Medieval high Wall with Arches*, 1878
Pencil; 125 × 87 mm
1952P3.7

B634 *Sketchbook: Entrance to Alleyway*, 1878
Pencil; 125 × 87 mm
1952P3.8

B635 *Sketchbook: Building Complex with Flight of Steps*, 1878
Pencil, over two pages; 125 × 171 mm
1952P3.9

B636 *Sketchbook: Mountain Range*, 1878
Pencil, over two pages; 125 × 171 mm
1952P3.10

B637 *Sketchbook: Study of Flight of Steps*, 1878
Pencil, over two pages; 125 × 171 mm
1952P3.11

B638 *Sketchbook: Four Birds in flight/ singing (Sparrows)*, 1878
Pencil with crayon, over two pages; 125 × 171 mm
Insc.: *copied from a Japanese screen*
1952P3.12

B639 *Sketchbook: Four Birds in flight and perching (Warbler and Sparrows)*, 1878
Pencil with crayon, over two pages; 125 × 171 mm
1952P3.13

B640 *Sketchbook: Four Birds, three in flight (*Top left: *Bunting? and Finches)*, 1878
Pencil with crayon, over two pages; 125 × 171 mm
1952P3.14

B641 *Sketchbook: Three Birds in flight (Imagined Finches)*, 1878
Pencil; 125 × 87 mm
1952P3.15

B642 *Sketchbook: Sketch of Dog or Wolf*, 1878
Pencil; 125 × 87 mm
1952P3.16

B643 *Sketchbook: Three Sketches of hind Legs of a Dog*, 1878
Pencil over two pages; 125 × 171 mm
1952P3.17

B644 *Sketchbook: Head Studies of a Dog*, 1878
Pencil; 125 × 87 mm
1952P3.18

B645 *Sketchbook: Two Head Studies of a Dog and 'Capitoline Wolf'*, 1878
Pencil; 125 × 87 mm
1952P3.19

B646 *Sketchbook: Study of 'Capitoline Wolf'*, 1878
Pencil; 125 × 87 mm
1952P3.20

B647 *Sketchbook: Head Study of 'Capitoline Wolf'*, 1878
Pencil; 125 × 87 mm
1952P3.21

B648 *Sketchbook: Study of floating Leaf*, 1878
Pencil; 125 × 87 mm
1952P3.22

B649 *Sketchbook: Study of a Bird on a Branch (Finch or Bunting?)*, 1878
Pencil; 125 × 87 mm
1952P3.23

B650 *Sketchbook: View of Montmajour, Provence*, 1878
Pencil, over two pages; 125 × 171 mm
Insc.: *Montmajour*
1952P3.24

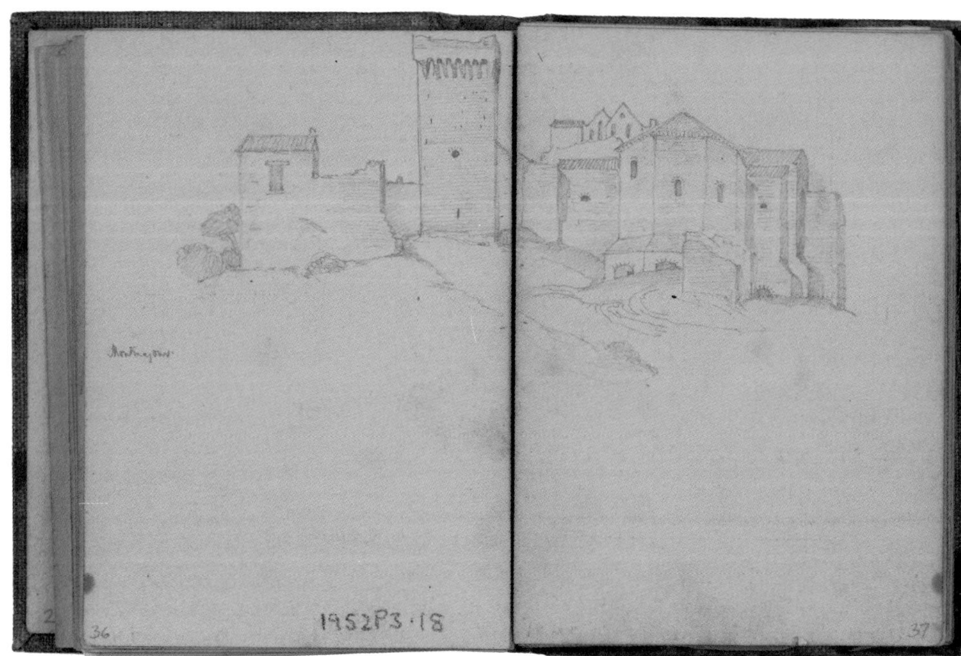

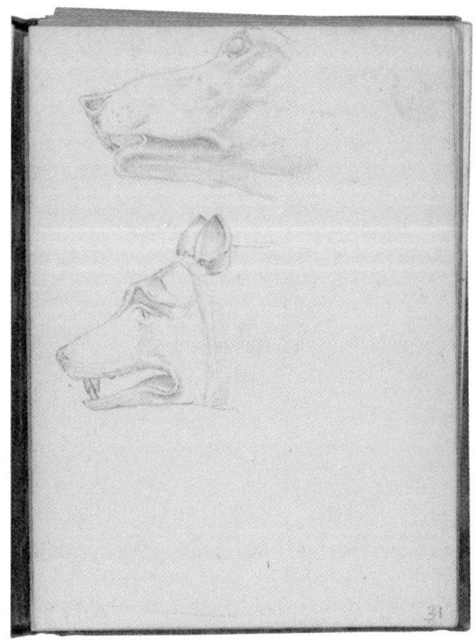

ABOVE LEFT:
Sketchbook: *Montmajour*, 1878 (cat. 48)

ABOVE: Sketchbook: Head Studies of a Dog and 'Capitoline Wolf', 1878 (cat. 48)

BELOW:
Sketchbook: Female: Costume, Helmet and Architectural Decoration, 1887–90 (B723)

BELOW RIGHT:
Sketchbook: Studies of Frieze/ Pattern Decoration, 1887–90 (B737)

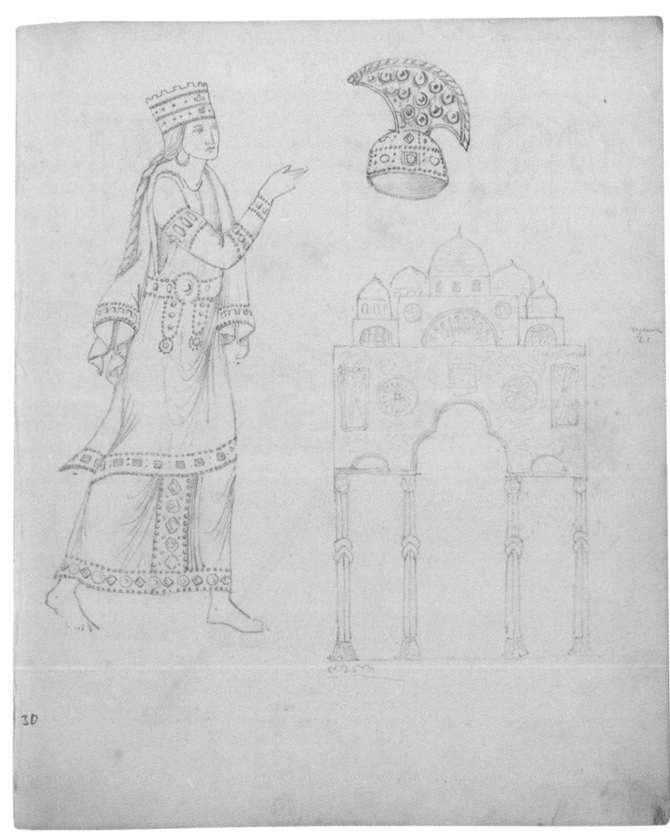

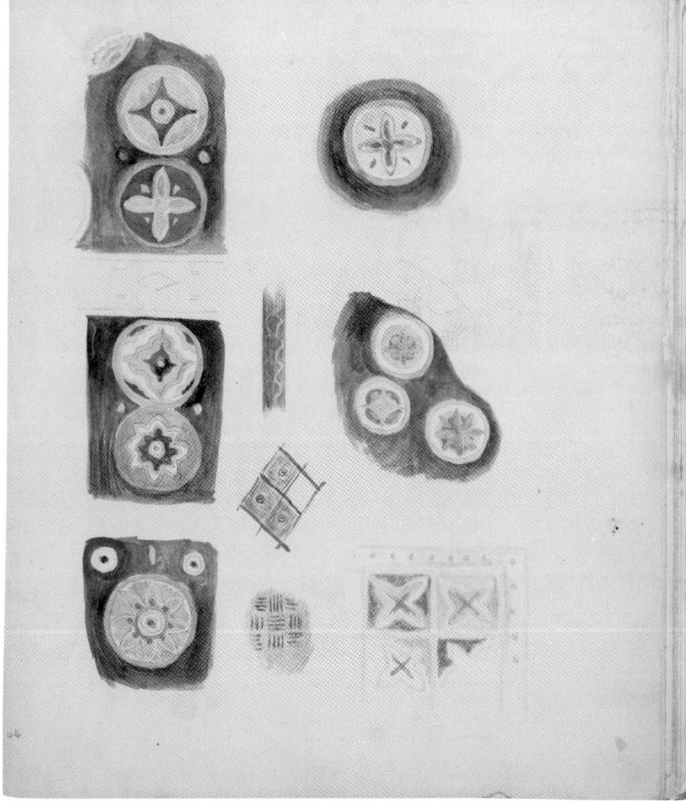

B651 *Sketchbook: Four Birds on Branches and in flight (Finches with Kingfisher)*, 1878
Pencil with crayon, over two pages; 125 × 171 mm
1952P3.25

B652 *Sketchbook: A Bird on a Branch (Mynah Bird?)*, 1878
Pencil with crayon; 125 × 87 mm
1952P3.26

B653 *Sketchbook: Two Birds, one in flight (Sparrows)*, 1878
Pencil with crayon; 125 × 87 mm
1952P3.27

B654 *Sketchbook: Peacock, with Bird on Branch (Finch or imagined Bird?)*, 1878
Pencil with crayon; 125 × 87mm
1952P3.28

B655 *Sketchbook: Bird (Finch or Bunting)*, 1878
Pencil with crayon; 125 × 87 mm
1952P3.29

B656 *Sketchbook: Two Birds, one in flight (Tit and Robin?)*, 1878
Pencil; 125 × 87 mm
1952P3.30

B657 *Sketchbook: Swooping Bird (Tit)*, 1878
Pencil with crayon; 125 × 87 mm
1952P3.31

B658 *Sketchbook: Three Birds singing (Sparrows)*, 1878
Pencil with crayon; 125 × 86 mm
1952P3.32

B659 *Sketchbook: Bird with bent Head (Sparrow)*, 1878
Pencil with crayon; 125 × 87 mm
1952P3.33

B660 *Sketchbook: Two swooping Birds (Sparrows and Finches?)*, 1878
Pencil with crayon; 125 × 87 mm
1952P3.34

B661 *Sketchbook: Flying Bird (Finch)*, 1878
Pencil with crayon; 125 × 87 mm
1952P3.35

B662 *Sketchbook: Bird in flight (Wren?)*, 1878
Pencil with touches of crayon; 125 × 87 mm
1952P3.36

B663 *Sketchbook: Bird in flight (imagined?)*, 1878
Pencil with crayon; 125 × 87 mm
1952P3.37

B664 *Sketchbook: Wader*, 1878
Pencil with crayon, over two pages; 125 × 171 mm
1952P3.38

B665 *Sketchbook: Plover in flight*, 1878
Pencil with crayon, over two pages; 125 × 171 mm
1952P3. 39

B666 *Sketchbook: Plover in flight*, 1878
Pencil with touches of crayon; over two pages; 125 × 171 mm
1952P3.40

B667 *Sketchbook: Wader in flight*, 1878
Pencil with crayon, over two pages; 125 × 171 mm
1952P3.41

B668 *Sketchbook: Bird in flight (Lapwing)*, 1878
Pencil with crayon; over two pages; 125 × 171 mm
1952P3.42

B669 *Sketchbook: Rail (?)*, 1878
Pencil with crayon; 125 × 87 mm
1952P3.43

B670 *Sketchbook: Cormorant (?)*, 1878
Pencil, 125 × 87 mm
1952P3.44

B671 *Sketchbook: Nude, draped and cast Studies, mostly for the Perseus Series*, c. 1877–82
Principally pencil, with white bodycolour on blue ground, bound in Roberson & Co. sketchbook, twenty-one drawings; 272 × 194 mm (overall size)
Insc.: on cover of sketchbook, *XII/ 5*[?]
1952P4

B672 *Sketchbook: Study of two Gorgons for 'The Death of Medusa II'*, 1875–79
Pencil; 262 × 177 mm
1952P4.1

B673 *Sketchbook: Nude Study of Perseus with separate Leg Study for 'The Call of Perseus'*, 1875–79
Pencil; 263 × 177 mm
1952P4.2

B674 *Sketchbook: Nude Leg Studies of flying Gorgons for 'The Death of Medusa II'*, 1875–79
Pencil; 263 × 175 mm
1952P4.3

B675 *Sketchbook: Studies of Hands and Arms for The Perseus Series*, 1875
Pencil; 263 × 177 mm
1952P4.4

B676 *Sketchbook Nude Study from Cast for The Perseus Series*, 1875–79
Pencil; 263 × 177 mm
1952P4.5

B677 *Sketchbook: Nude Study of Perseus*, 1875–79
Pencil; 263 × 175 mm
1952P4.6

B678 *Sketchbook: Studies of Arms and Hands holding Mirror and Sword for Perseus in 'The Finding of Medusa'*, 1875–79
Pencil; 263 × 177 mm
1952P4.7

B679 *Sketchbook: Study of Medusa for 'The Finding of Medusa'*, 1875–79
Pencil; 263 × 177 mm
1952P4.8

B680 *Sketchbook: Nude Study of a Man for 'Atlas Turned to Stone'*, 1875–79
Pencil; 263 × 177 mm
1952P4.9

B681 *Sketchbook: Two Studies of Medusa for 'The Finding of Medusa'*, 1875–79
Pencil; 263 × 177 mm
1952P4.10

B682 *Sketchbook: Nude Study of a Man for The Perseus Series*, 1875–79
Pencil; 263 × 177 mm
1952P4.11

B683 *Sketchbook: Four Studies of Nude and Feet possibly for 'The Doom Fulfilled'*, 1875–79
Pencil; 265 × 176 mm
1952P4.12

B684 *Sketchbook: Study for 'Stella Vespertina'*, 1875–79
Pencil; 263 × 176 mm
1952P4.13

B685 *Sketchbook: Study for 'Stella Matutina'(with foot on opposite page)*, 1875–79
Pencil; 263 × 177 mm
1952P4.14

B686 *Sketchbook: Nude Study of Medusa for 'The Death of Medusa I'*, 1875–79
White bodycolour with white chalk over pencil on blue watercolour background; 177 × 262 mm
1952P4.15

B687 *Sketchbook: Study of draped Medusa for 'The Death of Medusa I'*, 1875–79
Pencil; 263 × 177mm
1952P4.16

B688 *Sketchbook: Two Studies of draped Medusa for 'The Death of Medusa I'*, 1875–79
Pencil; 263 × 177 mm
1952P4.17

B689 *Sketchbook: Study of Gorgon with raised Arms and Hand Study for 'The Finding of Medusa'*, 1875–79
Pencil; 263 × 177 mm
1952P4.18

B690 *Sketchbook: Studies of Hands and a Putto for 'Earth'*, 1875–79
Pencil and chalk; 263 × 177 mm
1952P4.19

B691 *Sketchbook: Female Head Study*, 1875–79
Pencil; 263 × 177 mm
1952P4.20

B692 *Sketchbook: Female Head Study in profile to right*, 1875–79
Pencil; 263 × 177 mm
1952P4.21

B693 *Sketchbook: Byzantine and Romanesque Decoration*, c. 1887–94
Pencil with some watercolour and coloured pencils in bound Roberson & Co. sketchbook; 109 numbered pages; 279 × 227 mm
Insc.: *54/ everything in fairer key than finally intended/ amber varnish paint is turpentine throughout – then when quite dry mix final glaze colouring with amber varnish/ and use sparingly in the lights, if at all, freely in the darks – to a teaspoon full of varnish/ put really twice as much spirit of turpentine, and a teaspoon fresh of linseed oil to keep it from/ drying too quickly – mix all the glaze colours with a* [blocked out] *drop of this on the palette – it/ will seem to varnish a big picture – keep also a little bit to dip the brush in now &/ then/ Linseed Oil – can be kept open doors always with a hole in the cork, and the oil covered with a little water/ changed every 2 months – this refines it & revives the carbon* [in Burne-Jones's hand]/ *Studies from the Antique by Edward Burne-Jones Given by his daughter Margaret to his grand daughter Angela**
1952P6

B694 *Sketchbook: Details of Armour*, c. 1887–94
Pencil, sheet stuck into album; 311 × 197 mm
Insc.: *section*
1952P6.1

B695 *Sketchbook: Cloud/ Sky Study*, c. 1887–94
Pencil; 273 × 222 mm
Insc.: *deep purple clouds on green sky/ sky deepening to orange near the/ horizon*
1952P6.2

B696 *Sketchbook: Outline Study of Trees*, c. 1887–94
Pencil; 273 × 222 mm
1952P6.3

B697 *Sketchbook: Study of Frieze/ Pattern Decoration*, c. 1887–94
Pencil; 273 × 222 mm
1952P6.4

B698 *Sketchbook: Details of decorative Pattern/ Designs*, c. 1887–94
Pencil; some portions touched with sepia wash; 222 × 273 mm
Insc.: *Melanges III. plate 5/ Beati Misericordes Quo/ Ipsi Misodiam Conseut*
1952P6.5

B699 *Sketchbook: Two Studies of Archways*, c. 1887–94
Pencil; 273 × 222 mm
1952P6.6

B700 *Sketchbook: Studies of Frieze Decoration and Crozier*, c. 1887–94
Pencil; 273 × 222 mm
1952P6.7

B701 *Sketchbook: Study for Head of Crozier*, c. 1887–94
Pencil; 273 × 222 mm
1952P6.8

B702 *Sketchbook: Study for Head and Handle of Crozier*, c. 1887–94
Pencil; 273 × 222 mm
1952P6.9

B703 *Sketchbook: Two Studies of Crozier*, c. 1887–94
Pencil; 273 × 222 mm
1952P6.10

B704 *Sketchbook: Study of an ornamented Crozier*, c. 1887–94
Pencil; 273 × 222 mm
1952P6.11

B705 *Sketchbook: Study of Crozier*, c. 1887–94
Pencil; 273 × 222 mm
1952P6.12

B706 *Sketchbook: Studies of a 12th Century Warrior, Shield and Throne*, c. 1887–94
Pencil; 273 × 222 mm
Insc.: *Prudentium M.S. 283/ Bibl: Imperiale*
1952P6.13

B707 *Sketchbook: Study of ecclesiastical Costume*, c. 1887–94
Pencil; 273 × 222 mm
1952P6.14

B708 *Sketchbook: Costume, Hair and ornamented Decoration*, c. 1887–94
Pencil; 273 × 222 mm
Insc.: *See Book of Byzantine emperor p. 69/ all pearls/ See Emperor of Byzantium p. 69*
1952P6.15

B709 *Sketchbook: Studies of ornamented Decoration*, c. 1887–94
Pencil; 273 × 222 mm
Insc.: [inscriptions as part of ornamental decoration]
1952P6.16

B710 *Sketchbook: Study of Capital*, c. 1887–94
Pencil; 273 × 222 mm
1952P6.17

B711 *Sketchbook: Architectural Decoration*, c. 1887–94
Pencil; 273 × 222 mm
Insc.: various notes
1952P6.18

B712 *Sketchbook: Studies of Stonework*, c. 1887–94
Pencil; 273 × 222 mm
Insc.: *Syrie[?] centrale 65 vol 2*
1952P6.19

B713 *Sketchbook: Studies of Stonework*, c. 1887–94
Pencil; 273 × 222 mm
Insc.: *pl. 115/ vol. I page 45 preface*
1952P6.20

B714 *Sketchbook: Architectural Stonework*, c. 1887–94
Pencil; 273 × 222 mm
1952P6.21

B715 *Sketchbook: Arches*, c. 1887–94
Pencil; 273 × 222 mm
1952P6.22

B716 *Sketchbook: Arches*, c. 1887–94
Pencil; 273 × 222 mm
1952P6.23

B717 *Sketchbook: Architectural Detail*, c. 1887–94
Pencil; 273 × 222 mm
Insc.: *Siena plate XX*
1952P6.24

B718 *Sketchbook: Details of French Statues*, c. 1887–94
Pencil; 273 × 222 mm
1952P6.25

B719 *Sketchbook: Studies of French Statues of female Figures*, c. 1887–94
Pencil; 273 × 222 mm
1952P6.26

B720 *Sketchbook: Studies of French Statue of a female Figure and Two Harps*, c. 1887–94
Pencil; 273 × 222 mm
1952P6.27

B721 *Sketchbook: Study of Arches and a carved Column*, c. 1887–94
Pencil; 273 × 222 mm
1952P6.28

B722 *Sketchbook: Study of decorative Moulding, with SUPERBIA Poem*, 1887–90
Pencil; 273 × 222 mm
Insc.: *SUPERBIA/ Cetera qui supero – memet te ans cendere quero/ Sactantia/ Extello/ verbis me magna loquendo superbis,/ Inobedientia/ Nescio parere, michi/ jura recudo tenera./ Ypoerisis./ Quod videor grata mihi dat intus/ simulata./ Presumpcio./ Me credo tante quod sim par jure tonanti./ Contempcio./ Hesi pari reputo que meliora puto/ Pertinacia./ Nec male concepta mutabo nec male cepta./ INVIDIA./ Prospera cum video, protinus invideo./ Detraccio./ Detrapo dire si quid fieri puto recte/ Odium/ Est mihi solus amor quod nec amo nec amor./ Discordia./ Consona discordare facit discordia corda/ IRA/ Nulla fugit diva mea mens cum fervet in irce/ accidia./ Tristitiam genero, nil praeter te dia quero/ AVARITIA/ Estiat in cupido pro me sine lege cupido/ LUXURIA/ Servio sic/ ventri quod honestia recuso teneri.*
1952P6.29

B723 *Sketchbook: Female: Costume, Helmet and architectural Decoration*, 1887–90
Pencil; 273 × 222 mm
Insc.: *Agincourt LI*
1952P6.30

B724 *Sketchbook: Architectural and Frieze/ Pattern Decoration*, 1887–90
Pencil; 273 × 222 mm
Insc.: various notes (with mention of *Agincourt* plates)
1952P6.31

B725 *Sketchbook: Enamels*, 1887–90
Pencil; 273 × 222 mm
Insc.: *Sommerard 2. C V/ another beautiful Byzantine enamel V. I. chap XIV/ to begin next time with vol. 3*
1952P6.32

B726 *Sketchbook: Decorative Friezes*, 1887–90
Pencil with yellow, red and blue crayon; 273 × 222 mm
Insc.: *Viollet vol 1. 73*
1952P6.33

B727 *Sketchbook: Female Costume and Headdress Decoration*, 1887–90
Pencil; 273 × 222 mm
Insc.: *besants of gold hung on a dress/ besants of gold hung on a crown*
1952P6.34

B728 *Sketchbook: Detail of Building with curtained Entrance*, 1887–90
Pencil; 273 × 222 mm
1952P6.35

B729 *Sketchbook: Details of female Costume*, 1887–90
Pencil; 273 × 222 mm
1952P6.36

B730 *Sketchbook: Details of male Costume*, 1887–90
Pencil; 273 × 222 mm
Insc.: *gold ground & pearls/ stole*
1952P6.37

B731 *Sketchbook: Studies of French Shoes*, 1887–90
Pencil; 273 × 222 mm
Insc.: *stole . Viollet. v.3.pl. XI/ patterns of Jewels. Viol. v. 4 152.153*
1952P6.38

B732 *Sketchbook: Sketches of French Heraldic Creatures*, 1887–90
Pencil; 273 × 222 mm
1952P6.39

B733 *Sketchbook: Sketches of French Heraldic Creatures*, 1887–90
Pencil; 273 × 222 mm
Insc.: *from Kraken – Melanges 251. vol. III*
1952P6.40

B734 *Sketchbook: Sketches of French Heraldic Creatures*, 1887–90
Pencil; 273 × 221 mm
1952P6.41

B735 *Sketchbook: Studies of French Heraldic Creatures*, 1887–90
Pencil; 273 × 222 mm
1952P6.42

B736 *Sketchbook: Study of Heraldic Creatures*, 1887–90
Pencil; 273 × 222 mm
1952P6.43

B737 *Sketchbook: Studies of Frieze/ Pattern Decoration*, 1887–90
Pencil, crayon, watercolour and touches of gouache; 273 × 222 mm
1952P6.44

B738 *Sketchbook: Studies of Frieze/ Pattern Decoration*, 1887–90
Pencil with yellow and blue crayon; 273 × 222 mm
1952P6.45

B739 *Sketchbook: Studies of Weaponry*, 1887–90
Pencil, top left study heightened with blue crayon; 273 × 222 mm
1952P6.46

B740 *Sketchbook: Studies of Shields*, 1887–90
Pencil; 273 × 222 mm
1952P6.47

B741 *Sketchbook: Details of Armour and Weapons*, 1887–90
Pencil; 272 × 223 mm
Insc.: *detail*
1952P6.48

B742 *Sketchbook: Studies of Swords*, 1887–90
Pencil; 272 × 220 mm
1952P6.49

B743 *Sketchbook: Studies of Weaponry and Costume*, 1887–90
Pencil; 273 × 223 mm
1952P6.50

B744 *Sketchbook: Line of Arches and architectural Detail*, 1887–90
Pencil; 273 × 222 mm
1952P6.51

B745 *Sketchbook: Architectural Details*, 1887–90
Pencil; 273 × 222 mm
Insc.: *Cratasdovir/ Prvdi*
1952P6.52

B746 *Sketchbook: Details of Frieze/ Pattern Decoration*, 1887–90
Pencil; 273 × 222 mm
1952P6.53

B747 *Sketchbook: Details of architectural Corners and Decoration*, 1887–90
Pencil; 273 × 222 mm
1952P6.54

B748 *Sketchbook: Decorative Moulding*, 1887–90
Pencil; 273 × 222 mm
1952P6.55

B749 *Sketchbook: Studies for architectural Decoration*, 1887–90
Pencil; 273 × 222 mm
1952P6.56

B750 *Sketchbook: Studies of medieval Thrones*, 1887–90
Pencil; 273 × 222mm
1952P6.57

B751 *Sketchbook: Studies of carved Seat, Reliquary, Buttons and Candlesticks*, 1887–90
Pencil; 273 × 222 mm
Insc.: *Viol. I. 231/ another candlestick Viollet. 2.56/ button enamelled on leather/ another candlestick/ Viollet. 2. 56/ button*
1952P6.58

B752 *Sketchbook: Studies of medieval Belt Buckles*, 1887–90
Pencil; 273 × 222 mm
Insc.: *buckle for belt/ pearls*
1952P6.59

B753 *Sketchbook: Study of Breeches and Bishop's Vestment*, 1887–90
Pencil; 273 × 222 mm
Insc.: *a good pattern of stuff/ Viollet 3.28*
1952P6.60

B754 *Sketchbook: Details of Costume and Jewellery*, 1887–90
Pencil; 273 × 222 mm
952P6.61

B755 *Sketchbook: Costume Decoration and Crown*, 1887–90
Pencil; 273 × 222 mm
Insc.: *enamelled clasp*
1952P6.62

B756 *Sketchbook: Studies of Crown and Headdress*, 1887–90
Pencil; 273 × 222 mm
1952P6.63

B757 *Sketchbook: Details of Armour and Heraldic Decoration*, 1887–90
Pencil; 273 × 222 mm
1952P6.64

B758 *Sketchbook: Study of an ornamented Roundel*, 1887–90
Brown crayon, over pencil; 273 × 222 mm
1952P6.65

B759 *Sketchbook: Details of Dress Ornament*, 1887–90
Pencil, blue and yellow crayon; 273 × 222 mm
Insc.: *deep golden brown dress/ stripes of dim blue green/ band of brandished gold ornament – good for Eltirp* [?]
1952P6.66

B760 *Sketchbook: Studies of Ornament with fantastic Beasts*, 1887–90
Blue crayon with pencil; 273 × 222 mm
Insc.: *lions, griffins sphinxes* etc.
1952P6.67

B761 *Sketchbook: Details of Embroidery Decoration*, 1887–90
Pencil; 273 × 222 mm
Insc.: *white threads on purple ground/ applied leaf/ instead of disc or/ square*
1952P6.68

B762 *Sketchbook: Details of Ornament and Jewellery*, 1887–90
Pencil; 273 × 222 mm
1952P6.69

B763 *Sketchbook: Study of female Costume and Armour*, 1887–90
Pencil; 273 × 222 mm
1952P6.70

B764 *Sketchbook: Study of a medieval Knight with Helmet*, 1887–90
Pencil; 273 × 222 mm
1952P6.71

B765 *Sketchbook: Studies of Knights in Armour*, 1887–90
Pencil; 273 × 222 mm
1952P6.72

B766 *Sketchbook: Outline of female Figure*, 1887–90
Pencil and green crayon; 273 × 222 mm
1952P6.73

B767 *Sketchbook: Sketches of decorative Border and Outline of Shield*, 1887–90
Pencil with green crayon; 273 × 222 mm
Insc.: *black is used for red*
1952P6.74

B768 *Sketchbook: Studies of Helmets*, 1887–90
Pencil; 273 × 222 mm
Insc.: *pearls*
1952P6.75

B769 *Sketchbook: Studies of Helmets*, 1887–90
Pencil; 273 × 222mm
1952P6.76

B770 *Sketchbook: Bands of decorative Frieze*, 1887–90
Purple crayon; 273 × 222 mm
Insc.: *bands/ increasing in depth*
1952P6.77

B771 *Sketchbook: Details of Censer and decorative Border*, 1887–90
Pencil; 273 × 222 mm
Insc.: *censer*
1952P6.78

B772 *Sketchbook: Costume Pattern and woven Material*, 1887–90
Pencil with blue crayon; 273 × 222 mm
Insc.: *deep indigo*
1952P6.79

B773 *Sketchbook: Studies of medieval decorative Patterns*, 1887–90
Pencil heightened with blue, red, yellow, green and black crayon, with brown chalk; 273 × 222 mm
Insc.: *all darker colours/ on pic omit colour/ ground–/ indigo – deep salmon./ lake./ vermil–gray green equal/ strength?/ in 2 tints*
1952P6.80

B774 *Sketchbook: Studies of Tents*, 1887–90
Pencil; 273 × 222 mm
1952P6.81

B775 *Sketchbook: Studies of Knights on horseback, and Armour*, 1887–90
Pencil; 273 × 222 mm
1952P6.82

B776 *Sketchbook: Studies of Horses and Horsemen*, 1887–90
Pencil; 273 × 222 mm
1952P6.83

B777 *Sketchbook: Two Studies of Warhorses*, 1887–90
Pencil; 273 × 222 mm
Insc.: *8th cent*
1952P6.84

B778 *Sketchbook: Studies of Saddles*, 1887–90
Pencil; 273 × 222 mm
Insc.: *Bayeux/ 13 cent*
1952P6.85

B779 *Sketchbook: Studies of Horses and Saddles*, 1887–90
Pencil; 273 × 222 mm
1952P6.86

B780 *Sketchbook: Outline Studies of Shields and Sword*, 1887–90
Pencil; 273 × 222 mm
1952P6.87

B781 *Sketchbook: Studies of Shields and ornamental Archway*, 1887–90
Pencil; 273 × 222 mm
1952P6.88

B782 *Sketchbook: Details of Throne and robed Figure*, 1887–90
Pencil; 273 × 222 mm
Insc.: *Melanges Cahier vol. 2.157*
1952P6.89

B783 *Sketchbook: Study of Chalice and Candlestick*, 1887–90
Pencil; 273 × 222 mm
Insc.: *pearls/ enamels/ for ornamentation of enamels & filigree – see book on Byzantine emperor – p23/ (this I may use for work of chapel of S Grail)*
1952P6.90

B784 *Sketchbook: Stonework Details*, 1887–90
Pencil; 273 × 222 mm
Insc.: *well in Launcelot*
1952P6.91

B785 *Sketchbook: Ironwork and decorative Details*, 1887–90
Pencil; 273 × 222 mm
Insc.: *ironwork/ Beautiful stuff in Melange Vol 1 – at end/ band of flowers/ on dark green*
1952P6.92

B786 *Sketchbook: Study of an ornamented Door*, 1887–90
Pencil; 273 × 222 mm
1952P6.93

B787 *Sketchbook: Study of a Chalice*, 1887–90
Pencil; with touches of blue, yellow and red crayon; 273 × 222 mm
Insc.: *gold black/ & silver/ silver/ ground gold/ filigreed with interlaced byzantine work/ band everywhere silver/ letters/ black on silver/ Silver showing oftenest as gray black/ gold/ discs of silver/ drawing picked/ out in gold/ band of silver/ gold legend on/ silver black* [crossed out]*/ band of silver/ part 11 Geschichte der Deutschen Kunst Berlin 1888*
1952P6.94

B788 *Sketchbook: Study of Horseman and Horses' Hoofs*, 1887–90
Pencil; 273 × 222 mm
1952P6.95

B789 *Sketchbook: Studies of Ships*, 1887–90
Pencil; 273 × 222 mm
1952P6.96

B790 *Sketchbook: Details of Ships*, 1887–90
Pencil; 273 × 222 mm
1952P6.97

B791 *Sketchbook: Study of a Ship*, 1887–90
Pencil; 273 × 222mm
1952P6.98

B792 *Sketchbook: Study of two Knights fighting on horseback*, 1887–90
Pencil; 273 × 222 mm
1952P6.99

B793 *Sketchbook: Sketches of Drapery worn by Saints, and Knights on horseback*, 1887–90
Pencil; 273 × 222 mm
1952P6.100

B794 *Sketchbook: Study of Soldier fighting on horseback*, 1887–90
Pencil; 273 × 222 mm
1952P6.101

B795 *Sketchbook: Study of an Archer on horseback*, 1887–90
Pencil; 273 × 222 mm
1952P6.102

B796 *Sketchbook: Study of Two Soldiers fighting on horseback*, 1887–90
Pencil over two sheets; 273 × 435 mm
Insc.: *black horses or white*
1952P6.103

B797 *Sketchbook: Study of a medieval Knight on horseback carrying a Standard*, 1887–90
Pencil; 273 × 222 mm
Insc.: *black horses or white*
1952P6.104

B798 *Sketchbook: Study of a Knight on horseback*, 1887–90
Pencil; 273 × 222 mm
1952P6.105

B799 *Sketchbook: Two Sketches of Knight on horseback and a fallen Horse*, 1887–90
Pencil; 273 × 222 mm
1952P6.106

B800 *Sketchbook: Sketch of wounded Knight on horseback*, 1887–90
Pencil; 273 × 222 mm
1952P6.107

B801 *Sketchbook: Sketches of Two Figures on horseback*, 1887–90
Pencil, just spreading onto second page; 273 × 222 mm
1952P6.108

B802 *Sketchbook: Apollo and Daphne*, 1887–90
Pencil; 273 × 222 mm
1952P6.109

The Song of Solomon

B803 *The Song of Solomon: 'Awake, O North Wind!'*, 1876
Pencil on stiff toned paper; 339 × 182 (i.), 356 × 214 mm (p.)
Insc.: *SVRGE: AQVILO: ET: VENI: AVSTER: PERFLA: HORTVM; MEVM: ET: FLVANT: AROMATA: ILLIVS/ QVAM: PVLCHRA: ES: ET: QVAM DECORA: CHARISSIMA: IN DELICIIS*
1927P463

B804 *The Song of Solomon: 'Who is this that cometh out of the wilderness?'*, 1876
Pencil on stiff toned paper; 350 × 203 mm
Insc.: *QVAE.EST.ISTA.QVAE.ASCENDIT. DE.DESERTO.DELICIIS.AFFLVENS.INNIX A.SVPER.DILECTVM.SVVM/ E B J*
Presented by Mrs George Frederick Watts, 1924 (1924P92)

B805 *The Song of Solomon: Sketch*, 1876
Pencil; 293 × 139 (i.), 306 × 154 mm (p.)
1904P189

B806 *The Song of Solomon: Study of a Zephyr for 'Sponsa de Libano'*
Autotype after chalk drawing in National Museums and Galleries on Merseyside, c. 1891; 421 × 331 mm (sight)
Insc.: *E B J*
Presented by H. S. Turner, accessioned in 2006 (2006.0871)

B807 *Spring/Flora*, pub. 1900
Photogravure; 400 × 275 (i.), 670 × 510 mm (p.)
P.: 1900 (1900P69)

Stained Glass Design

B808 *Stained Glass Design: Adam*, 1862
Indian ink and wash over pencil; 600 × 315 mm
1904P500

B809 *Stained Glass Design: Two Angels*, 1862
Indian ink and wash over pencil with touches of white bodycolour; 885 × 385 mm
Insc.: *Pencil*
1904P547

B810 *Stained Glass Design: Angels and Children*, 1865
Brown chalk over pencil on Whatman paper; 171 × 113 (i.), 187 × 128 mm (p.)
Insc.: *flowers*; preliminary small sketch for B811
1927P595

B811 *Stained Glass Design: Angels and Children*, 1865
Indian ink and sepia, with coloured chalks, watercolour and bodycolour over pencil squared up; 958 × 675 mm
1900P179. See B810

B812 *Stained Glass Design: Angel holding the Moon*, 1862–63
Indian ink and sepia wash over pencil on paper, laid on second sheet; 600 × 553 mm
Insc.: *FP 2*
1904P515

B813 *Stained Glass Design: Angel playing a Horn*, 1862–63
Indian ink and sepia wash over pencil on cut-out sheet, laid down on second sheet; 550 × 515 (i.), 545 × 600 mm (p., sight)
Insc.: *FP13*
1904P514

B814 *Stained Glass Design: Angels playing Harps*, 1862
Indian ink and sepia over pencil; 1023 × 494 mm
1904P545

B815 *Stained Glass Design: Angels playing Organs*, 1862
Indian ink over black chalk and pencil; 1020 × 505 mm
Insc.: *SP 60/ SP60*
1904P546

B816 *Stained Glass Design: Angel playing on Bells*, 1862
Indian ink and wash over pencil and red-brown chalk, on various sections of paper; 900 × 900 (i.), 940 × 940 mm (p.)
Insc.: *F.P.88*
1904P502

B817 *Stained Glass Design: Angel playing on Bells*, 1862
Indian ink, wash and pencil; 888 × 900 (i.), 939 × 935 mm (p.)
1904P503

B818 *Stained Glass Design: Angel playing on Bells*, 1862
Indian ink and wash over pencil, on various sections of paper; 852 × 849 (i.), 940 × 937 mm (p.)
1904P504

B819 *Stained Glass Design: Angel playing on Bells*, 1862
Indian ink and wash over pencil, laid down on various sections of paper; 900 × 900 (i.), 938 × 938 mm (p.)
Insc.: *FP3*
1904P505

B820 *Stained Glass Design: Angel playing on Bells*, 1862
Indian ink with sepia wash over pencil; 850 × 850 (i.), 940 × 940 mm (p.)
Insc.: *LP85/ FP88*
1904P506

B821 *Stained Glass Design: Angel playing on Bells*, 1865
Pencil, sepia wash and chalk; 325 × 325 mm
1904P507

B822 *Stained Glass Design: Angel playing on Bells*, 1865
Pencil, sepia wash and chalk; 325 × 328 mm
1904P508

B823 *Stained Glass Design: Angel playing on Bells*, 1865
Pencil and chalk; 325 × 325 mm
Insc.: *Te Deum Laudamus*
1904P509

B824 *Stained Glass Design: Angel playing on Bells*, 1865
Pencil and chalk on paper; 325 × 325 mm
Insc.: *Amino Confido*
1904P510

B825 *Stained Glass Design: Angel playing on Bells*, 1865
Pencil on paper; 325 × 327 mm
Insc.: *Venite Exultemus Dom*
1904P511

B826 *Stained Glass Design: Angel playing on Bells*, 1865
Pencil, chalk and wash on paper; 325 × 325 mm
Insc.: *Domine*
1904P512

B827 *Stained Glass Design: Angel playing on Pipes*, 1862–63
Indian ink and sepia wash over pencil, laid down on second sheet; 525 × 600 (i.), 550 × 603 mm (p.)
Insc.: *F.P. 10-*
1904P513

B828 *Stained Glass Design: The Angels of the Hierarchy: Seraphim*, 1873
Wash, watercolour, bodycolour, with pencil; 1190 × 567 (i.), 1222 × 599 mm (p.)
Insc.: *No 1* [illegible] *for all the patterns and made a little larger* [illegible] *all must be* [illegible] *finished in that way* [illegible] *and the* [illegible] *gown/ Wings light pink and white White dress shielded with flesh – nimbus full R(ed) censer gold flesh* [illegible]*/ No leave out the sandals* [underscored twice]*/ Feet to touch it/ this line is the upper edge of the screen* [?]*/ Jesus/ No 1 top row/ Seraph A Censer* [illegible]*/ bright red rays/* [top of nimbus; an arrow pointing down]
1927P411.1

B829 *Stained Glass Design: The Angels of the Hierarchy: Cherubim*, 1873
Wash with watercolour, pencil and bodycolour; 1205 × 570 (i.), 1220 × 595 mm (p.)
Insc.: [illegible] *full of eyes/ the omni center* [?] *of God/ feet to touch this line/ No leave out sandals/ blue dress/ 36 wh*[i] *t*[e] [illegible]
1927P411.2

B830 *Stained Glass Design: The Angels of the Hierarchy: Thrones*, 1873
Wash, with watercolour and bodycolour over pencil; 1189 × 565 (i.), 1220 × 600 mm
Insc.: *No 3/ top row/ A throne and scales/ Thrones/ The Justice of God/ nimbus/ orange wings/ dress white in primer throne gold/ No leave out sandals* [underscored twice]*/ feet to touch this line/ on oblong piece of pattern let ink* [illegible] *the white dress/ gold*
1927P411.3

B831 *Stained Glass Design: The Angels of the Hierarchy: Potentates [Powers]*, 1873
Wash, bodycolour, watercolour and pencil; 1180 × 567 (i.), 1200 × 600 mm (p.)
Insc.: *nimbus/ fire R*[ed]*/ purple/ the feet to touch this line/* [illegible] *all white/ Potentates/ generally an animal* [illegible] *underfoot or a fiend chained*
1927P411.4

B832 *Stained Glass Design: The Angels of the Hierarchy: Dominions*, 1873
Wash and bodycolour over pencil; 1185 × 568 (i.), 1220 × 598 mm (p.)
Insc.: *the church with sceptre/ used to be a pope* [illegible] *world/ crown golden/ purple/ pattern the cape & the space in* [illegible] *or green/ His feet to touch/ white/ full Red/ R*[ed]*/ white silver pall/ technical/ colour notes*
1927P411.5

B833 *Stained Glass Design: The Angels of the Hierarchy: Principates [Principalities]*, 1873
Wash, watercolour and bodycolour over pencil; 1197 × 569 (i.), 1220 × 599 mm (p.)
Insc; [illegible] *or whiten/ W*[hite]*/ arrange with pattern/ blue/ white fig pattern/ blue/ lined green/ feet to touch this line/ Principates/ a ring with cross sceptre/ No 6 on lower row*
1927P411.6

B834 *Stained Glass Design: The Angels of the Hierarchy: Virtutes [Virtues]*, 1873
Wash and bodycolour over pencil; 1197 × 575 (i.), 1228 × 600 mm (p.)
Insc.: *nimbus/ purple/ white/ feet* [illegible] *to touch this line/ light paint ruby/ pattern this/ white & orange*
1927P411.7

B835 *Stained Glass Design: The Angels of the Hierarchy: Archangeli*, 1873
Sepia wash and watercolour, with bodycolour over pencil; 1195 × 567 (i.), 1225 × 600 mm (p.)
Insc.: *ornament the nimbus well/ black & blue wings/ grass & flowers/ grass & flowers to the wall/ leggings cloth/ armour stops at the knee pieces/ feet to touch this line/ mail very carefully/ done/ deepen*
1927P411.8

B836 *Stained Glass Design: The Angels of the Hierarchy: Angeli*, 1873
Sepia wash and bodycolour over pencil; 1200 × 583 (i.), 1220 × 598 mm (p.)
Insc.: *W*[hite]*/ feet* [illegible] *to touch this line/ W*[hite – crossed out]*/ light bright blue/ golden wings / R*[e]*d* [illegible]
1927P411.9

B837 *Stained Glass Design: The Angels of the Hierarchy: Imago Dei*, 1873
(*In the Image of God: Adam*)
Wash and pencil; 1215 × 585 (i.), 1220 × 600 mm (p.)
Insc.: *feet to touch this line*
1927P411.10

B838 *Stained Glass Design: Two Angels*, 1862
Wash, Indian ink and coloured chalks over pencil; 1468 × 465 mm
Insc.: *TR:50117* [?]
1900P188

B839 *Stained Glass Design: The Annunciation*, 1862
Sepia wash, Indian ink, and watercolour over pencil; 750 × 750 mm
Insc.: *AVE: MARIA : GRATIA: PLENA : DOMINUS : EST: TECUM*
1931P64

B840 *Stained Glass Design: The Ascension*, 1884
after Burne-Jones cartoon now in the National Gallery of Victoria
Pen and ink with watercolour on paper; 235 × 117 (i.), 461 × 334 mm (p.)
Insc.: *Birmingham/ St Philips Ch/ Scale 1/2' = 1'/ The Property of Morris & Co/ Merton Abbey/ Surrey/ Property of Morris & Co.**
Presented by Philip B. Chatwin, 1943 (1943P12)

B841 *Stained Glass Design: The Baptism of Christ*, 1864–65
Pencil, squared up for transfer; 550 × 470 mm (i.)
1904P516

B842 *Stained Glass Design: The Baptism of Christ*, 1865
Pencil and chalk on three sheets of paper; 1810 × 378 mm
Insc.: *TR:SP 42*
1900P183

B843 *Stained Glass Design: Joshua commanding the Sun and Moon to stand still for 'The Battle of Beth-Horon'*, 1863
Sepia wash and chalk on paper; 1860 × 560 mm
1898P54

B844 *Stained Glass Design: Nude Studies of Joshua for 'The Battle of Beth-Horon'*, 1863
Pencil; 135 × 225 mm
Insc.: *'Joshua'/ Lyndhurst window/ E.B.J.* *
1927P540

B845 *Stained Glass Design: Nude Study for Joshua for 'The Battle of Beth-Horon'*, 1863
Pencil; 240 × 102 mm
Insc.: *'Joshua'/ E.B.J./ Lyndhurst window/ window**
1927P541

B846 *Stained Glass Design: Two Nude Studies of Joshua for 'The Battle of Beth-Horon'*, 1863
Pencil; 113 × 157 mm
Insc.: *'Joshua'/ E.B.J./ Lyndhurst window/ window**
1927P542

B847 *Stained Glass Design: Nude Study of Joshua for 'The Battle of Beth-Horon'*, 1863
Pencil; 201 × 68 mm
Insc.: *'Joshua'/ Lyndhurst/ E B J.**
1927P543

B848 *Stained Glass Design: Nude Study of Joshua for 'The Battle of Beth-Horon'*, 1863
Pencil; 169 × 123 mm
Insc.: *Joshua/ E B J./ Lyndhurst**
1927P544

B849 *Stained Glass Design: The Building of the Ark*, 1863
Sepia wash and brush over pencil; 535 × 534 mm
1901P9

B850 *Stained Glass Design: The Building of the Temple*, 1863
Sepia and brush with wash over pencil; 535 × 535 mm
1901P10

B851 *Stained Glass Design: Charity/Caritas standing on Envy*, 1865–66
Pencil; 352 × 86 mm
Insc.: *Charity/* E.B.J*
1927P534

B852 *Stained Glass Design: Charity/Caritas standing on Envy*, 1865–66
Pencil on tracing paper;
237 × 178 mm
1979P210

See *Chaucer* section for *'Legend of Good Women'* designs

B853 *Stained Glass Design: Christ blessing Children*, 1862
Indian ink, sepia wash and watercolour over pencil on various sheets of paper;
955 × 400 (i.), 955 × 1555 mm (p.)
Insc.: *In Heaven Their Angels Do/ Always Behold the Face of My Father/ Which is in Heaven/* SP29
1904P544

B854 *Stained Glass Design: Christ blessing Children*, c. 1866–69
Pencil, pen and ink; 136 × 95 (i.), 146 × 103 mm (p.)
verso: pencil sketch of same subject, reversed
1927P537

B855 *Stained Glass Design: Christ blessing Children*
Platinum print by Frederick Hollyer after pencil drawing dated to c. 1886–87; 246 × 220 (i.), 292 × 247 mm (p.)
Insc.: TOP/ *Christ Blessing Children/ Copyright/ Frederick Hollyer/ London/ S572*
1927P537.1

B856 *Stained Glass Design: Christ cleansing the Temple*, 1876–78
Black chalk and pencil; 910 × 777 (i.), 934 × 807 mm (p.)
1927P413

B857 *Stained Glass Design: Christ in Majesty*, 1861
Indian ink and wash over pencil, with amended attachments;
492 × 490 mm
Insc.: *white/ red/ purple (blue)/ light blue/ green*
1904P531

B858 *Stained Glass Design: Christ in Majesty*, 1862
Sepia wash with red and blue chalk; 935 × 807 mm
Insc.: *border/ Co/ Ho/* E/ O/ G/ OD/ I/ F/ OH/ A/ OJ
1901P11

B859 *Stained Glass Design: Christ in Majesty*, 1863
Indian ink, wash, over pencil;
710 × 545 mm
1904P530

B860 *Stained Glass Design: Christ in Majesty*, 1863
Indian ink and sepia over pencil;
510 × 450 mm
1904P532

B861 *Stained Glass Design: Drapery Study for 'Christ in Majesty'*, 1865–66
Pencil and red-brown chalk;
261 × 194 mm
1904P144

B862 *Stained Glass Design: Study for 'Christ in Majesty'*, 1865–66
Pencil and red-brown chalk;
246 × 194 mm
1904P145

B863 *Stained Glass Design: Christ's Entry into Jerusalem*, 1883
Watercolour, pencil and pastel;
2235 × 1015 mm (i.)
1927P412

B864 *Stained Glass Design: Study of Head for Christ*, 1865–67
Pencil; 121 × 105 mm
Insc.: E B J
1927P565

B865 *Stained Glass Design: Christ on the Cross*, 1877
Centre light for a triptych, see B951 and B958
Pencil on paper mounted on six sheets; 3444 × 750 mm (i., sight)
Presented by Wilfred Buckley CBE in memory of his father, 1926 (1927P2)

B866 *Stained Glass Design: The Cleansing of Namaan*, 1865
Pencil, with outlines in Indian ink and sepia wash;
1807 × 377 mm
Insc.: TR:SP *41*
1900P182

B867 *Stained Glass Design: David and Melchisedek*, 1865
Brown chalk over pencil on Whatman paper; 178 × 91 (i.), 190 × 108 mm
Insc.: *flowers*
1927P596

B868 *Stained Glass Design: David playing the Harp (Drapery Study)*, 1865–66
Pencil and red chalk on cream laid paper, laid onto card;
318 × 174 (i.), 328 × 182 mm (p.)
1904P143

B869 *Stained Glass Design: David, Earl of Huntingdon*, 1888
Black chalk on three sheets;
1410 × 830 (i.), 1493 × 914 mm (p.)
Prov.: J. R. Holliday, bought from Morris & Co., 11 July 1901
Presented by John Feeney, 1901 (1901P34)

B870 *Stained Glass Design: The Deliverance of St Peter from Prison*, 1863
Sepia and Indian ink, partly coloured in watercolour;
1851 × 555 mm
Insc.: F/ QG/ ROMA/ *all stone work to mal* [cut off] *to thoroughly to* [cut off] *the proper* [cut off]/ *mail/ r/ */ mail/* R/ *flesh/* R/ HW/ W-S/ S: PETRUS: APOST/ *o/ o/* R
Presented by Charles Fairfax Murray, 1898 (1898P51)

B871 *Stained Glass Design: Elijah calling Fire from Heaven*, 1863
Sepia wash, Indian ink, and red chalk over pencil; 1862 × 557 mm
1898P53

B872 *Stained Glass Design: Elijah in the Wilderness*, 1874
Watercolour and bodycolour;
1768 × 610 mm
Presented by Sir John Holder, Sir John Middlemore and John Feeney, 1898 (1898P18)

B873 *Stained Glass Design: Enoch, King David, Christ, Solomon, Elijah, St Thomas, Caritas, St Michael, Justitia, and St Paul*, 1874
Pencil on two sheets of cream-toned paper; 337 × 373 mm
Insc.: **/ */ charity/ all white/ Michael/ */ Justice/ red orange*
1927P440

B874 *Stained Glass Design: Eve*, 1862
Indian ink and sepia wash over pencil; 598 × 314 mm
1904P501

B875 *Stained Glass Design: Ezekiel and Isaiah*, 1865
Brown chalk over pencil on Whatman paper; 174 × 88 (i.), 189 × 105 mm (p.)
Insc.: *flowers*
1927P597

B876 *Stained Glass Design: Study for Faith/ Fides standing on Unbelief*, 1865–66
Pen-and-ink with pencil and watercolour; 352 × 87 mm
Insc.: *Faith/* E B J.*
1927P532

B877 *Stained Glass Design: Faith/Fides standing on Unbelief*, 1865–66
Pencil on tracing paper;
250 × 176 mm
Found unaccessioned in 1979 (1979P208)

B878 *Stained Glass Design: The Flight into Egypt*, 1862
Sepia wash and brush, with chalk;
800 × 678 mm (p.)
1901P7

B879 *Stained Glass Design: 'The Flight into Egypt' – Angels leading the Way*, 1862
Sepia and Indian ink with wash and chalk over pencil; 790 × 670 mm
1901P8

B880 *Stained Glass Design: Fra Angelico*, 1870
Black chalk with bodycolour and sepia wash over pencil on two sheets; 1412 × 490 mm (sight)
Insc.: *centre light/* FP*178*
Presented by Charles Fairfax Murray, 1900 (1900P187)

B881 *Stained Glass Design: Frey*, 1883–84
Black with white chalk and touch of blue chalk on three sheets;
1805 × 717 mm
Insc.: NEWPORT USA/ FREY
1927P410

B882 *Stained Glass Design: The Garland Weavers: Full-Length Figure Study*, c. 1862–66
Coloured chalks, laid down;
340 × 159mm
Insc.: E B J/ *1862/* E B J
1927P454

B883 *Stained Glass Design: The Garland Weavers: Hand Studies*, 1866–67
Pencil on Whatman paper;
381 × 281 mm
Insc.: F/ G/ N
1927P553

B884 *Stained Glass Design: The Garland Weavers: Drapery Study*, 1866–67
Pencil, with red chalk;
388 × 190 mm
1904P25

B885 *Stained Glass Design: The Garland Weavers: Drapery Study*, 1866–67
Pencil; 325 × 174 mm
1904P26

B886 *Stained Glass Design: The Garland Weavers: Drapery Study*, 1866–67
Pencil, laid down; 336 × 198 mm
1904P27

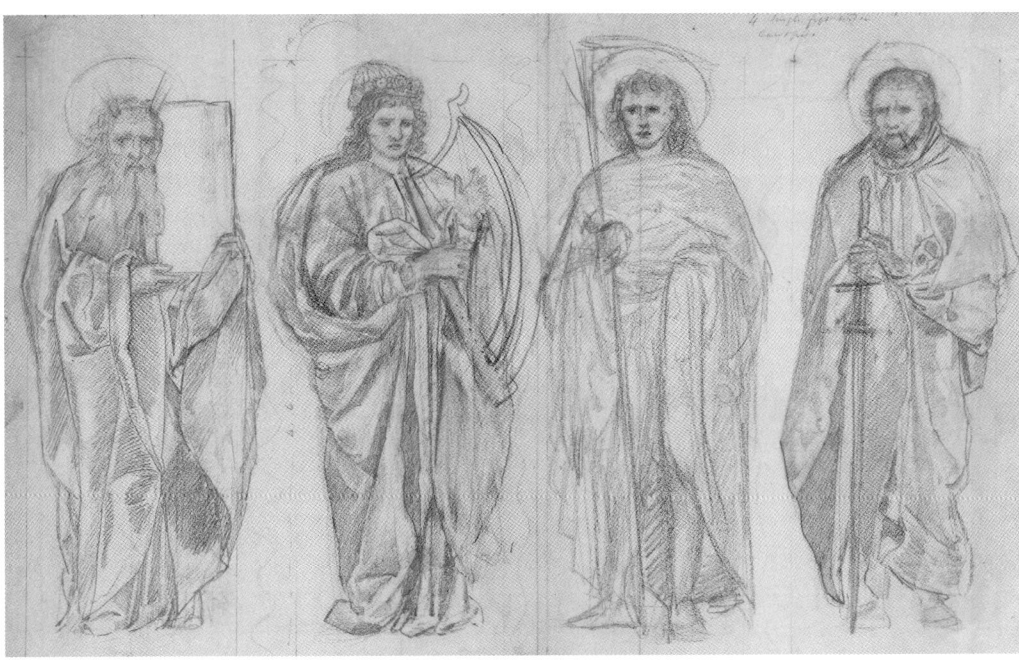

B908 (cat. 29), detail

B887 *Stained Glass Design: The Garland Weavers: Drapery Study*, 1866–67
Pencil with red chalk; 305 × 185 mm
1904P28

B888 *Stained Glass Design: The Garland Weavers: Drapery Study*, 1866–67
Pencil; 319 × 190 mm
1904P29

B889 *Stained Glass Design: The Garland Weavers: Drapery Study*, 1866–67
Pencil, with red chalk; 336 × 179 mm
1904P30

B890 *Stained Glass Design: The Garland Weavers: Drapery Study of a Girl plucking Flowers*, 1866–67
Pencil; 335 × 181 mm
1904P31

B891 *Stained Glass Design: The Garland Weavers: Drapery Study*, 1866–67
Pencil with chalk; 304 × 163 mm
1904P32

B892 *Stained Glass Design: The Garland Weavers: Drapery Study*, 1866–67
Pencil; 285 × 125 (i.), 340 × 168 mm (p.)
1904P33

B893 *Stained Glass Design: George Wishart*, 1888–89
Black chalk on three sheets; 1405 × 829 (i.), 1483 × 917 mm (p.)
Prov.: J. R. Holliday bought from Morris & Co., 11 July 1901
Presented by John Feeney, 1901 (1901P37)

B894 *Stained Glass Design: Gudrida, Wife of Thorstein*, 1883–84
Black, brown and blue chalk with touches of colour; 1815 × 723 mm (sight)
Presented by Mrs Middlemore, 1930 (1930P1135)

B895 *Stained Glass Design: Hope/Spes trampling on Despair*, 1864–66
Pencil on tracing paper; 278 × 176 mm
Insc.: *Spes*
Found unaccessioned in 1979 (1979P209)

B896 *Stained Glass Design: Hope/Spes standing on Despair*, 1865–66
Pen and ink with pencil over watercolour; 275 × 87 mm
1927P533

B897 *Stained Glass Design: Studies for Hope/Spes*, 1865–66
Pencil and red-brown chalk; 355 × 227 mm
Insc.: *E B.J./ hope**
verso: pencil sketch of left hand
1927P535

B898 *Stained Glass Design: Hope/Spes*, 1873
Indian ink, sepia wash, white bodycolour over pencil on paper laid on canvas; 1423 × 526 (i.), 1481 × 602 mm (arched frame)
Insc.: *Meole Brace centre light/ Top/ L.P. 109* [crossed out] *59/* [diagram with three lights & rose window, arrow pointing down] *Hope/ Sacrifice of Noah/ Simeon not yet invested/ faint* [cut off] *gree*[n] *leaves/ clouds painted/ carefully as before/ deep grass & flowers/ feet at* [faint]
1927P429

B899 *Stained Glass Design: King David*, 1863
Sepia, pencil, red chalk and watercolour, heightened with white chalk; 923 × 362 mm
Insc.: *TR:FP*
1900P184

B900 *Stained Glass Design: King Robert the Bruce*, 1888
Black chalk on three sheets; 1406 × 835 (i.), 1480 × 900 mm (p.)
Prov.: J. R. Holliday, bought from Morris & Co., 11 July 1901
Presented by John Feeney, 1901 (1901P33)

B901 *Stained Glass Design: The Last Judgment*, 1874–80
Wax crayon, left to right: 3050 × 950, 3050 × 855, 3050 × 950 mm (i.)
Insc.: *E B J 1874*
Presented by Rt Hon. William Kenrick and J. R. Holliday, 1898 (1898P19)

B902 *Stained Glass Design: The Last Supper*, 1865
Pencil; 294 × 346 (i.), 377 × 511 mm (p.)
Insc.: *1865*
1904P529

B903 *Stained Glass Design: Leif Erickson*, 1883–84
Black chalk on three sheets of Whatman paper; 1820 × 720 mm (sight)
Presented by Mrs Middlemore, 1930 (1930P1134)

B904 *Stained Glass Design: The Madness of Sir Tristram*, 1862
Working copy after Burne-Jones with background by Burne-Jones.
Indian ink, pencil and chalk on paper; 580 × 560 (i.), 620 × 580 mm (p.)
Insc.: *W Hastings/ found in home/ 60 1/ 2 58/ S.P. 80/ to fill up with this/ copy* [E B J's hand]*/ The back is put in by E B J.**
Presented by Charles Fairfax Murray, 1912 (1912P38)

B905 *Stained Glass Design: The Magdalen anointing Christ's Feet*, 1863
Sepia and black ink over pencil; 777 × 585 mm (sight)
Insc.: *the drape to be/ white on/ a matted ground/ to be richly patterned/ lining lining/ to be x covered with pattern/ outside of cloak/ lining/ all the pavement/ lining of sleeve/ x end of dress/ cushion/ lining/ Judas with a black & carrots nimbus/ nimbus richly patterned/ patterned – St John*
Presented by Charles Fairfax Murray, 1913 (1901P13)

B906 *Stained Glass Design: Mars*, 1878
Bodycolour and watercolour; 823 × 481 mm
Insc.: *MARS TERRERVS*
1898P20

B907 *Stained Glass Design: Drapery Study for Moses*, 1865–66
Pencil on cream paper; 318 × 176 mm
1904P142

B908 *Stained Glass Design: Moses, David, St John the Baptist and St Paul*, 1866
Brown-red chalk over pencil on two sheets; 554 × 770 mm
Insc.: *4 inch scale/ 1866/ Moses/ 4 figs/ Moses, David, St John Bapt,*

St Paul other piece under canopy above/ 4.6/ David/ 1.5/ let these be drawn out by light window/ very faintly/ St John Bapt/ Viga Glam's Saga/ 4 single figs under canopies/ Hill Glasgow/ St Paul/ verso: *E B Jones/ 4 single figures under canopy/ Glasgow*
1904P217

B909 *Stained Glass Design: The Nativity*, 1863
Sepia and coloured chalks; 782 × 468 mm
Presented by Charles Fairfax Murray, 1901 (1901P14)

B910 *Stained Glass Design: The Nativity*, 1864–65
Pencil, Indian ink and wash; 600 × 472 mm
Insc.: *Let this nimbus be quite round/ And covered with pattern-same with the other nimbuses-let them be/ quite round.*
1904P533

B911 *Stained Glass Design: The Nativity: An Angel with two Shepherds*, 1886
Chalk and charcoal on three sheets of paper; 2018 × 482 mm
1927P421

B912 *Stained Glass Design: The Nativity: Two Angels*, 1886
Chalk and charcoal on three sheets of paper; 2018 × 483mm
1927P422

B913 *Stained Glass Design: The Nativity: Virgin and Child*, 1886
Chalk and charcoal on three sheets of paper; 2018 × 483 mm
1927P420

B914 *Stained Glass Design: Noah building the Ark*, 1874
Red chalk over pencil on paper laid on canvas; 519 × 415 mm
Insc.: *Building the Ark* [followed by a rough diagram showing the position of the panel in the lower part of a light]
1927P425

B915 *Stained Glass Design: Odin*, 1883–84
Black chalk, charcoal with bodycolour on three sheets; 1808 × 710 mm
Insc.: *ASGARD*
1927P409

B916 *Stained Glass Design: Study of Patience, Obedience and Docility*, 1875
Pencil with Indian ink; 603 × 758 mm
Insc.: *top of etc/ front of foreground/ Patientia/ Obedientia/ obedientia/ Docilitas/ docilita*
verso: *These designs will go by the side of the 3 theological virtues designed by you so long ago. I send you one of them to remind you of the fashion thereof. These also should have the* [ ] *vices under foot*
1927P430

B917 *Stained Glass Design: Provost Halliburton*, 1888
Black chalk on three sheets; 1408 × 834 (i.), 1489 × 912 mm (p.)
Prov.: J. R. Holliday, bought from Morris & Co., 11 July 1901
Presented by John Feeney, 1901(1901P36)

B918 *Stained Glass Design: Prudence and Fortitude*, 1875
Pencil with tracery outlines in black pen and ink; 669 × 468 mm
Insc.: *SFDP 38/ No 5*
1927P433

B919 *Stained Glass Design: Queen Mary Stuart*, 1888–89
Black chalk and pencil on three sheets; 1410 × 831(i.), 1486 × 911 mm (p.)
Prov.: J. R. Holliday, bought from Morris & Co., 11 July 1901
Presented by John Feeney, 1901 (1901P38)

B920 *Stained Glass Design: The Resurrection: Study of sleeping Soldier*, 1861–62
Pencil; 129 × 128 mm
Insc.: *E.B.J./ Resurrection/ Resurrection**
1927P589

B921 *Stained Glass Design: The Resurrection: Study of Soldier*, 1861–62
Pencil; 111 × 152 mm
Insc.: *E.B.J./ Resurrection/ Resurrection **
1927P590

B922 *Stained Glass Design: The Resurrection*, 1861–62
Indian ink and wash over pencil, on various sheets on paper; 1145 × 597 mm
1904P535

B923 *Stained Glass Design: Ruth*, 1879
Black chalk, pencil and touches of brown chalk on two sheets; 1567 × 535 mm
Insc.: *FP 372/ Ruth/ Kirkcaldy/ darkish green under* [illegible]*/ light blue/ nimbus red*
1927P419

B924 *Stained Glass Design: The Sacrifice of Abel*, 1874
Black chalk touched with brown chalk; 620 × 807 mm
1927P427

B925 *Stained Glass Design: The Sacrifice of Abraham*, 1874
Black chalk; 577 × 670 mm
Insc.: *Leigh tracery no. 18. Right.*
1927P428

B926 *Stained Glass Design: The Sacrifice of Noah*, 1874
Black and brown chalk; 573 × 667 mm
Insc.: *Leigh tracery no. 17. left./ 15.5.74/ blue background*
1927P426

B927 *Stained Glass Design: A Seraph*, 1862
Sepia wash and Indian ink with touches of bodycolour over pencil on various sheets of paper; 1095 × 233 mm
Insc.: *Eyes all/ round*
1904P536

B928 *Stained Glass Design: Sir William Wallace*, 1888–89
Black chalk on three sheets of cream paper; 1412 × 832 (i.), 1488 × 911 mm (p.)
Prov.: J. R. Holliday, bought from Morris & Co., 11 July 1901
Presented by John Feeney, 1901 (1901P35)

B929 *Stained Glass Design: The Song of Solomon: 'I charge you, O Daughters of Jerusalem'*, 1862–63
Sepia brush and ink, with coloured chalks over pencil; 569 × 467 mm
Presented by Charles Fairfax Murray, 1900 (1900P173)

B930 *Stained Glass Design: The Song of Solomon: 'My Mother's Children were angry with me'*, 1862–63
Sepia and brush; 575 × 458 mm
Insc.: *b/ r*
Presented by Charles Fairfax Murray, 1900 (1900P174)

B931 *Stained Glass Design: The Song of Solomon: 'I opened to my Beloved'*, 1862–63
Sepia brush and ink, and pencil; 576 × 570 mm (i.)
Presented by Charles Fairfax Murray, 1900 (1900P175)

B932 *Stained Glass Design: The Song of Solomon: 'As the Lily among Thorns'*, 1862–63
Sepia wash and brush, with chalks over pencil; 1000 × 480 mm
Presented by Charles Fairfax Murray, 1900 (1900P176)

B933 *Stained Glass Design: The Song of Solomon: 'The Watchman that went about the City'*, 1862–63
Sepia wash and brush, with pencil; 580 × 464 mm (i.)
Insc.: *grove wall* [faintly written]*/ y/ g/ Green*
Presented by Charles Fairfax Murray, 1900 (1900P177)

B934 *Stained Glass Design: The Song of Solomon: 'As the Apple Tree among the Trees of the Wood'*, 1862–63
Sepia wash and brush, with chalks over pencil; 1000 × 482 mm
1900P178

B935 *Stained Glass Design: The Song of Solomon: 'I Sleep, but my Heart waketh'*, 1862–63
Indian ink and sepia over pencil; 530 × 465 (i.), 594 × 480 mm (p.)
Insc.: *this is ground/ and may be any colouring/ place patterns anywhere you like – in lead lines/ Chapter 5 verse 2*
1904P542

B936 *Stained Glass Design: The Song of Solomon: 'Whither is thy Beloved gone, O thou fairest among Women'*, 1862–63
Indian ink and sepia wash over pencil; 574 × 468 mm
Insc.: *Chapter 6 verse 1*
1904P543

B937 *Stained Glass Design: St Alban*, 1864
Indian ink and sepia over pencil and chalk, squared up; 1085 × 360 mm
Insc.: *FP66/ St Alban*
1904P537

B938 *Stained Glass Design: St Bertha*, 1879
Black chalk on two sheets of paper; 1642 × 535 mm
Insc.: *Bertha Regina/ St Helens Welton*
1927P417

B939 *Stained Glass Design: St Boniface and St Richard*, 1865
Brown chalk over pencil on Whatman paper; 171 × 114 (i.), 187 × 130 mm (p.)
Insc.: *flowers*
1927P600

B940 *Stained Glass Design: Drapery Study for St Catherine*, 1865–66
Pencil and red-brown chalk, laid down on second sheet; 342 × 153 mm
1904P151

B941 *Stained Glass Design: Study of St Cecilia teaching St Frideswide*, 1859
Pen and ink and sepia wash on blue paper; 181 × 199 mm
Insc.: *St Cecilia teaching St Frideswide, Oxford window/ E.B.J.**
1927P536

B942 *Stained Glass Design: Nude Study for St Christopher*, 1867
Pencil and touches of brown chalk; 355 × 203 mm
1904P153

B943 *Stained Glass Design: St Christopher and the Infant Christ*, 1867
Pencil; 395 × 159 mm
1904P152

B944 *Stained Glass Design: Nude Study for St Christopher*, 1867
Pencil on cream paper, laid down on second sheet; 425 × 283 mm
1904P154

B945 *Stained Glass Design: St Constantine*, 1879
Black chalk; 1725 × 532 mm
Insc.: *Constantinvs Imp/ St Helens Welton*
1927P415

B946 *Stained Glass Design: St Edith, Queen and Abbess*, 1863
Sepia wash and Indian ink, with red chalk; 1495 × 303 mm
Presented by Charles Fairfax Murray, 1898 (1898P55)

B947 *Stained Glass Design: St Ethelbert*, 1879
Black chalk; 1725 × 533 mm
Insc.: *Ethelbertus rex*
1927P414

B948 *Stained Glass Design: St Helena*, 1879
Black chalk on two sheets of paper; 1623 × 531 mm
Insc.: *S/ HeLena/ Imp trix*
1927P416

B949 *Stained Glass Design: St John the Evangelist and St Peter*, 1865
Brown chalk over pencil on Whatman paper; 174 × 86 (i.), 191 × 110 mm (p.)
Insc.: *flowers*
1927P598

B950 *Stained Glass Design: Study for St John the Evangelist*, 1865
Pencil; 312 × 148 mm
1904P150

B951 *Stained Glass Design: St John the Evangelist*, 1877
Right light for triptych, see B865 and B958
Pencil; 1950 × 710 mm (i., sight)
Presented by Wilfred Buckley CBE in memory of his father, 1926 (1927P4)

B952 *Stained Glass Design: Drapery Study for St John the Baptist*, 1865–66
Black and white chalk on brown paper, left edge on a second sheet of brown paper; 322 × 171 mm
1904P148

B953 *Stained Glass Design: Drapery Study for St John the Baptist*, 1865–66
Black and white chalk on brown paper; 410 × 214 mm
1904P158

B954 *Stained Glass Design: St Luke*, 1866
Black with blue chalk; 873 × 350 (i.), 873 × 350 mm (p.)
Insc.: *St Luke Painter/ two? light window/ bottom of pavement/ bottom of grass/ lower this foot to* [cut off] *and the red* [cut off]
1900P186

B955 *Stained Glass Design: St Mark the Evangelist*, 1863–64
Sepia and Indian ink, squared up in pencil; 930 × 305 mm (i.). For insc. see cat. 22
Presented by Charles Fairfax Murray, 1900 (1900P185)

B956 *Stained Glass Design: Head Study of Maria Zambaco for St Mark the Evangelist*, 1869–71
Pencil; 293 × 238 mm
Insc.: *E.B.J.*/ to AC*
1927P455

B957 *Stained Glass Design: St Mark the Evangelist*, 1874
Sepia wash, Indian ink and bodycolour over pencil on paper laid on board; 493 × 209 (i.), 1230 × 505 mm (p.)
Insc.: *ark centre tier/ K/ sibyl/* [extremely faint notes]*/ lining/ outside/ outside/ 107* [in white, maker's mark]*/ Morris & C* [cut off] *dont* [sic, cut off]*/ endin* [cut off] *from right*
1927P423

B958 *Stained Glass Design: St Mary the Virgin*, 1877
Left light for triptych, see B865 and B951
Pencil on paper mounted on four sheets of paper with black wash border; 1910 × 710 mm (i., sight)
Presented by Wilfred Buckley CBE in memory of his father, 1926 (1927P3)

B959 *Stained Glass Design: St Mary the Virgin*, 1879
Black chalk and pencil touched with brown chalk; 1567 × 538 mm
Insc.: *FP 371/ Top of Nimbus*
1927P418

B960 *Stained Glass Design: Nude Study for St Matthew*, 1873
Pencil on paper; 254 × 178 mm
1927P530

B961 *Stained Glass Design: Draped Study for St Matthew*, 1873
Pencil on paper; 250 × 175 mm
1927P531

B962 *Stained Glass Design: St Nicholas and St Stephen*, 1865
Pencil, brown and red chalk on Whatman paper; 175 × 186 (i.), 190 × 108 mm (p.)
Insc.: *flowers*
1927P599

B963 *Stained Glass Design: St Nicholas: Study for Cope*, 1865–66
Pencil with blue crayon; 258 × 138 mm
1904P146

B964 *Stained Glass Design: St Paul*, 1861–62
Indian ink and brush over chalk and pencil; 388 × 564 (i.), 175 × 170 mm (p.)
Insc.: *This was the first design made/ by E B Jones for Morris and Co**
1904P540

B965 *Stained Glass Design: St Peter*, 1861–62
Indian ink and wash with chalk; 181 × 188 (i.), 388 × 562 mm (p.)
Insc.: *St Peter/ This was the first design made/ by EB Jones for Morris and Co**
1904P539

B966 *Stained Glass Design: St Stephen*, 1864
Sepia and brush over pencil, squared up; 1013 × 362 mm
1904P538

B967 *Stained Glass Design: The Stoning of St Stephen*, 1863
Sepia, with red chalk; 1847 × 557 mm
Presented by Charles Fairfax Murray, 1898 (1898P52)

B968 *Stained Glass Design: Nude Studies for 'The Stoning of St Stephen'*, 1863
Pencil; 353 × 181 mm
Insc.: *Stoning of Stephen/ Lyndhurst Window/ E.B.J.**
1927P539

B969 *Stained Glass Design: St Ursula*, 1868
Watercolour and sepia, heightened with bodycolour; 1265 × 420 mm
Bequest of J. R. Holliday, 1927, accessioned in 1931 (P1931P63)

B970 *Stained Glass Design: Thor*, 1883–84
Black chalk on three sheets; 1811 × 710 mm
Insc.: *NEWPORT USA/ THOR*
1927P408

B971 *Stained Glass Design: Thorfinn Karlsefne*, 1883–84
Black chalk with touches of colour on three sheets of Whatman paper; 1814 × 720 mm
Bequest of Mrs Middlemore, 1930 (1930P1136)

B972 *Stained Glass Design: The Tiburtine Sibyl*, 1875
Pencil, black chalk and pastel, heightened with gold paint; 1116 × 453 (i.), 1270 × 565 mm (frame)
1927P424

B973 *Stained Glass Design: Drapery Study for Tobias and the Angel*, 1862–63
Pencil; 268 × 134 mm
1904P147

B974 *Stained Glass Design: The Tomb of Tristram and Iseult*, 1863
Indian ink and sepia wash over pencil; 587 × 560 (i.), 618 × 583 mm (p.)
Insc.: *blue/ blue/ blue/ blue/ bloo* [sic]*/ blu* [sic]*/ blew* [sic]/ [the following covered by the frame] *1863/ Tristram's Tomb/ potion/ jealousy/ marriage/ Tristram* [ ] *tomb/* [ ] *Tennyson's 'King's Idylls'/ SP*[ ]
Presented by Charles Fairfax Murray, 1912 (1912P37)

B975 *Stained Glass Design: The Transfiguration of Christ*, 1874
Pencil; 2360 × 500 (c.), 2304 × 500 (l.), 2305 x 500 mm (r.) (sight)
1927P407

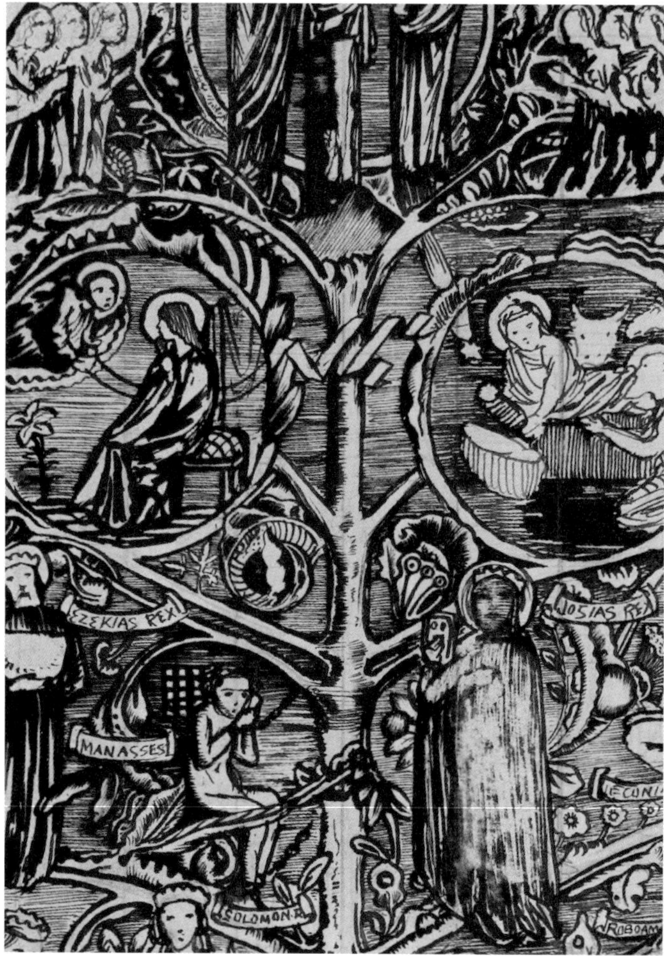

B976 (cat. 4), detail

B976 *Stained Glass Design: The Tree of Jesse*, 1860–61
Sepia pen and ink over pencil on cream-toned paper;
307 × 420 mm
Insc.: *Left light* [top to bottom]*: SAMSON/ JOSHUA/ GIDEON/ JACOB/ NOEH* [sic]*// Middle light* [top to bottom]*: INRI/ EZEKIAS REX/ MANASSES/ JOSIAS REX/ ECUNIAS/ ACHAZ/ SOLOMON R/ DAVID REX/ ROBOAM/ IN THE BEGINNING/ IN THE DAYS/ GENERATION OF JESUS OF THE/ THE BEGINNING OF THE GOSPEL OF JESUS CHRIST//*
Right light [top to bottom]*: JOAHN BAPTISTA/ MALACHI/ MALACHI/ MICAH/ EZEKIEL/ DAVID/ JEREMIAS/ ESAIAS*
1927P437

B977 *Stained Glass Design: Virgin and Child*, 1861–62
Sepia wash with brush, over pencil; 619 × 622 mm
Presented by Charles Fairfax Murray, 1900 (1900P181)

B978 *Stained Glass Design: Virgin and Child*, 1868
Sepia wash and watercolour over pencil; 1270 × 435 mm
Insc.: *head/ wherever obs* [cut off] *send it back* [cut off] *will finish/ Lin* [cut off]*/ border*
Presented by Charles Fairfax Murray, 1901 (1901P12)

B979 *Stained Glass Design: Virgin Mary*, 1863
Sepia wash and brush, over pencil, drawn on grid; 917 × 364 (i.), 950 × 430 mm (p.)
Insc.: [squared up for transfer; each square, on both sides, are numbered, horizontally from 1–7, and vertically from 1–22]/ *make the window just* [cut off] *5 in & make a* [cut off] *if necessary/ 191/*
Presented by Charles Fairfax Murray, 1900 (1900P180)

B980 *Stained Glass Design: Wars of the Roses: Edward IV, Henry VI and St George with Allegory*, c. 1862–64
Watercolour with pen and ink over pencil; 354 × 662 mm
Insc.: *ARS/ REX EDWARDUS/ SANCTUS GEORGIUS/ REX HENRICUS/ SCIENTIA*
1927P438

B981 *Stained Glass Design: The Worship of the Golden Calf*, 1866
Pencil; 630 × 531 mm
1904P541

B982 *Stained Glass Design: The Worship of the Lamb*, 1864–65
Pencil; 300 mm (circular)
Presented by Charles Fairfax Murray, 1910 (1910P85)

B983 *St Cecilia*, pub. 1900
Photogravure; 258 × 130 (i.), 670 × 510 mm (p.)
P.: 1900 (1900P47)

St George Series

B984 *St George*, pub. 1900
Photogravure; 510 × 160 (i.), 670 × 510 mm (p.)
P.: 1900 (1900P67)

B985 *St George Series: 'The King's Daughter/ The Princess in the Garden'*, pub. 1900
Photogravure; 277 × 157 (i.), 340 × 210 mm (p.)
P.: 1900 (1900P58)

B986 *St George Series: Study of the Princess for 'The Princess in the Garden'*, 1865–66
Red-brown chalk (right edge cut); 283 × 123 mm
1904P102

B987 *St George Series: Sketch for 'The Princess in the Garden'*, 1865–66
Pencil: 89 × 57 mm
Insc.: *E.B.J.**
1927P503

B988 *St George Series: Drapery Study of the Princess for 'The Princess in the Garden'*, 1865–66
Pencil and brown-red chalk; 288 × 140 mm
1904P105

B989 *St George Series: 'The Petition to the King'*, pub. 1900
Photogravure; 280 × 480 (i.), 510 × 670 mm (p.)
1900P59

B990 *St George Series: Composition Sketch for 'The Petition to the King'*, 1865–66
Pencil; 90 × 171 mm
Insc.: *E.B.J.**
1927P502

B991 *St George Series: Study of Seated King for 'The Petition to the King'*, 1865–66
Red chalk and pencil;
287 × 195 mm
1904P59

B992 *St George Series: Sketches of King for 'The Petition to the King'*, 1865–66
Pencil on cream paper;
89 × 246 mm
Insc.: *E.B.J.**
1927P508

B993 *St George Series: Study of Seated King for 'The Petition to the King'*, 1865–66
Black and white chalks on brown paper; 227 × 341 mm
1904P95

B994 *St George Series: Study of Chamberlain for 'The Petition to the King'*, 1865–66
Red chalk and pencil;
302 × 161 mm
1904P60

B995 *St George Series: Drapery Study of kneeling Figure for 'The Petition to the King'*, 1865–66
Pencil; 180 × 103 mm
Insc.: *Story of S George/ The bones brought to King/ E.B.J.**
1927P491

B996 *St George Series: Drapery Study of kneeling Figure for 'The Petition to the King'*, 1865–66
Pencil on cream-toned paper;
245 × 238 mm
Insc.: *Story of S. George the bones/ of their victim brought to/ the King/ E.B.J.**
1927P489

B997 *St George Series: Study of kneeling Figure for 'The Petition to the King'*, 1865–66
Pencil on cream-toned paper;
281 × 218 mm
Insc.: *Story of S George. the bones brought/ to the King/ E.B.J.**
1927P490

B998 *St George Series: Study of kneeling Figures for 'The Petition to the King'*, 1865–66
Pencil; 281 × 313 mm
Insc.: *Story of St George The bones brought/ to the King/ E.B.J.**
1927P488

B999 *St George Series: The Princess draws the fatal Lot*, pub. 1900
Photogravure; 276 × 478 (i.), 510 × 670 mm (p.)
1900P60

B1000 *St George Series: Composition Sketch for 'The Princess draws the fatal Lot'*, 1865–66
Pencil on cream paper; 90 × 158 mm
Insc.: E.B.J. *
1927P500

B1001 *St George Series: Sketch of the Princess and an Attendant for 'The Princess draws the fatal Lot'*, 1865–66
Pencil; 66 × 91 mm
Insc.: E.B.J.*
1927P501

B1002 *St George Series: Study of the Princess for 'The Princess draws the fatal Lot'*, 1865–66
Pencil and red chalk; 301 × 166 mm
1904P67

B1003 *St George Series: Study of the Princess for 'The Princess draws the fatal Lot'*, 1865–66
Red chalk and pencil; 312 × 149 mm
1904P64

B1004 *St George Series: Study of Princess and a female Attendant for 'The Princess draws the fatal Lot'*, 1865–66
Red chalk and pencil; 315 × 224 mm
1904P61

B1005 *St George Series: Study of a female Attendant for ' The Princess draws the fatal Lot'*, 1865–66
Red chalk and pencil on cream paper; 239 × 85 mm
1904P63

B1006 *St George Series: Two Studies of female Attendants for 'The Princess draws the fatal Lot'*, 1865–66
Red chalk and pencil; 315 × 217 mm
1904P62

B1007 *St George Series: Two Studies of female Attendants for 'The Princess draws the fatal Lot'*, 1865–66
Pencil, with red chalk; 230 × 228 mm
1904P68

B1008 *St George Series: Study of the Priest for 'The Princess draws the fatal Lot'*, 1865–66
Pencil and brown chalk on cream-toned paper; 333 × 163 mm
Insc.: *Story of St George/ The princess drawing the lot../* E.B.J.*
1927P487

B1009 *St George Series: Study of Temple Priest's Head for 'The Princess draws the fatal Lot'*, 1865–66
Pencil; 67 × 53 mm
Insc.: E.B.J.*
1927P499

B1010 *St George: 'The Princess led to the Dragon'*, pub. 1900
Photogravure; 278 × 252 (i.), 670 × 510 mm (p.)
1900P61

B1011 *St George Series: Composition Sketch for 'The Princess led to the Dragon'*, 1865–66
Pencil with chalk on cream-toned paper; 88 × 97 mm
Insc.: E.B.J.*
1927P504

B1012 *St George Series: Four Studies of female Attendants for 'The Princess led to the Dragon'*, 1865–66
Pencil with red chalk; 204 × 249 mm
1904P70

B1013 *St George Series: Study of female Attendant for 'The Princess led to the Dragon'*, 1865–66
Pencil and red chalk; 278 × 116 mm
1904P72

B1014 *St George Series: Study of female Attendant for 'The Princess led to the Dragon'*, 1865–66
Pencil and red chalk; 295 × 156 mm
1904P69

B1015 *St George Series: Study of female Attendant for 'The Princess led to the Dragon'*, 1865–66
Pencil and red chalk; 301 × 136 mm
1904P71

B1016 *St George Series: Study of female Attendant for 'The Princess led to the Dragon'*, 1865–66
Pencil and red chalk on cream-toned paper; 267 × 131 mm
1904P74

B1017 *St George Series: Study of female Attendant for 'The Princess led to the Dragon'*, 1865–66
Brown chalk with pencil; 314 × 139 mm
Insc.: *Story of St George/* E.B.J.*
1927P484

B1018 *St George Series: Two Studies of female Attendants for 'The Princess led to the Dragon'*, 1865–66
Pencil and red chalk; 282 × 200 mm
1904P75

B1019 *St George Series: Nude Studies of two Soldiers for 'The Princess led to the Dragon'*, 1865–66
Black chalk, heightened with white chalk on brown felt paper; 304 × 205 mm
1904P73

B1020 *St George Series: 'The Princess chained to the Tree'*, pub. 1900
Photogravure; 276 × 242 (i.), 670 × 510 mm (p.)
P.: 1900 (1900P62)

B1021 *St George Series: Composition Sketch for 'The Princess chained to the Tree'*, 1865–66
Pencil with brown chalk; 89 × 97mm
Insc.: E.B.J.*
1927P505

B1022 *St George Series: Study of the Princess for 'The Princess chained to the Tree'*, 1865–66
Pencil; 224 × 98mm
1904P65

B1023 *St George Series: Study of the Princess's Drapery for 'The Princess chained to the Tree'*, 1865–66
Pencil and red chalk; 222 × 86 mm
1904P66

B1024 *St George Series: 'St George slaying the Dragon'*, pub. 1900
Photogravure; 280 × 345 (i.), 510 × 670 mm (p.)
1900P63

B1025 *St George Series: Composition Sketch for 'St George slaying the Dragon'*, 1865–66
Brown chalk on paper; 160 × 189 mm
Insc.: E.B.J./ *St George and the Dragon**
1927P492

B1026 *St George Series: Two Composition Sketches of St George for 'St George slaying the Dragon'*, 1865–66
Pencil on grey-toned paper; 113 × 162 mm
Insc.: E.B.J.*
1927P497

B1027 *St George Series: Slight Sketch for 'St George slaying the Dragon'*, 1865–66
Pencil on grey-toned paper; 55 × 58 mm
Insc.: E.B.J.*
1927P498

B1028 *St George Series: Studies for 'St George slaying the Dragon'*, 1865–66
Pencil; 145 × 305 mm
Insc.: *St George & the Dragon/* E.B.J.*
1927P496

B1029 *St George Series: Nude Study for 'St George slaying the Dragon'*, 1865–66
Black and white chalk on brown paper; 370 × 458 mm
1904P12

B1030 *St George Series: Nude Study of St George for 'St George slaying the Dragon'*, 1865–66
Red chalk; 328 × 240 mm
1904P83

B1031 *St George Series: Nude Study of St George for 'St George slaying the Dragon'*, 1865–66
Pencil drawing with red chalk; 325 × 257 mm
1904P84

B1032 *St George Series: Nude Study of St George for 'St George slaying the Dragon'*, 1865–66
Red chalk; 329 × 248 mm
1904P82

B1033 *St George Series: Nude Study of St George for 'St George slaying the Dragon'*, 1865–66
Red chalk and pencil, background heightened in red chalk, laid down; 336 × 280 mm
1904P85

B1034 *St George Series: Nude Study of St George for 'St George slaying the Dragon'*, 1865–66
Red chalk on cream-toned paper; 328 × 238 mm
1904P81

B1035 *St George Series: Nude Study of St George for 'St George slaying the Dragon'*, 1865–66
Red chalk; 280 × 228 mm
1904P80

B1036 *St George Series: Study of St George's Cloak for 'St George slaying the Dragon'*, 1865–66
Black and white chalk on brown paper; 202 × 152 mm
1904P78

B1037 *St George Series: Studies of Arms and Hands for 'St George slaying the Dragon'*, 1865–66
Black chalk heightened with white on brown paper; 333 × 237 mm
Insc.: *Story of St George/* E.B.J.*
1904P91

B1038 *St George Series: Study of the Princess for 'St George slaying the Dragon'*, 1865
Black chalk with touches of red chalk; 276 × 259 mm
1904P76

B1039 *St George Series: Study of Princess's Drapery for 'St George slaying the Dragon',* 1865–66
Pencil; 183 × 266 mm
Insc.: *Story of St George/* E.B.J.*
1927P485

B1040 *St George Series: Study of Princess's Sleeves for 'St George slaying the Dragon'*, 1865
Black chalk heightened with red chalk; 253 × 212 mm
Insc.: *x outside* (twice)
1904P77

B1041 *St George Series: 'The Return of St George and the Princess'*, pub. 1900
Photogravure; 280 × 360 (i.), 510 × 670 mm (p.)
1900P64

B1042 *St George Series: Composition Sketch for 'The Return of St George and the Princess'*, 1865–66
Pencil with red chalk; 91 × 114 mm
Insc.: E.B.J.*/ *Carpets for windows*
1927P507

B1043 *St George Series: Study of St George for 'The Return of St George and the Princess'*, 1865–66
Pencil; 115 × 108 mm
Insc.: *Return of S George/* E.B.J.*
1927P494

B1044 *St George Series: Two Studies of female Attendant scattering Flowers for 'The Return of St George and the Princess'*, 1865–66
Black and white chalk on brown paper; 384 × 249 mm
1904P86

B1045 *St George Series: Feet Studies for female Attendant scattering Flowers and Musicians for 'The Return of St George and the Princess'*, 1865–66
Black and white chalks on brown paper, laid down on second sheet; 362 × 484 (i.), 398 × 548 mm (p.)
1904P218

B1046 *St George Series: Studies of female Attendant scattering Flowers for 'The Return of St George and the Princess'*, 1865–66
Black and white chalk on brown paper; 365 × 289 mm
1904P90

B1047 *St George Series: Sketch of two female Attendants for 'The Return of St George and the Princess'*, 1865–66
Pencil; 120 × 104 mm
Insc.: *Return of S George/ with Princess/* E.B.J.*
1927P493

B1048 *St George Series: Four Studies of Arms and Hands for 'The Return of St George and the Princess'*, 1865–66
Black chalk, heightened with white on brown paper; 360 × 305 mm
1904P79

B1049 *St George Series: Drapery Study of Girl playing Pipes for 'The Return of St George and the Princess'*, 1865–66
Black and white chalks on brown paper; 390 × 190 mm
1904P89

B1050 *St George Series: Nude Study of Girl playing Pipes for 'The Return of St George and the Princess'*, 1865–66
Red chalk; 293 × 152 mm
1904P87

B1051 *St George Series: Nude Study of Girls playing Pipes for 'The Return of St George and the Princess'*, 1865–66
Red chalk; 253 × 137 mm
1904P88

B1052 *St George Series: Head Study of St George for 'The Return of St George and the Princess'*, 1865–66
Red chalk over pencil; 131 × 109 mm
Insc.: *Return of/ St George study/ for head of St/* E.B.J.*
1927P495

B1053 *St George Series: Study of Sleeve Drapery for 'The Return of St George and the Princess'*, 1865–66
Pencil; 267 × 221 mm
1904P94

B1054 *Studies of Helmet, female Profile and Ostrich Feathers*, 1865–67
possibly related to *'The Return of St George'*
Black and white chalks; 280 × 367 mm
1904P92 (also see B545)

B1055 *St George Series: Drapery Study*, 1865–66
Pencil on cream-toned paper; 209 × 222 mm
Insc.: *Story of St George/* E.B.J. *
1927P486

B1056 *St George Series: Composition Sketch for St George and Princess Sabra* (unused), 1865–66
Pencil; 91 × 110 mm
1927P506

St Theophilus and the Angel

B1057 *St Theophilus and the Angel*, pub. 1900
Photogravure; 192 × 262 (i.), 272 × 332 mm (p.)
1900P32

B1058 *St Theophilus and the Angel: Composition Sketch*, 1863
verso: *Study for 'Ezekiel and the Boiling Pot'*
Pencil, with chalk; 139 × 164 (i.), 178 × 189 mm (p.)
Insc.: *Theophilus & the Angel/ Ezekiel & the boiling pot**
1927P511 (See B273)

B1059 *St Theophilus and the Angel: Rough Composition Sketch*, 1863
Pencil; 141 × 123 mm
Insc.: *Theophilus/* E.B.J. *
1927P514

B1060 *St Theophilus and the Angel: Composition Sketch*, 1863
Pencil; 105 × 131 mm
Insc.: *Theophilus/* E.B.J.*
1927P512

B1061 *St Theophilus and the Angel: Composition Sketch*, 1863
Pencil; 137 × 234 (i.), 168 × 245 mm (p.)
Insc.: E.B.J./ *Theophilus and the Angel/ Tannhauser**
1927P510

B1062 *St Theophilus and the Angel: Composition Sketch*, c. 1865–66
Pencil, squared up; 254 × 351 mm
Insc.: *Theophilus & the/ Angel/* E.B.J.*
1927P509

B1063 *St Theophilus and the Angel: Study of St Theophilus*, 1863–65
Pencil and red-brown chalk; 292 × 151 mm
1904P169

B1064 *St Theophilus and the Angel: Drapery Study for St Theophilus*, 1863–67
Pencil and red-brown chalk; 319 × 176 mm
1904P162

B1065 *St Theophilus and the Angel: Study for St Theophilus*, 1863–67
Pencil and red-brown chalk; 317 × 176 mm
1904P163

B1066 *St Theophilus and the Angel: Study for St Theophilus*, 1863–67
Brown chalk; 229 × 136 mm
1904P182

B1067 *St Theophilus and the Angel: Three Studies of St Theophilus*, 1863–67
Pencil and red-brown chalk; 319 × 485 mm
1904P183

B1068 *St Theophilus and the Angel: Study for Hand of Theophilus*, 1863–67
Pencil; 195 × 189 mm
Insc.: *E. BURNE JONES* [E B J'S hand]/ *MDCCCLXIII–VII/ Study for the hands of Theophilus**
1927P513

B1069 *St Theophilus and the Angel: Drapery Study of the Angel*, 1863–65
Red brown chalk; 285 × 130 mm
1904P159

B1070 *St Theophilus and the Angel: Drapery Study of the Angel*, 1863–67
Pencil; 375 × 119 mm
1904P166

B1071 *St Theophilus and the Angel: Drapery Study of the Angel*, 1863–67
Pencil and Chinese white on green-toned paper; 342 × 117 mm
1904P167

B1072 *St Theophilus and the Angel: Nude Study of the Angel*, 1863–67
Red chalk; 227 × 104 mm
1904P165

B1073 *St Theophilus and the Angel: Nude Study of the Angel*, 1863–67
Red-brown chalk with pencil; 315 × 124 mm
1904P178

B1074 *St Theophilus and the Angel: Nude Study of the Angel*, 1863–67
Pencil over red-brown chalk; 216 × 85 mm
1904P164

B1075 *St Theophilus and the Angel: Two Studies of the Angel*, 1863–67
Pencil and brown chalk; 333 × 190 mm
1904P168

B1076 *St Theophilus and the Angel: Study of the Angel*, 1863–66
Pencil; 157 × 70 mm
Insc.: *Theophilus and the Angel/ E.B.J.**
1927P515

B1077 *St Theophilus and the Angel: Study for the Body of St Dorothea*, 1863–67
Pencil; 132 × 360 (i.), 149 × 360 mm (p.)
1904P176

B1078 *St Theophilus and the Angel: Nude Study for the Executioner*, 1863–67
Red-brown chalk and pencil; 262 × 114 mm
1904P177

B1079 *St Theophilus and Mourner: Study of a Mourner*, 1863–67
Pencil with red-brown chalk; 285 × 134 mm
1904P170

B1080 *St Theophilus and the Angel: Study of a Mourner*, 1863–67
Red-brown chalk; 313 × 119 mm
1904P171

B1081 *St Theophilus and the Angel: Study of a Mourner*, 1863–67
Red-brown chalk; 285 × 131 mm
1904P172

B1082 *St Theophilus and the Angel: Study of a Mourner*, 1863–66
Pencil; 270 × 139 mm
1904P174

B1083 *St Theophilus and the Angel: Study of a Mourner*, 1863–67
Pencil with touches of brown chalk; 271 × 117 mm
1904P175

B1084 *St Theophilus and the Angel: Study of a Mourner*, 1863–67
Brown chalk over pencil; 311 × 152 mm
1904P181

B1085 *St Theophilus and the Angel: Drapery Study of a Mourner*, 1863–67
Red-brown chalk; 318 × 172 mm
1904P180

B1086 *St Theophilus and the Angel: Drapery Study of a Mourner*, 1863–67
Red-brown chalk; 279 × 161 mm
1904P179

B1087 *St Theophilus and the Angel: Drapery Study of a Mourner*, 1863–67
Pencil and red-brown chalk; 247 × 118 mm
1904P161

B1088 *St Theophilus and the Angel: Drapery Study of a Mourner*, 1863–67
Red-brown chalk; 285 × 106 mm
1904P160

B1089 *St Theophilus and the Angel: Drapery Study of a Mourner*, 1863–67
Pencil and red-brown chalk; 268 × 156 mm
1904P173

B1090 *St Theophilus and the Angel: Sketch for the Mourners*, 1863–66
Red chalk on paper; 148 × 173 mm
1927P516

B1091 *St Theophilus and the Angel: Study of a Court Lady*, 1863–67
Pencil and white chalk on brown paper, laid down on sheet of brown paper; 188 × 199 mm
1904P185

B1092 *St Theophilus and the Angel: Study of a Court Lady*, 1863–67
Pencil and white chalk on brown paper; 187 × 120 mm
1904P184

B1093 *St Theophilus and the Angel: Study of a Court Lady*, 1863–67
Pencil and white chalk on brown paper, laid down on sheet of brown paper; 182 × 107 mm
1904P186

B1094 *St Theophilus and the Angel: Study of a Court Lady*, 1863–67
Pencil and white chalk on brown paper, laid down on sheet of brown paper; 188 × 119 mm
1904P187

The Star of Bethlehem

B1095 *The Star of Bethlehem*, 1888–91
Watercolour and bodycolour with scraping on ten sheets of J. Whatman Turkey Mill Kent paper dated 1882 or 1883; 2570 × 3860 mm
Insc.: *E B J 18/ 90*
Commissioned by the Corporation of Birmingham, 1887 (1891P75)

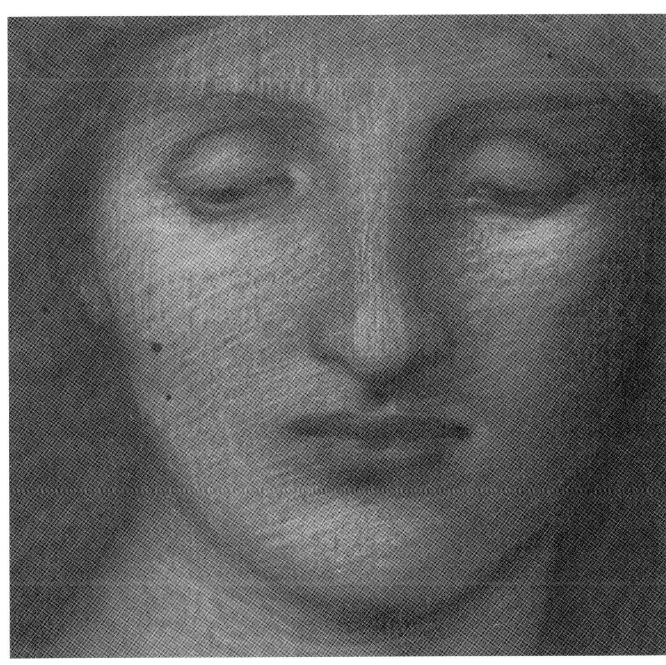

B1097 (cat. 55), detail

B1096 *The Star of Bethlehem: Study for Balthazar, the King of Nubia*, 1887
Black chalk, heightened with white and gold medium; 348 × 163 mm
Insc.: *E B.J/ 1887*
Presented by Alderman C. F. Gaunt, 1916 (1916P33)

B1097 *The Star of Bethlehem: Study for the Angel's Head*, 1890
Red and white chalk on brown paper; 375 × 290 mm
Insc.: *E B J 1890*
Bequest of J. R. Holliday, 1927, and accessioned in 1931 (1931P62)

B1098 *Still-Life: Study of Onions*, c. 1871–75 (or earlier)
Watercolour with bodycolour; 185 × 325 mm
1927P547

B1099 *Summer Snow*, pub. *Good Words*, 1863, p. 380
Wood engraving, engraved by the Dalziel Brothers for an unsigned poem
Insc.: *The Summer Snow* (printed)
The artist is named in the index as *Christopher Jones* (the name given to Burne-Jones's son who died in infancy in 1863)
Probably from the collection of J. R. Holliday, 1927 (1978P548.1)

B1100 *Tapestry Design: The Quest of the Holy Grail: Study for 'The Attainment'*, 1890–91
Bodycolour with gold paint on paper; 516 × 1593 mm
1949P6

B1101 *Tapestry Design: The Quest for the Holy Grail: Study for 'The Summons'*, 1891–94
Sepia, watercolour and bodycolour on buff paper; 654 × 1211 mm
1994P22
See *Chaucer* section for *'Legend of Good Women'* Tapestry Designs

B1102 *Temperance/ Temperantia*, pub. 1900
Photogravure; 515 × 215 (i.), 670 × 510 mm (p.)
1900P71

B1103 *The Temple of Love: Study of a Putto*, 1868–75
Pencil on cream-toned paper; 134 × 130 mm
1927P560

B1104 *The Temple of Love: Three Studies of Putti*, 1868–75
Pencil; 135 × 155 mm
1927P561

B1105 *Thisbe*, c. 1864
Pencil with black chalk; 317 × 235 mm
Insc.: *At every time when they durste so* [above image]/ *But what is that that love cannot espie/ Ye lovers two if that i shall not lie,/ ye founden first this little narrow clift/ and with a sword as soft as any shrift, they let their wordes through the clifte pace/ and tolden, while they stonden in the place/ All their complaint of love, and all their wo/ At every time when that they dursten so/ Thisbe of Babylon.*
Presented by Edward Robert Hughes, 1909 (1909P63)

Tile Design

B1106 *Tile Design: Pyramus and Thisbe – Pyramus Draws His Sword to Slay Himself*, 1865–66
Sepia ink and brown wash over pencil on cream-toned paper; 297 × 213 (i.), 316 × 240 mm (p.)
Insc.: *And at the laste this Piramus ys come/ But al to long, allas, at home was hee:/ The moone shoone, men myente wel ysee,/ And in his way, as that he come ful faste/ Hise eighen to the grounde adoun he caste.//* verso: *cape face shifting out with hand/ handsome face/ eyes flat/ hands on shoulder*
1927P592

B1107 *Tile Design: Study of Pyramus for 'Pyramus and Thisbe'*, 1865–66
Pencil on cream-toned paper; 274 × 173 mm
1927P593

B1108 *Tile Design: The Marriage Feast at Cana (I)*, 1866
Pencil with chalk, squared up for transfer each numbered 1–15; 267 × 267 (i.), 290 × 293 mm (p.)
Insc.: *all to be richly covered with grass & flowers*
1927P434

B1109 *Tile Design: The Marriage Feast at Cana (II)*, 1866
Pencil and brown chalk, squared up; 266 × 266 mm
Insc.: *Supper at Cana/* E.B.J. *
1927P435

B1110 *Tile Design: The Supper at Emmaus*, 1866
Pencil, squared up and numbered 1–21; 268 × 266 (i.), 292 × 292 mm (p.)
Insc.: *carry on the frieze/ pillars like the one* [illegible] *cap* [cut off]/ *flowers/ some to* [illegible] *over from the steps*
1927P436

B1111 *Tile Design: Theseus and the Minotaur in the Labyrinth*, 1861
Pencil, sepia wash, pen and ink; 260 × 255 mm
1927P594

Troy Triptych

B1112 *Troy Triptych: Composition Study*, 1870–72
Watercolour, bodycolour and pencil; 780 × 810 mm
Presented by Philip Burne-Jones, 1922 (1922P179)

B1113 *Troy Triptych: Helen Captive in Burning Troy*, 1870–72
Watercolour and bodycolour; 1035 × 368 mm
Purchased in 1898 (1898P21)

B1114 *Troy Triptych: Study of Two Putti*, 1870–72
Sepia wash and white bodycolour over pencil on brown paper; 406 × 610 mm
Presented by Mrs J. W. Mackail, 1922 (1922P184)

B1115 *Troy Triptych: Study of Two Putti*, 1870–72
Sepia wash and white bodycolour over pencil on brown paper; 406 × 610 mm
Presented by Mrs J. W. Mackail, 1922 (1922P185)

B1116 *Troy Triptych: Study of Two Putti*, 1870–72
Sepia wash and white bodycolour over pencil on brown paper; 407 × 610 mm
Insc.: *Brown Paper*
Presented by Mrs J. W. Mackail, 1922 (1922P186)

B1117 *Venus Concordia: Study of the Three Graces*, 1895
Charcoal and pastel on paper; 1325 × 667 mm
Purchased in 1898 (1898P22)

B1118 *Venus Epithalamia*, pub. 1900
Photogravure; 271 × 191 (i.), 670 × 510 mm (p.)
P.: 1900 (1900P25)

B1119 *Wheel of Fortune*, pub. 1900
Photogravure; 500 × 252 (i.), 670 × 510 mm (p.)
1900P84

B1120 *Wheel of Fortune: Studies of the Hands and Feet of the Slave*, 1875–83
Pencil; 262 × 158 mm (sight)
1927P449

The Wine of Circe

B1121 *The Wine of Circe*, pub. 1900
Photogravure; 310 × 470 (i.), 510 × 670 mm (p.)
P.: 1900 (1900P65)

B1122 *The Wine of Circe: Early Composition Sketch*, 1863
Pencil; 127 × 247 (i.), 154 × 263 mm (p.)
Insc.: *Wine of Circe/* E.B.J *
1927P524

B1123 *The Wine of Circe: Sketches*, 1863
Pencil on thick cream card; verso: sepia; 190 × 178 mm
Insc.: E.B.J./ *Circe**
1927P525

B1124 *The Wine of Circe: Study for Drapery of Circe*, 1863–69
Pencil on cream paper; 218 × 109 mm
1904P133

B1125 *Wine of Circe: Study of Drapery for Circe*, 1866–69
Pencil on cream paper, cut out and laid down; 190 × 95 (i.), 218 × 108 mm (p.)
1904P134

B1126 *The Wine of Circe: Study of Drapery*, 1866–69
Pencil with touches of red chalk on cream paper, laid down; 372 × 261 mm
1904P132

B1127 *The Wine of Circe: Two Drapery Studies*, 1866–69
White chalk and pencil on brown paper, laid down on second sheet of brown paper, and then on card; 299 × 476 mm
1904P130

B1128 *The Wine of Circe: Drapery Studies for crouching Figure of Circe*, 1866–69
Black and white chalks on brown paper, laid down on another sheet of grey-brown paper; 258 × 323 mm
1904P138

B1129 *The Wine of Circe: Nude Study for Circe*, 1866–69
Black chalk on brown paper, laid down on second sheet of brown paper; 240 × 227 (i.), 286 × 267 mm (p.)
1904P137

B1130 *The Wine of Circe: Nude Study for Circe*, 1866–69
Black chalk with touches of white on brown paper, cut out and laid down on second brown sheet; 270 × 285 mm
1904P136

B1131 *The Wine of Circe: Two Nude Studies*, 1866–69
White chalk with touches of black chalk on brown paper; 279 × 362 mm
1904P135

B1132 *The Wine of Circe: Study for the upper part of Circe*, 1866–69
Pencil and red-brown chalk on cream paper; 96 × 181 mm
1904P131

B1133 *Winter: Study of flying Drapery*, 1866–67
Black and white chalks on brown paper; 291 × 277 mm
1904P128

B1134 *Winter?: Flying Drapery Study*, 1864–67
Pencil; 238 × 182 mm
1904P129

B1135 *The Wizard*, pub. 1900
Photogravure; 273 × 163 (i.), 670 × 510 mm (p.)
P.: 1900 (1900P96)

B1136 *A Wood Nymph*, pub. 1900
Photogravure; 297 × 297 (i.), 670 × 510 mm (p.)
P.: 1900 (1900P77)

B1137 *Zephyrus and Psyche*, pub. 1900
Photogravure; 248 × 176 (i.), 670 × 510 mm (p.)
P.: 1900 (1900P33)

The following list comprises missing works that were accessioned but not recorded in the 1939 *Catalogue of Drawings*, as well as two drawings that are currently missing:
Pygmalion and the Image (photogravure, 1899P58)
Flamma Vestalis (etching, 1931P325)
Female Drapery Study (white chalk, 1904P41)
Female Nude Study (white chalk, 1904P227)
Drapery Study (pencil, 1904P40)
Nude Study, Feet and Hands (pencil, 1904P213)
Stained Glass Design: The Last Judgment (watercolour, 1971P71)
Troy Triptych: Five Studies for the Frieze (sepia, 1922P183)

Index

Adam 49
Adoration of the Kings, The (with Annunciation) 49, 63
Alps, France, Birds and Dogs 56–8, 79
Altar of Hymen 63
Amy Gaskell Bonham 63
Angel of the Martyrs (with violin) 63
angels 63, 69, 84–5, 88
Annecy 79
Annunciation, The 12, 28, 40, 63, 85
Apollo and Daphne 84
architectural and street scenes 79, 82, 83, 84
Ariadne and Lucretia 51–2
armour and weapons 81, 82, 83
Arnold, Thomas 8
Arthur in Avalon 16
Ascension, The 85
Astrologia 29, 52, 63
Atlas turned to Stone 56, 79
Aurora 32, 63
Awake, O North Wind!/ Sponsa de Libano 32, 56, 84,

Backgammon Players, The 12, 63
Baldwin, Alfred 32
Baleful Head, The 56, 78–9
Balfour, Frances 31
Baptism of Christ, The 85
Bartley, Mary 14
Bath of Venus, The 16, 63
Battle of Beth-Horon, The 85
Beguiling of Merlin, The 29, 63
Bell, Malcolm 16, 54
Benson, W. A. S. 56
bewigged figure 49, 63
Biblical subjects 86, 87, 88, 89, 90
Birch, Charles 9
birds 79, 81
Blessed Damozel, The 12, 28, 63
Botticelli, Sandro 15, 25, 52
Briar Rose series 25, 31, 36, 63
Bridges, Richard 62
Brown, Ford Madox 10, 16, 49, 51
Browning, Robert 11
Building of the Ark, The 85
Building of the Temple, The 85
Buondelmonte's Wedding 28
Burden, Elizabeth 54
Burden, Jane *see* Morris, Jane
Bürger, G. A. 8, 9
Burne-Jones, Georgiana (Lady) 8, 9, 12, 28–9, 34, 40, 51, 55, 58, 59
Burne-Jones, Margaret 31, 32
Burne-Jones, Philip 28, 37, 38*n*
Byron, George Gordon Lord 8
Byzantine and Romanesque Decoration 59, 81

Caiva, Antonia 29
Car of Love, The 29, 59, 63, 83
caricatures 58, 63–4
Carlyle, Thomas 10
Cassavetti, Demetrius 29
Cassavetti, Euphrosyne Ionides 29
Caswell, Mr 9
Catherwood, Frederick 9, 11
Chant d'Amour, Le 31, 52, 64
Charity/ Caritas 55, 61, 64, 86
Chaucer, Geoffrey 15, 29, 51–2, 53, 55, 64–5
Childe Roland 11
Christ, life of 77, 86, 87, 88, 89
Cinderella 50, 65
Clark, Thomas 9, 12–14
clouds 82
Cockerell, Sydney 35, 37n, 38n, 40
Coleridge, Samuel Taylor 8
Colonna, Francesco 15
Combe, Thomas 10
Corbould, E. H. 9
Cornforth, Fanny 12, 28, 50
Coronio, Aglaia 55
costume 82, 83
see also drapery
Court of Phineus 56, 79
Cox, David 9–10
Crane, Walter 55
Crivelli, Carlo 16
crozier 82
Cruikshank, George 9, 11
Cupid and Psyche Series 15, 29, 36, 52, 62, 65–9, 79

Dadd, Richard 9
Dalziel Brothers 50, 58
Dalziels' Bible Gallery 58, 69
Danaë 69
dancing girl 69
David, Earl of Huntingdon 86
Days of Creation, The 16, 50, 55, 69
de Beaumont, Robin 51
de la Motte Fouqué, Friedrich 11
Death of Medusa, The 81
decorative patterns 59, 81, 82, 83, 84
Deer by a Fountain 77
Defence of Guenevere, The 11
della Robbia, Luca 50
Depths of the Sea, The 31, 69
Dickens, Charles 9
Dies Domini 56, 69
Dixon, Richard Watson 8
dogs and wolves 79
Doom Fulfilled 56
Dorigen of Bretaigne 29, 69
Dorothy Drew 70
Dossi, Dosso 31

drapery 51, 54, 56, 63, 64–5, 69, 70–1, 73, 74, 75, 78, 79, 81, 84, 87, 88, 89
Dream of Sir Lancelot at the Chapel of the San Graal, The 70
Dürer, Albrecht 11–12

Earth 81
Earthly Paradise, The (project) 15–16, 29, 52
Edward Burne-Jones 70
Elliott, David 36
embroidery *see* needlework
Entombment, The 70
Eros and Psyche 62
Etty, William 9, 14
Eve 49
Evening Star, The 70
Ezekiel and the boiling Pot 50, 51, 70

Fair Rosamund and Queen Eleanor 12, 70
Fairy Family, The 10, 40, 70
Faith/ Fides 29, 72, 86
Fall of Lucifer, The 70
Fates, The 14, 36, 70
Feast of Peleus, The 16, 70
Feeney, John 37*n*
Finding of Medusa, The 81
Flamma Vestalis 72
Flower Book, The 37, 72–3
Foster, Myles Birket 51
Fra Angelico 86
Frey 86

Galatea 29
Garden of the Hesperides, The 31, 73
Garden of Pan, The 73
Garland Weavers, The 36, 50, 86–7
Gaskell, Amy 32
Gaskell, Helen Mary 31, 32
George Wishart 87
Georgiana Burne-Jones 51, 73
Gertrude Lewis 73
Gilbert, W. S., and Sullivan, Arthur 31
Gilchrist, Alexander 50
Gillott, Joseph 9
Giorgione 12, 50
Gladstone, Mary 31
Goblin Wrestler 58, 64
Going to the Battle 28
Golden Stairs, The 31, 73
Goss, Rev. John 10
Graham, Cicely 32
Graham, Frances (later Horner) 31–2
Graham, William 31

Green Summer 12, 52, 73
Grimm, Jakob and Wilhelm 11
Gudrida, Wife of Thorstein 87

Hall, S. C. 9
hands 55, 64, 65, 69, 70, 71, 74, 81, 91, 92
Harris, Mrs William 62
Hart, John Napthali 51
Hartley, Harold 51
Hauptman, Dr William 58
heads 54–5, 59, 63, 64, 71, 74, 78, 81
Heart of the Rose, The 73
heraldic creatures 82
Hill of Venus, The 15, 73
Holden, Angus 56
Holliday, J. R. 34, 35–6, 62
Hollyer, Frederick 61
Holy Grail tapestries 16, 59
Hood, Thomas 9
Hope/ Spes 51, 73, 87
Horner, Sir John Fortescue 32
horses 73, 83, 84
Hours, The 14, 74
Howard, George 54
Howell, Charles Augustus 27, 54
Hughes, Arthur 10
Hunt, Venetia 32
Hunt, William Holman 10

Idyll, An 12, 49, 50, 74
Ionides, Luke 33*n*

James, Henry 10, 25
Jane Morris 74
Jekyll, Gertrude 59
Jews, caricatures 58, 64
Jones, Augusta 29, 52, 63, 71
Jones, Elizabeth Coley 28, 32

Kaines Smith, S. C. 37*n*
Keats, John 8, 9
Keene, Bessie 29, 32
Keene, Mrs 29
Keightley, Thomas 11
Kelmscott Chaucer 61
Kenrick, William 34, 35, 59
King Cophetua and the Beggar Maid 25, 58, 59, 74
King David 51
King Mark and La Belle Iseult 12, 74
King René's Honeymoon 49, 74
King Robert the Bruce 87
King Sigurd the Crusader – A Norse Saga 74
knights 28, 83, 84
Knight's Farewell, The 28

Ladies and Animals sideboard 12, 74
Ladies and Death 28
'Lady of Shalott, The' 10
Lament, The 14–15, 36, 52, 74
Landscape 50, 74
Lapse of the Year, The 74–5
Last Judgment, The 35, 56
Last Sleep of Arthur in Avalon, The 59
Laus Veneris 7, 31, 75
leaf 79
Lee, James Prince 8, 9
Legend of Good Women, The 15, 29, 51–2, 54, 55, 64–5
legs 81
Leif Ericson 87
Leigh, J. M. 14
Leighton, Barbara, *Edward Burne-Jones Painting 'The Star of Bethlehem'* 59
Leighton, Frederic 14
letters 75
Letters to Katie 31
Lewis, George 31
Lewis, Gertrude 31
Lewis, Katie 31, 32, 36
Lewis, Matthew 'Monk' 8
Leyland, Frederick 14
Linnell, John 9
Lippi, Filippino 25
Love among the Ruins 75
Love disguised as Reason 75
Love is Enough 75
Love leading the Pilgrim 75
Lucretia 15, 29, 51, 54, 75
Lucretia, Hippolyte and Helen 54
Luna 75

Macdonald, Agnes 28, 32, 71
Macdonald, Alice 28
Macdonald, Georgiana *see* Burne-Jones, Georgiana
Macdonald, Harry 28
Macdonald, Louisa 28, 32
Mackail, J. W. 32
Maclaren, Archibald 10–11, 40
Maclise, Daniel 9
Madness of Sir Tristram, The 87
male studies 75
 see also nudes
Malory, Thomas 11
Man Embracing a Tree 54, 75
Manet, Edouard 7
Manzoni, Alessandro 8
Margaret Burne-Jones 75
Maria Zambaco 29, 54–5, 75–6, 89
Marshall, Peter Paul 51
Mary, Virgin 51, 88, 89, 90
Masque of Cupid, The 29, 76
Masque of the Four Seasons, The 29, 55, 76
Maxse, Violet and Olive 32
Meadows, Kenny 9
Merciful Knight, The 12, 50–1, 76
Michelangelo Buonarroti 16, 25
Mill, The 76
Millais, John Everett 10, 36, 51
Mirror of Venus, The 76
Mona Lisa homage 32
Montmajour 79
Moore, Albert 14, 15
Morning of the Resurrection, The 76
Morris & Company Revised Index of Stained Glass Cartoons 76
Morris & Company Windows Books 76–7
Morris, Jane (née Burden) 28, 40, 54
Morris, May 31
Morris, William 10, 11, 12, 15, 16, 28, 29, 40, 49, 50, 51, 52, 55
Mortuary Design: Gravestone and Plot 77
Moses, David, St John the Baptist and St Paul 52
mountains 79
Müller, W. J. 9
Munera Pulveris 15
murals 12, 77
Murray, Charles Fairfax 34–6, 61, 62
Muses leaving the dying Poet, The 77
Music 77

Nativity, The 77
needlework/ embroidery designs 64, 70, 77, 93
 see also tapestries
Newman, John Henry 10
Norma (model) 29
Norton, Charles Eliot 15
nudes 51, 52, 54, 56, 70, 71–2, 73, 74, 78, 81

Odin 88
'Ossian' 8
Ovid 55

Palmer, Samuel 50
Pan and Psyche 77
Paris and Helen 77
Parnassus 77
Passing of Venus, The 25, 54, 77
Patience, Obedience and Docility 88
Paton, Noel 9
Perseus Series 16, 56, 77, 78, 79, 81
Phidias 12
Philip Comyns Carr 77
Phyllis and Demophoön 16, 25, 29–31, 37, 54, 55, 77
Pilgrim at the Gate of Idleness, The 77
Pilgrim in the Garden of Idleness, The 70, 77
Poesis/ Poetry 77
Poynter, Edward 14, 32
Price, Cormell 8
Princess in the Garden, The 52
Prioress's Tale, The 77
Provost Halliburton 88
Prudence and Fortitude 88
Punch 58
Pygmalion and the Image 15, 16, 29, 56, 58, 77–8

Queen Mary Stuart 88
Rape of Proserpine, The 25, 78
Redgrave, Richard 9
Rembrandt van Rijn 7
René, King of Anjou 49
Reserva (model) 29
Ring Given to Venus, The 15, 78
Robertson, Graham 7, 32
Rock of Doom, The 56, 79
Romaunt of the Rose 56, 79
Rooke, T. M. 25
Rose Garden, The 29, 78
Rossetti, Dante Gabriel 9, 10, 11, 12, 14, 16, 28, 29, 31, 34, 36, 49, 51, 52
Ruskin, John 8, 10, 11, 12, 14, 15, 16, 25, 27, 51, 52
Russell, R. R. 56

St Frideswide window, Christ Church, Oxford 12, 89
St George Series 14, 36, 52, 75, 90–2
St John the Evangelist 54–5, 89
St Mark the Evangelist 29, 51, 56, 89
St Theophilus and the Angel 14, 15, 36, 50, 92–3
saints 84, 86, 88, 89, 90
Sale, Lady 8, 9
Sandys, Frederick 52
Sandys, Mary 52
Sargent, John Singer 33*n*
Schnorr von Carolsfeld, Julius 58
Schoenherr, Douglas 35
Scott, Sir Walter 8, 11
Sea Nymph, A 78
Seddon, John P. 12, 49
Self-Caricature 55
self-portraits 55, 63, 64
Selsley, cartoons 12
Sewter, A. C. 16, 35
Shakespeare, William 8
ships 84
Sibylla Delphica 78
Silver, Miss 29
Sir William Wallace 88
Sirens, The 25, 32, 58, 61, 78
sketchbooks 56–8, 78–84
Sleigh, Bernard 27
Smith, Ellen 29
Smith, R. Catterson 61
Soane, Sir John 9
Solomon, Simeon 29, 58
Song of Solomon, The 16, 29, 32, 50, 84, 88
Sotheby, Alfred Francis 59
Soul Attains, The 56, 58
Southey, Robert 11
Spartali, Marie 31
Sponsa de Libano/ Awake, O North Wind! 32, 56, 84
Spozzi, Charles 9–10
Spring/ Flora 84
stained-glass designs 12, 16, 34–6, 49, 50, 51, 52, 54–6, 75, 76–7, 84–90
Stanhope, John Roddam Spencer 49, 50
Star of Bethlehem, The 8, 25, 35, 59, 61, 73, 93
Star of Bethlehem 61, 73
Stella Matutina 56
Stella Vespertina 56, 81
Still-Life: Study of Onions 93
Stillman, William J. 31
Stoning of St Stephen, The 51, 89
Stunner, A (verso: *Girl with Ringlets*) 49, 63
Summer 29
Summer Snow 93
Swinburne, A. C. 25

tapestry designs 16, 59, 93
Temperance/ Temperantia 29, 93
Temple of Love, The 93
Tennant, Margot and Laura 31
Tenniel, John 9
Tennyson, Alfred Lord 10, 58
tents 83
Thirkell, Angela 36, 51, 58, 62
Thisbe 94
Thor 89
Thorfinn Karlsefne 89
Thorpe, Benjamin 8
Three Ostrich Feathers 77
Tiburtine Sibyl, The 89
tile designs 12, 94
Titian 12
Tomb of Tristan and Iseult, The 89
Tree of Forgiveness 55
Tree of Jesse, The 40
trees 82
Troy Triptych (project) 16, 37, 40, 94
Turner, J. M. W. 9, 10

Venus 29
Venus Concordia 25, 94
Venus Epithalamia 29, 94
Vespertina Quies 32

Wallis, Sir Whitworth 37*n*
Ward, E. M. 9
Wars of the Roses 90
Watts, George Frederic 12, 14, 29, 35, 52, 54
Waxen Image, The 11, 28
Webb, Philip 35, 51
Wedding Procession of Sir Degrevaunt, The 77
Wheel of Fortune 94
Whistler, J. A. McN. 7, 14, 15
Whitley, A. E. 34, 52, 62
Wildman, Stephen 58
William Morris as an ancient Poet 63
Wine of Circe, The 14, 15, 29, 94
Winter 29, 94
Wise and Foolish Virgins, The 28
Wizard, The 32, 94
Wood Nymph, A 94
Wortley, Mary Stuart 31

Yonge, Charlotte 11

Zambaco, Demetrius 29
Zambaco, Maria Cassavetti 29–31, 32, 54–5, 56, 75–6, 78, 89
Zephyrus and Psyche 94